STAGE DANCING

THE ART OF

STAGE DANCING

NED WAYBURN

BELVEDERE

LC 80-69259
ISBN 0-87754-250-3

Cover design and lettering by
Thomas Morris — Sharpshooter Studios

Belvedere Publishers, Inc.
c/o Chelsea House Publishers
70 West 40th Street, New York 10018

GREETINGS!

Someway I don't care for the word "Preface." As I think the matter over, I'm not sure that I ever read a preface to any book; and this fact suggests to me that possibly others would pass by this page in my book if I dubbed it by that much-worn and very trite word. So I've hailed you all with a much more cheery and stimulating title for my opening page; and perhaps, in consequence, some may read it.

My Greetings are specially extended to certain chosen groups of people: First, to all students of the past, the present, and those hoped for in the future; second, to the hundreds of teachers of the art of dancing who esteem my original methods of instruction sufficiently to care

about what I may print on the subject; and third, to a public that has sat "in front" at any or many of my productions, and enjoyed them, and is, in consequence, interested to know something about the hard work, the thought and the skill, necessary to bring about such pleasing results.

Lest so narrow a limit to my Greetings may be misunderstood, on second thought I will extend my Greetings to that world of people who love life and beauty and happiness; who appreciate honest effort to make living more enjoyable and brighter; who love laughter and smiles and the good things that go with them.

And if all that kind of people will read and appreciate my book, I shall not miss the others.

But still, to them, as well as to you, I extend

Greetings!

NED WAYBURN

As a writer of books, I confess myself
to be a good stage craftsman.

I have never before attempted author-
ship, and this volume is simply a spontaneous outpouring of my personal love
and knowledge of a great art that has
filled my years with joy and happiness,
and some renown in the theatrical world.

To have been one modest part of an instrument that has piped to pleasure many

millions of my fellows, is surely justification for personal satisfaction. How this playing has been done, how it is being done today in greater degree than ever before, is what I have in mind to tell a curious public.

And so I became an author for this once, and what you may discover that I lack in literary ability, let me trust you will find compensated for in the plainness and simplicity of the facts, incidents and reminiscences that I relate. If not the manner, at least the matter is worthy of your approval.

My story is presented in the first person, and this is because I find it easiest to write from a personal viewpoint—not, I hope, as the result of any special desire to see the letter I in print. A more experienced author would be able to write this book with less suggestion of ego in its pages, I have little doubt, and so I have called this explanatory word An Apology that you may understand why things are as they are, and not demand of the tyro the same quality of literary excellence that you would be justified in expecting of the better qualified writer.

To paraphrase one of my earliest school-boy speeches,—"If this be an apology, make the most of it."

CONTENTS

FRED AND ADELE ASTAIRE

SCENE FROM "NED WAYBURN'S SYMPHONIC JAZZ REVUE"

"BY THE SOUTH SEA MOON," FOLLIES OF 1922

DOLLY SISTERS

LOUISE GROODY

The
ART
of
STAGE
DANCING

NED WAYBURN

THE ART OF STAGE DANCING

Overture

A BIT OF ANCIENT HISTORY

E VERY age has had its ways of dancing; every people has expressed it s e l f in some form of rhythmic motion.

The dance originally was the natural expression of the simple emotions of a primitive people. Triumph, defeat, war, love, hate, desire, propitiation of the gods of nature, all were danced by the hero or the tribe to the rhythm of beaten drums.

Over six thousand years ago Egypt made use of the dance in its religious ritual. At a very early period the Hebrews gave dancing a high place in their ceremony of worship. Moses bade the children of Israel dance after the crossing of the Red Sea. David danced before the Ark of the Covenant. The Bible is replete with instances showing the place of the dance in the lives of the people of that time.

Greece in its palmy days was the greatest dancing nation the world has ever known. Here it was protected by priesthood and state, practiced by rich and poor, high and lowly born. One of the nine muses was devoted to the fostering of this particular art. Great ballets memorialized great events; simple rustic dances celebrated the

19

coming of the flowers and the gathering of the crops. Priestesses performed the sacred numbers; eccentric comedy teams enlivened the streets of Athens. Philosophers taught it to pupils for its salutary effect on body and mind; it was employed to give soldiers poise, agility and health.

The dance was undoubtedly among the causes of Greek vigor of mind and body. Physicians prescribed its rhythmic exercise for many ailments. Plato specifies dancing among the necessities for the ideal republic, and Socrates urged it upon his pupils. The beauty of harmonized movements of healthy bodies, engendered by dancing, had its effect on the art of Greece.

Since the days of classic Greece, scenery, music and costume have created effects then undreamed of, but notwithstanding the lack of incidental factors, the greatness and frequency of municipal ballets, the variety of motives that dancing was made to express, combine to give Greece a rank never surpassed as a dancing nation.

The Greek stage of this age was rich in scope, and for its effects drew upon poetry, music, dancing, grouping and posing.

Then came the Dark Ages of history, and in a degraded world dancing was saved and taken under the protection of the Christian church, where it remained for the greater part of a thousand years. The vehicle that carried the ballet through this period was known as the "spectacle." These sacred spectacles, in grouping, evolution, decoration and music, possessed qualities that entitle them to a respectable place in the annals of opera ballet. The steps were primitive, but they sufficed for the times.

However, the organization of the first real opera ballet conforming to standards of modern excellence did not come till the latter part of the fifteenth century, when

Cardinal Riario, a nephew of Pope Sixtus IV, composed and staged a number of important ballet productions.

But the greatest development of the modern type of ballet received its impetus under the reign of Louis XIV of France, who founded the national ballet academy at Paris in 1661, and often played prominent parts himself. Under this influence great performers began to appear, artists whose work, by grace of beauty alone, attested that perfection in ballet technique was approaching.

The growth of the ballet since the time of Louis XIV has been the contribution of individual artists, who by giving expression to their own original ideas have thus advanced the art to the pinnacle attained by the modern Russian ballet of today.

The above outline of the history of the dance is made brief intentionally, with no attempt to touch upon the various forms of dancing as practiced by the many nations and tribes. Numerous books have been written covering all aspects of this subject, and giving in detail the steps and rhythms of the people of every age, and of every continent and the isles of the sea; and as matters of interest, education and research they are competent and complete, and especially edifying to the student of Terpsichore.

But the subject that interests us is not concerned with ancient lore nor with historical data, however delightful they may be. I am writing for the American of today about present-day matters in the American theatrical world, and to that end choose to ignore all other phases of the subject.

In our day the development of the dance has reached its greatest heights, in both the social circle and the stage picture.

The advance made in stage dancing within the last generation has been very pronounced, yet so gradual has been this growth and improvement, that only the elders of the present time can visualize its progress, and that only by a backward look to the period of paucity and monotony that ruled in their junior years, and contrast the dearth of then with the abundance of now.

For really, whether in our multitude of revues or in our many musical shows, the dance, the pose, the rhythm and the melody that enhance our delight are all parts of the modern art of stage dancing. And it is of this art that the writer seeks to tell the story in the present volume.

Both the theatre and the dance have had their abundant historians. The dance is ages older than the theatre. The time of the coming of the dance to the theatre and their fitting union ever after has been recorded. They have advanced together hand in hand through the years since their first meeting and are closer companions at this hour than ever before.

Stage dancing is no longer the haphazard stepping of feet to music that it was in the beginning. From its earlier crude efforts it has developed into a modern art, a profession of the first class, calling for brain and ability at their very best, its devotees giving years of labor to perfecting themselves in their chosen art.

MODERN STAGE DANCING

MODERN stage dancing differs from social or ballroom dancing in that it is the kind of dancing that one can commercialize.

Most of the artistic and financial successes of the stage today are built upon music and dancing. We find these two essential elements in opera, revue, musical comedy, pantomime and vaudeville, while the place of the dance in moving pictures may well be recognized. Should the old-time minstrel show come back, as it is certain to do, there will be added another name to the list of active entertainments that call for a union of music and dancing to insure their prosperity.

The Follies, the Frolics, the Scandals, the Music Box, the Vanities, the Passing Shows—by whatever name the modern revue is spread before an eager public, the basis of its appeal is always the same. And when the Junior Leagues—the various charity organizations and the social and college clubs of our cities stage a performance that shall appeal to the interest of their public, and consequently gather in the shekels to their coffers, these amateur organizations turn naturally to music and dance and spectacle as the mediums with the widest appeal; an appeal to both the performer and the spectator.

Incidentally, let me say that the appeal of music and the dance to the performer, whether on the professional or the amateur stage, is not given the consideration to which it is entitled. Perhaps nobody in the audience cares whether or not the dancer is enjoying the dance. But let me tell you, the dancer is having just as good a time up there on the stage as you are down in front; and probably you never gave the matter a thought!

The dancers' enjoyment of the art is an essential factor in the causes that lead to the popularity of our modern type of stage entertainment. To have acquired proficiency in their chosen profession the dancers have labored strenuously and long, and now the reward of years of effort is theirs. They love their art as well as its emoluments. By industry and perhaps frugality they have acquired an independent career for life. They have made much of their opportunities. They have a right to be happy. And they are.

Probably no man ever lived who knows personally so many dancing folks as I do, and among all my stage acquaintances and friends I can count on a very few fingers the number that I would not class as supremely happy in their profession, and those few who might be considered as unhappy are made so by circumstances entirely apart from the stage, or, in a few instances, because of their own folly and indiscretions. The stage world is a happy world in the main. Its rewards are abundant in friendships as well as in cash, and the happiness radiated to you from behind the foot-lights is the direct result of the happiness that permeates the very being of the smiling favorite of the gods whose efforts to please you have met with your approbation. So the pleasure of dancer and spectator are in a degree mutual, which in great measure explains the fascination that the dancing show has for the public.

In nearly every amateur stage performance in my long experience there have been present some few who exhibited natural ability as dancers, and possessed foundation requirements for professional stage work. In cases where these favored ones have placed themselves under my instruction their improvement has been rapid and sure.

There is no such thing as an untrained successful dancer; there never has been; there never will be. Given that one has the ability requisite to a knowledge of the dance, the rest comes from active training, and nothing else. And by "ability" I do not mean experience, but rather that natural talent to step to music and observe tempo and rhythm that every dancer must possess. It is a talent inborn in the dancer, and needs only proper development under competent instruction to bring out all the possibilities that are in one. Beyond that, and after the days of instruction are over, the only limit is the personality, the mental ability and the originality of the dancer himself, and these we encourage in every possible manner, for that way lies the electric sign in front of a Broadway Theatre, and all that goes with it in glory and gold.

It is to the amateur dancer of today that the professional stage looks for its recruits. There never before has been so great a demand for stage dancers as exists now, and the supply for both solo and ensemble work barely suffices. Talent naturally is encouraged by this condition of the market for its wares, and all who take advantage of this popularity and qualify for the better grade positions will find little difficulty in securing what they are entitled to.

I am anxious to get over with one part of this book that seems necessary to its complete understanding by a reading public, and that is the very personal subject of myself, its author. I am going to permit entrance into these pages of a brief biography of Ned Wayburn for two distinct reasons: First, to establish by what route I came to be an authority on stage-craft and stage dancing; and second, by a recital of my personal struggle and effort and final success, to encourage all young men and young women of ambition to themselves enter upon the stage of our great calling, with every hope of future success.

To that end, I am permitting a friend to come on the stage with his story of my stage career and experience.

As I look back upon my own history, it seems like a romance. And it is; a romance in real life; every word of it true, and the entire scenario as wonderful as anything in the movies.

ANN PENNINGTON

THE THREE REILLY'S—ALICE, GRACIE AND JOHNNY

EVELYN LAW

LINA BASQUETTE

NED WAYBURN—AN INSPIRATION

By Carleton B. Case

EVERY line of endeavor has its outstanding leaders. The men and women who do great things in a grand way ever command our admiration. We like to hear about their public careers and the intimate side of their exceptional lives is of decided interest to us. This I think is especially true where the noted ones are among our public entertainers, the player-folk, who bring so much joy and happiness into the world out of nothing—creators of innocent pleasure.

Long years before this was penned, and while yet my locks were innocent of the whiteness that now typifies my years, I was closely associated with the family of Wayburn. I was a man in Chicago when Ned Wayburn was a boy in the same city, starting on what was destined to become a truly remarkable career.

I know Ned Wayburn well. He is a king and a thoroughbred, as man or as manager, and to know him is to esteem him.

His fame is peculiar in that it is based so largely

on the success of other people—the actors and dancers whom he has discovered or directed and so helped to become stars of the first magnitude. To name them by hundreds is easy; to number all who are approaching stardom or who, now well placed on the professional stage, have materially profited by his aid and instruction, will go into the thousands. Surely such a record of achievement is ample cause for pride.

Ned Wayburn possesses an almost uncanny faculty of discerning latent talent in the line of his profession. You may not know one dance step from another, yet his discerning eye will detect a possibility for you in some branch of the dancing art that results will later prove as correct as they are surprising to yourself.

I have heard him tell of Evelyn Law, that when she first came to the studio she exhibited a tap and step dance as her specialty.

"This type of dancing was totally unsuited to her," said Ned, "and I told her so. And I also told her what her 'line' was. She took my advice, and today she leads the world in that type of dancing, and her salary has four figures in it every week."

The man who can do that is a genius, and Ned Wayburn has done it many, many times.

There is one outstanding fact in his entire career as producer of shows and director of the education of his pupils in his dancing studios: He insists that everything and everybody about him shall be "the best." His studios are fitted up "the best," regardless of cost. Sixty thousand dollars he paid for the fittings and furnishings of the two floors contained in his perfect establishment for teaching dancing at Columbus Circle, Broadway and Sixtieth Street, New York. His instructing staff must be "the best." His pupils must be "the best." I mean by that, not that the pupils are so qualified when they enter, but that when they are ready to graduate from his institution into the professional life of the stage, then they must be "the best"; nothing else will do.

So, too, in his own stage productions, and he has several, and more are in prospect. They are nowhere slighted. The best cast, music, dancing, costumes, scenery—everything—always. Ned never was a piker. He wasn't born that way. Lavish some consider him, but he finds his luxuriant presentations are appreciated by the line in front of the box office. He couldn't put on a "cheap" show if he wanted to. One goes to a Ned Wayburn show with the assurance of getting his money's worth in beauty and pleasurable entertainment. It pays; and the financial test is after all the one criterion by which to form a final judgment in things theatrical.

Now I am going to give some details of the inspiring career that began with an ambitious boy possessed of an artistic temperament, a love of music and of the beautiful, and who was at the same time a "hustler" and a born executive—a career developed by experience, still in progress and not yet at its culmination. As you read, it will seem almost incredible that one man, still comparatively young, could in so brief a period have accomplished so much that calls for great mental stress and extraordinary physical activity.

Ned Wayburn was born in Pittsburgh, Pennsylvania, where his parents were socially prominent. Later the Wayburn family moved to Atlanta, Georgia, and thence to Chicago. During his school days he first attracted attention as an amateur athlete, winning recognition as a fast runner, trick skater, tennis player, center rush on various football teams, and finally as a semi-professional baseball pitcher and home-run hitter. While employed in his father's manufacturing plant in Chicago, he took part in many amateur theatricals, and became noted as a dramatic coach for charity entertainments and clubs, leading cotillions and taking part in many society and club entertainments.

It was at that time that his success in directing and writing dialogue for amateur theatricals attracted the attention of Hart Conway, of the Chicago School of Acting, who promptly engaged him as assistant. At the same time, he had the privilege of seeing and studying the greatest stars and the best attractions at the Chicago Grand Opera House, where he began at the very bottom of the ladder as an usher in the gallery, balcony and main floor. Finally he became chief usher—then sold tickets for the gallery—took tickets at the main door. The late Aaron Hoffman, famous playwright, was opera glass boy at that time with him, and the well-known star, Taylor Holmes, was one of his ushers! Eventually he became Assistant Superintendent of that theatre.

To gain additional experience, Ned worked as a "super" with many different attractions, including the companies of Olga Nethersole, Otis Skinner, Walker Whiteside, Julia Stuart, etc., finally playing small parts in the legitimate and Shakespearian drama.

Having displayed a natural aptitude as a director while holding "prompt books" at rehearsals, he became a dramatic director and actor of eccentric comedy and character parts. Then his natural instinct for dancing asserted itself, and he became a specialty dancer, practicing from three to eight hours a day to perfect his dancing, incidentally developing his talent as a musician.

The late Col. John Hopkins saw Ned Wayburn at a society benefit performance in Chicago, and induced him

to play one week's engagement. Thus Ned Wayburn
made his first professional appearance at Hopkins' Theatre, State Street, Chicago, being billed as "Chicago's
Leading Amateur"— a singing and dancing "black-faced"
comedian, doing a "ragtime piano" specialty, and dancing act. This led to other engagements. The "piano
specialty," which he originated, started the "ragtime"
craze. He played in and around Chicago and the middle
west. He came East to New York, and was booked by
the late Phil Nash, on the Keith Circuit, billed as "The
Man Who Invented Ragtime." In his piano specialty
he created the idea of playing the classics in "Ragtime,"
being the first person on the stage to play "Mendelssohn's
Wedding March," "Oh Promise Me," "Star-Spangled
Banner," etc., in syncopated rhythm or "Ragtime." He
was also the first on the stage to do imitations of the harp,
bagpipe, mandolin, banjo, etc., on the piano. His act was
much imitated all over the world.

Upon reaching New York he met with misfortune.
There was no piano for him at his opening performance
and his original act had been stolen and performed in New
York ahead of his appearance. This culminated in a period
without work. Finally he found himself walking Broadway from one Thursday morning until late Saturday
night, with neither food nor money!

Having looked forward so much to New York and what
he expected it to bring him, he was at first discouraged
and inclined to give up and go back home with each succeeding rebuff, but he made up his mind to stick it out, no
matter what he had to do until he got on in a first class
company. After months of patient canvassing of all managers' and agents' offices where he was denied recognition,
he was finally given an opportunity, through an acquaint-
ance who heard him play in a 26th St. theatrical boarding

house, to demonstrate his ability in a try-out for the most popular star on Broadway at the time, May Irwin. She immediately recognized his ability and gave him an engagement at $25.00 per week, to introduce ragtime to Broadway. (He was receiving $125.00 per week when he first came to New York.) He wrote for Miss Irwin the first ragtime song, "Syncopated Sandy." He was so hard up at the time that he sold a one-half interest in this song to a man named Stanley Whiting for $25.00, so this man could have his name on the song as co-author. For an entire season she sang it and he played it in the performances of "The Swell Miss Fitzwell" at the old Bijou Theatre, New York City (Broadway between 30th and 31st Sts.). "Syncopated Sandy" sold over 1,000,000 copies. It was used to teach people to play ragtime. All Mr. Wayburn ever received out of its publication was a $15.00 advance royalty, which he was glad to get. He also helped write the third act of "The Swell Miss Fitzwell," and re-wrote the second act, including some of the musical numbers, for which he received no royalty. Incidentally, he was promoted to the position of stage director by Miss Irwin, and wrote some of her most successful songs, receiving a salary of $30.00 per week. He taught society to play ragtime and to cakewalk. However, he had confidence in his ability and worked hard to gain experience. He canvassed the music stores while en route with the company and sold sheet music which helped defray his expenses, and he saved his spare pennies. Finally, he signed up with Mathews and Bulger, a very popular team of stars.

From that moment the star of success glowed brightly for Ned Wayburn. For two years following he toured the United States and Canada with Dunne and Ryley's musical comedy success, "By the Sad Sea Waves," which he helped write and stage, introducing "ragtime," now known as "Jazz," to America in nearly every city of over 5,000 population. Gertrude Hoffmann was one of his dancing girls in the chorus of this show.

Being a born musician he turned his talents, in his spare time, to writing songs, many of which became quite popular, and from which he derived considerable revenue. "He Ain't No Relation of Mine," "Spend Your Money While You Live 'Cause You're Gonna Be a Long Time Dead," "Ragtime Jimmie's Jamboree," etc., etc.

Mr. Wayburn then staged George M. Cohan's first musical play, "The Governor's Son," and George Ade's first musical play, "The Night of the 4th," the latter at Hammerstein's Victoria Theatre, New York, with Joseph Coyne and Harry Bulger as the featured comedians. Thus began an unending succession of triumphs as a theatrical producer and stage director.

Mr. Wayburn was engaged by Oscar Hammerstein as producing stage director for Hammerstein's Victoria Theatre Paradise Roof Gardens, at 42nd Street and 7th Avenue, where the Rialto Theatre now stands, where he had charge three summers and staged the very first "girl" acts, including Ned Wayburn's "Jockey Club" with the Countess Von Hatzfeldt, which toured to the Pacific Coast and back to New York, booked by Martin Beck.

He was then engaged by Sire Bros. as producing stage director for their New York Theatre and Roof Gardens where he, a mere boy, staged and directed the greatest company of stars ever assembled under one roof, including Jessie Bartlett Davis, Mabelle Gilman, Virginia Earle, Marie Dressler, Nina Farrington, Thomas Q. Seabrooke, Dan McAvoy, Junie McCree, Louis Harrison, Marion Winchester, Emma Carus, etc., etc. "The Hall of Fame" was one of many productions staged for them.

He then became producing stage director for Klaw and Erlanger. During the next four years produced and helped to create:

"The Billionaire" with Jerome Sykes, "Bluebeard" with Eddie Foy, "The Rogers Brothers in London," "The Rogers Brothers in Paris," "The Rogers Brothers in Ireland," "The Rogers Brothers in Panama," "The Ham Tree" with McIntyre and Heath, "Mother Goose" with Joseph Cawthorne, "Humpty-Dumpty," "The White Cat," "The Pearl and the Pumpkin," "Little of Everything" with Fay Templeton and Pete Dailey, and many other productions for the New Amsterdam Theatre and Roof, also for the New York Theatre Roof, acting as general stage director of both. He leased and managed the New York Theatre Roof Gardens, where he conceived and produced some very successful headline vaudeville acts, among them, "Ned Wayburn's Minstrel Misses," and "Ned Wayburn's Rain-dears," which afterward played the Keith circuit and other vaudeville theatres to previously unequaled success.

Left Klaw and Erlanger to engage in the vaudeville producing field for himself through the encouragement of B. F. Keith, E. F. Albee, Percy G. Williams, William Hammerstein, F. F. Proctor and Martin Beck. Owned and produced the following headline acts: "The Futurity Winner," "The Star Bout," "The Rain-dears," with Neva Aymar; "The Dancing Daisies," with Dorothy Jardon; "The Phantastic Phantoms," with Larry and Rosie Ceballos; "The Side Show," with Harry Pilcer, and about 100 other big acts. Produced his own musical comedy attraction, "A One Horse Town."

For Mortimer H. Singer at the La Salle Theatre, Chicago, produced the following Musical Comedies: "The Time, the Place and the Girl," starring Cecil Lean—and which ran 464 consecutive performances to "standing room only"; "The Girl Question," "The Golden Girl," "The Goddess of Liberty," "Honeymoon Trail," "The Girl at the Helm," "The Heart Breakers," etc.

Founded "Ned Wayburn's Training School for the Stage," which first occupied the American Savings Bank Building, 115 West 42nd Street, between Broadway and 6th Avenue, New York City, and then expanded to the entire five-story building at 143 West 44th Street, next to the Hudson Theatre and opposite the Lambs Club. John Emerson, President of the Actor's Equity Association, and Zelda Sears, author of "The Lollypop," and many other successes, were then members of his faculty.

For the Shuberts and Lew Fields staged "The Mimic World," at the Casino Theatre, New York. For Lew Fields (of Weber and Fields), at the Broadway Theatre and Herald Square Theatre staged: "The Midnight Sons," "The Jolly Bachelors," "The Hen Pecks," "The Summer Widowers," "The Never Homes," "The Wife Hunters," "Tillie's Nightmare," starring Marie Dressler; Lew Fields in "Old Dutch," Victor Herbert's "The Rose of Algeria," etc.

For the Messrs. Shubert at the Casino Theatre, N. Y., the following musical comedies: "The Girl and the Wizard," starring Sam Bernard; "Havana," with James T. Powers (made the American version of this libretto); "The Prince of Bohemia," with Andrew Mack, and "Mlle. Mischief," starring Lulu Glaser.

Staged and appeared in "The Producer," written by William Lebaron, a headline vaudeville production (fifty people) which opened at Hammerstein's Victoria Theatre, New York City, and played for months in vaudeville, headlining in all principal eastern cities.

Staged "The Military Girl," starring Cecil Lean and Cleo Mayfield, at the Ziegfeld Theatre in Chicago. Engaged by Lee and J. J. Shubert as producer for New York Winter Garden, created a policy for that theatre and a formula for musical productions still used there; staged "The Passing Show of 1912," "The Honeymoon Express," with Al Jolson and Gaby Deslys, "Broadway to Paris," "The Passing Show of 1913," etc.

For the English manager, Albert de Courville, at the Hippodrome, London, England, at the highest terms ever paid a stage director, he directed George Robey, Ethel Levey, Harry Tate, Billy Merson, Shirley Kellogg, and other famous continental stars.

He staged "Hullo Tango" (ran over one year), "Zig-Zag" (ran one and one-half years), "Box of Tricks," "Joybells," etc.

Opened offices in London, producing "The Honeymoon Express," which ran five years in London and the provinces; produced "Dora's Doze," at Palladium Music Hall, and leased Middlesex Music Hall, London, to stage his own musical productions with American, French and English stars, in association with Oswald Stoll, but was obliged to stop productions there when war was declared.

* * *

Next he staged and presented his own production of a farce, "She's In Again," at Gaiety Theatre, New York City; also put on his own $150,000 production of "Town Topics," with Will Rogers, at the Century Theatre, New York, for which playhouse he created a Continental Music Hall policy.

It was soon after this that he accepted an engagement as producer and general stage director for Florenz Ziegfeld and staged the "Follies of 1916," "Follies of 1917," "Follies of 1918," and "Follies of 1919."

In addition to the above, Mr. Wayburn devised and staged for Mr. Ziegfeld nine successful Midnight Frolics and two Nine O'Clock Revues atop the New Amsterdam Theatre, New York, during this time.

For Mesmore Kendall, devised and staged the opening presentation for the Capitol Theatre, New York City, September, 1919, including an elaborate and very successful revue.

For Dillingham and Ziegfeld, at Century Theatre, New York, he devised and staged the sensationally successful second act finale to "The Century Girl" (1916), where the 50-foot circular revolving stage was employed so ingeniously in the "Uncle Sam" finale.

Staged "Miss 1917" at the Century Theatre, New York, with Irene Castle, Elsie Janis and 40 other stars.

For Lew Fields: "The Poor Little Ritz Girl."

For A. L. Erlanger and B. C. Whitney: "The Ed Wynn Carnival," at the New Amsterdam Theatre, N. Y.

For A. L. Erlanger: "Two Little Girls in Blue" (with the Fairbanks Twins, Oscar Shaw and Evelyn Law), at the George M. Cohan Theatre, N. Y.

Founded Ned Wayburn Studios of Stage Dancing and Ned Wayburn Booking Offices.

Staged F. Ziegfeld's production, starring Will Rogers, also "Follies of 1922," which ran 67 consecutive weeks in New York City and about 40 weeks on tour. No other "Follies" up to this time ever ran over 16 weeks in New York. Produced many vaudeville acts, among them, "Ned Wayburn's Dancing Dozen." Arranged motion-picture presentations for the Famous Players-Lasky Theatres. In association with Ben Ali Haggin produced several tableaux, including "Simonetta," "Dubarry," and "The

Green Gong," which were presented in many of the principal cities. Staged the musical comedy "Lady Butterfly," at Globe Theatre, New York.

Staged the Anatol Friedland headline girl act for the Keith-Albee and Orpheum vaudeville circuits, and "The Birth of Venus," a series of beautiful tableaux which were shown in many principal motion picture and vaudeville theatres. Staged for Florenz Ziegfeld "Follies of 1923," at New Amsterdam Theatre, New York, which attraction played to the largest week's receipts of any Follies ever produced at New Amsterdam Theatre.

Staged the following headline vaudeville productions:

"NED WAYBURN'S HONEYMOON CRUISE"

—an elaborate junior musical comedy, adapted for vaudeville, with a cast of dancers, principals and ensemble, composed entirely of pupils of the Ned Wayburn Studios. This act, the highest priced in vaudeville, started on tour in January, 1924, and broke all box-office records of the Poli Theatres in New England, as well as those of many other theatres on the Keith-Albee Circuit, including the premiere vaudeville theatre of the world, Keith-Albee Palace Theatre, New York, and the new $7,000,000 Earle Theatre in Philadelphia. It is still breaking records, and is one of the most sought-after acts in vaudeville.

"NED WAYBURN'S DEMI-TASSE REVUE"

—another headline act, composed entirely of pupils of the Ned Wayburn Studios. Now on the Keith-Albee and Orpheum Circuits.

The opening engagement at Bridgeport broke the attendance record of the Palace Theatre there and the same results followed at New Haven, Hartford and Worcester, when the audiences and newspaper critics alike declared the Revue even better than Ned Wayburn's "Honeymoon Cruise," which had previously held the attendance records in those cities.

"NED WAYBURN'S SYMPHONIC JAZZ REVUE"

Another new production, also composed of pupils of the Ned Wayburn Studios—touring the principal motion picture theatres in the Middle West and also Keith-Albee and Orpheum Circuits.

Staged the dances for Geraldine Farrar in an Operatic Fantasie—"Carmen" (all the dancers in this production being pupils of the Ned Wayburn Studios).

SOCIETY, UNIVERSITY AND PRIVATE ENTERTAINMENTS

For Mrs. William K. Vanderbilt, 2nd, devised and staged her "Mah Jong Fete" at the Hotel Plaza, New York, for the Big Sisters charity, December, 1923, and her "Persian Jazz Fete," December, 1924.

The Princeton Triangle Club's Musical Comedy, "Drake's Drum" last year and "The Scarlet Coat" this year.

The Filene Store's musical comedy, "The Caddie Girl," Colonial Theatre, Boston, in April, 1924, and "Barbara Lee," in April, 1925, presented at the Tremont Theatre, Boston, for one week, with Leah Ainsworth, a Ned Wayburn pupil, in the title role.

Penn. State College Thespian Club's Show, "The Magazine Cover Girl" last year, and "Wooden Shoes" this year.

The Third Annual Masonic Fashion and Home Exposition at Madison Square Garden, New York, May, 1924.

Elaborate entertainments for the Willys-Overland Company, at the Hotel Biltmore, New York (three years).

Jewelers' 24-Karat Club Annual Entertainment at the Waldorf-Astoria Hotel, New York (three successive years).

"Own Your Own Home Exposition," at Trenton, New Jersey.

Shriner's Frolic, at Washington, D. C.

Kansas City "Junior League Follies" (December, 1924).

Atlanta "Junior League Follies" (February, 1925).

A Musical Revue for the New York Edison Co., 1925 (so successful it had to be repeated).

The Providence Junior League Show, 1925.

The New Haven "Junior League Nautical Bal Cabaret," 1925.

The Vincent Club Musical Comedy, "Fez," in Boston (April, 1925).

"The Chatterbox Revue" in Rochester (April, 1925).

The Massachusetts "Tech" Show, "The Duchess of Broadway" (1925),—and a great many other society, charity, masonic and church entertainments.

It is out of this amazingly wide and varied experience that Ned Wayburn evolved the courses in stage dancing, stage-craft and showmanship which are being taught with such great success today at the Ned Wayburn Studios.

Ned Wayburn is known to thousands as the genius who staged the very best editions of "The Follies" and "Midnight Frolics" at the New Amsterdam Theatre, N. Y. But in the world of the theatre—among those who *know*—he is recognized as America's foremost creator, producer and director of musical comedies, revues, headline vaudeville productions, motion picture presentations, fétes and every other form of entertainment that features beautiful, original or spectacular dancing.

His versatility knows almost no limit. His wealth of theatrical experience runs the gamut from his own first appearance as an amateur actor and coach to a succession of triumphs as producing director of the most gorgeous theatrical presentations both here and abroad.

Added to his practical stage-craft there is the vital flame of imaginative genius, a creative faculty that clearly stamps all his work. It is this, as well as his extraordinary executive ability and his all-embracing knowledge of stage technique, that makes him the most sought-after of all directors. It also explains the distinct advantage which pupils of the Ned Wayburn Studios have over all others, in that they are being constantly sought for desirable engagements because of the thorough way in which they are trained, both physically and mentally, in dancing.

THE NED WAYBURN METHOD OF TRAINING

THERE are five basic types of stage dancing that I teach, covering the modern field in full, and supplying the pupil with a complete knowledge of all the steps needed for a successful stage career.

These five types consist of:

Musical Comedy Dancing,

Tap and Step Dancing (Clogging),

Acrobatic Dancing,

Exhibition Dancing (Ball-room),

Modern Americanized Ballet Dancing.

The last named includes all the best variety of ballet dances, such as toe, classical, character, interpretive, oriental, folk, national, covering Spanish, Russian, Greek, Javanese, etc.

Instruction is given in any or all of the above to beginners, advanced amateurs, professionals and teachers, and is preceded in every case by the Ned Wayburn Foundation Technique, which includes my limbering and stretching process, and is one of the most important courses ever devised for the, student of dancing in that it saves years of study. This original technique is described in a succeeding chapter.

In addition to the types of dancing mentioned above, we also give instruction in the art of making up for the stage.

Accompanying the technical instruction, each class and pupil receives without cost the benefit of the valuable stage-craft, managerial and producer's knowledge that I have acquired during my years of activity in the theatrical world. This is given in occasional lectures or inspirational talks before the class. Students also, when duly fitted, will be informed as to where and how to obtain engagements, correct forms of contract to be entered into, and other valuable business information concerning the practical side of selling their services to the best advantage, saving them much time and possible embarrassment and loss.

In all probability, if you love dancing and aspire to make it a career, you possess an innate sense of rhythm. You feel the swing of music and love to move your body to the strains of a lilting melody. The first great possessions of the successful stage dancer are a love of harmonious sounds and a sense of rhythmic motion. If you haven't these, you might better abandon the idea of studying with me as far as any hope is concerned of my developing you into a stage artist. While you would find much to enjoy and to benefit your health and appearance in taking my dancing exercises, if you are minus the very first dancing essentials you could not expect us to advance you beyond your own limitations.

Another important qualification for the stage dancer, which if not possessed at its fullest may be acquired under our instruction, is a sense of direction. This sense of direction is of maximum importance in stage dancing, because, as you can readily understand, since you have your audience in front of you and to your left and your right, you must do your dances so that they will appeal to all sections of your audience. And there are certain stage directions which you must know in order to grasp my method of instruction.

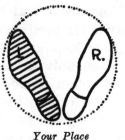

Your Place

That you may get absolute precision in direction, let us proceed as follows: Imagine that you are standing on a stage, in a circle the diameter of your own feet; we will call that circle "your place."

Divide the stage into eight different directions. You are now facing the "front." Face the "left," the "back," the "right," and then "front" again. That makes four directions—front, left, back and right. Face half-way to the left—that is called "left oblique." Face half-way to the back—that is called "left oblique back." Now face back. Face half-way to the right—that is called "right oblique back." Now face half-way to the front. That is called "right oblique." That makes eight different directions, very easy to memorize and never forgotten after once learned, and you will employ them in your stage work every day. That they may become familiar with the necessary directions, students are

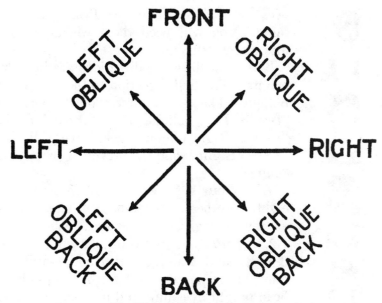

The Eight Different Directions

given brief instructions at their first lesson, as I stand before them and take the turns with them and announce the name of each direction as I take it.

Left Turn

In making the turn from wall to wall, when you turn to the left around, you should turn on the right heel, which thus acts as a pivot and keeps you in "your place"; like this — left oblique, left, left oblique back, back, right oblique back, right, right oblique, and front. In going around to the right turn on the left

Right Turn

Turning the Head

heel. Fix these directions firmly in your mind. You will need them when you get into stage dancing.

The eight different directions are in eight counts. The first direction to the left is left oblique. That is counted "one." Left is "two." Left oblique back, "three." Back, "four." Right oblique back, "five." Right, "six." Right oblique, "seven." Front is "eight."

All of our steps are taught in counts of eight. We begin to count from one and go as far as eight, then repeat. We count, 1,2,3,4,5,6,7,8, or we count "1-and, 2-and, 3-and, 4-and, 5-and, 6-and, 7-and, 8-and," as may be required. After the steps have been taught by counts and learned properly, through much patient practice, they are fitted to music.

Without turning the rest of the body, turn the head sharply to the left wall, so that your face is square to the wall. You are now looking left. Look front. Look to the right (square around). Look front. Look left oblique. Front. Right oblique. Front. Now throw the head back and look up (without straining the muscles of the neck) —hold the head at an angle of about 45 degrees. Your head should not be tilted to one side, but straight back. Now look "front" again—now "down," now "front." There is a difference between *turning* it to the left or right and *inclining* to left or right. Incline your head to the left shoulder—hold your face up a little and keep it square to the front—chin high—now incline your head to the right shoulder—up straight—now turn it to the left (around as far as you can)— turn it front—turn it to the "right"—turn it "front—throw it "back"—look up, now "front"—drop "down" and now "front."

THE LESSON TO A CLASS IS AS FOLLOWS

Now, be careful to keep your lines straight up and down, directly behind one another. Let those in the first line *across* raise the right hand. Second line across

Inclining the Head

raise hands up; third line across, and fourth line across. This is called across stage (indicating left to right). This is called up and down stage (indicating front to back), and going down this way (to the footlights) is moving down-stage. Going toward the back wall is moving up-stage or back-stage.

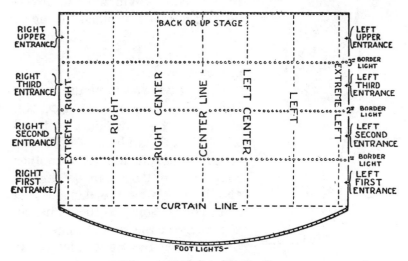

Diagram of Modern Theatre Stage

CONCERNING ENTRANCES AND EXITS

If you come in sight of the audience from that side (indicating left) you are making an entrance from the left. If you leave in that direction, you are making an exit to the left. It is an artistic feat to make a good exit. It requires not only specialized training, but also practical experience in front of an audience. It may be a vocal exit, a dramatic or spoken exit, or a dancing exit, and one must reach a decided climax at the exit. If the dance consists of eight steps, properly spaced, the most effective steps are put in where they will provoke applause. The last or finish step must get the most applause or the dancer fails. So we put a climactic "trick" step in for a finish, and then we top that with the exit, and the exit must be a *surprise*. Otherwise, the dance has not built up from the time the dancer makes an entrance and gets the attention of the audience. So making an effective exit is really a difficult thing to do. You are taught in the advanced instruction how to enter and exit properly.

Correct
Standing Position

One draws the applause on the eighth step by assuming a certain attitude or by "striking a picture" which asks the audience for the applause, and on the exit another round of applause can be earned, and in this way the dance "gets over," or is "sold" to the audience, as we say in the show business.

Now face the right, please. If you make an exit on that side you

are making an exit to the right. If you come on from that side (meaning if you come in sight of the audience from that side) you are making an entrance from the right.

The proper way to stand to learn my kind of stage dancing is with the left toe pointed left oblique, and the right toe right oblique. Have your knees together, heels together, with the weight equally distributed between the feet, hands down at the side, arms relaxed, heads up and direct your gaze straight ahead on a line with your eyes.

Never recognize anyone over the footlights. Always look straight front on a line with the eyes. Never look at the floor when dancing unless specifically so instructed. To look at the floor while dancing gives an audience the impression that you have no confidence in yourself and that you are laboring to perform your dance.

In dancing, the head and arms and upper part of the body (torso or trunk) are as important as the feet and legs.

Movements of Eyes Only

The eyes are the most expressive agent of the body.

Now, without turning your head, using your eyes only, look left oblique, look front, look right oblique, front, look left oblique down, look front, look left oblique up, look front, look right oblique down, look right oblique up, look front.

Most of my instruction is based on the eight different directions which you have been told about, and on the four different parts of the foot, which you must also understand thoroughly. This makes it easy to analyze any dancing steps that we teach.

These four different parts of the foot are:

1, the toe, or end of the shoe.

2, the ball of the foot (the half sole).

3, the heel.

4, the flat of the foot.

Tapping the toe of the left foot to the floor makes the first count; stamping the ball of the left foot, the second count; the heel of the left, the third count; and the flat of the entire foot the fourth count. These four different parts of the foot become an exercise by counting 1, 2, 3, 4, with the left foot, and 5, 6, 7, 8, with the right foot, beginning with the right toe on the count of 5. This exercise if practiced faithfully will give flexibility to the muscles and ligaments that control the entire foot, all of which are used in musical comedy dancing, for the American tap, step and specialty work (clogging), for social or ball-room

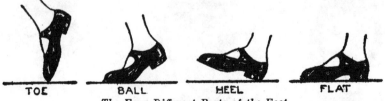

TOE   BALL   HEEL   FLAT

The Four Different Parts of the Foot

dancing, for exhibition dancing, as well as in the acrobatic dancing work, and for my Americanized ballet training, including toe dancing.

Do this exercise first with the left foot, then with the right foot, to the count of 1, 2, 3, 4, 5, 6, 7, 8, and practice it often, till it becomes a perfectly natural action. It is the basis of the best "bread and butter" dancing steps, as you will discover in later lessons.

In doing this exercise, remember that in dropping the toe to the floor it must be placed *straight* back, and not left or right oblique back; straight back from the "place" where you stand. The knees should be kept together. When you stamp the ball of your foot, the feet are directly opposite each other.

I want you to note that each of the four movements of this exercise has a distinct sound. The dropping of the

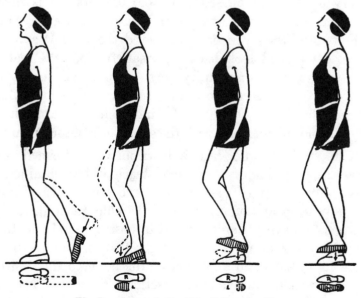

The Development of a "Tap" Dancing Step

toe, the stamping of the ball of the foot, of the heel, and of the flat foot, each creates a separate and distinct sound. I have named these sounds "taps," and it is the various combinations of these sounds that are used so effectively in musical comedy dances, in tap, step, and American specialty dancing (sometimes called clogging), as well as in some of our choicest acrobatic dancing.

Some of our pupils are apt at tap and step dancing, others are more apt at ballet dancing, musical comedy or acrobatic dancing. Some of our young ladies take four classes a day; some take three; others two; and still others but one class a day. In addition to this, there are pupils, among them a great many young gentlemen, who take private lessons in their chosen style of dancing every day while some only take one private lesson a week.

Try to perfect yourselves as solo dancers. It is there that fame and fortune await you. You may not appreciate it now, but when you have mastered the Ned Wayburn courses, you will look back with satisfaction and realize the wonderful opportunity my simple courses have afforded you. There is no other school in the world that teaches the five basic types of dancing in the same thorough, rapid manner and with the same satisfactory results.

The student who has industriously performed the essential preliminary work as I teach it has obtained a satisfactory mastery of the body, and has a large range of movement at command; is now able to control the source of movement and to relax opposing muscles so that the movement may follow through; that is, may continue from its initiative in any part of the body to the desired climax, without muscular obstruction. The entire body is now ready and responsive to any call upon it, and the act of dancing becomes a pleasure and a joy it never was before, and never would have been but for the preliminary work as I have arranged it for the making of beautiful and efficient dancers.

The result is a harmony of rhythmical coördination that will echo far beyond the dancing courses and into the various activities of one's whole life.

The great freedom and abandonment of movement now acquired is not a combination of erratic movements and gestures distributed at random. The freedom gained is the result of perfect control, not in any degree the result of unguided abandon. My dancers know how to work because they are sure of themselves; the controlled individual is the free individual.

But the dancer has gained more than mastery of movement. Valuable as are strength and skill, even more so is the resultant balance and soundness of the nervous system that directly results from such rhythmical coördination, fitting one for meeting the complex and often disturbing demands of life. Now, too, in the process of acquiring such a splendid state of general physical well-being, the pupil has absorbed and acquired some understanding of the power and the wonder of a physical self, and will proudly treat this newly discovered self with respect and consideration.

The mental gains as the result of this work have a right to consideration, also. The handicap of self-consciousness is largely overcome by the complete mastery of the movements of the body; the mind becomes freed, the mental horizon enlarged, as the direct result of body and nerve control.

The delight of free and expressive movement with a body that responds joyously to the slightest impulse of thought and feeling, develops a new resource of pleasure, and in perfection of bodily response is found a new source of beauty with endless promise for the future.

If you begin the courses with the feeling, "make me a dancer if you can," and act with indifference throughout the instruction that is given for your benefit, you are doomed to failure. No one succeeds unless they want to and work very hard.

You are here to prepare for an honorable calling, a beautiful, respected and profitable profession, that when once you acquire will remain at your disposal all your life. Most of our pupils recognize this and sincerely strive, with our help, to perfect themselves through incessant patient practice. We have no intention ever to let a small minority of indifferent, "I don't care" pupils, hold back the ambitious ones. Those who merit success shall have every opportunity always.

You, no doubt have been to good shows, seen good dancing and attractive posing and grouping, with rich scenery, proper lighting and appropriate music, and have wished that you, too, might share in the applause of the audience for your own merit as a dancer.

I want to help you become what so many others of my scholars have become, the best in their line of endeavor.

I am enthusiastic about my part of the work, and ask and expect you to be just as enthusiastic as I am. Really, you should have *more* enthusiasm than I have, since it is *you* who are to go before the audiences and get the applause and the pay, and not me. Whether or not you are enthusiastic about your work will show in your results. Your degree of interest and improvement is recorded, so I know just what you are accomplishing.

You must expect to get tired, really "tired out," in your earliest lessons and practice. That is what has invariably happened to all others before you, who are drawing down the fat salaries today. I expect it, and should be surprised indeed if any student proved to be an exception. In fact, if you do not tire, and perspire and pant after an hour of working your every muscle in a set of movements new to them, then you surely are not getting the benefit that the exercises are intended to promote. Soreness during your first four or five lessons is a sign of your having taken the lessons earnestly and honestly and actively, as you should in your own interest. The soreness will work out and be gone for good after a few lessons. Please get sore! Then I know you are all right.

But do not overdo at any time, now or later, in class work, private lessons, or home practice, and especially be careful while you are new at the work, and the novelty of it tempts your ambition to keep on and on. Alternate work and rest, strenuous toil and complete relaxation, is the ideal way to build yourself into beauty and strength and suppleness by my method, without danger of straining or injury.

In the classroom, if a pupil needs to sit and rest a bit occasionally it is permitted. But do not let our consideration for your comfort become an excuse for mere laziness! There are lazy girls as well as lazy men in the world, I have heard, and it is barely possible that one or two might decide to take my courses sometime. If they do, our required work will give them inspiration, as well as perspiration, and enable them to overcome an inclination to indolence that they must master if they hope to succeed as dancers—or in any other vocation.

Let me encourage you by saying, what I know to be true, that you will harden yourself in a few days' time so that the muscles of your body will pleasantly respond to your demands without crying out loud when called upon.

Just keep at it. Don't get discouraged because it wearies you on the start. If you could see our advanced pupils going through their routines, and how easily they perform the same simple exercises you are required to do in the beginning, their muscles ready, trained and responsive, and every motion of their bodies a pleasure to them and a satisfaction after patient practice, you would be encouraged and would be able to smile at the few temporary discomforts of a few sore muscles. But do not be too ambitious and work to the point of exhaustion.

CECIL LEAN

FAIRBANKS TWINS

OSCAR SHAW

VIVIENNE SEGAL

NED WAYBURN STAGE DANCES

I HAVE already named the five basic types of stage dancing taught in my courses. In this chapter I shall describe them in detail in such a manner that anyone can distinguish them from one another.

No doubt when you have seen dances of the new type executed on the theatrical stage you may have been unable in some cases to correctly classify them. That is not at all surprising, since the classification is my own, as well as some of the steps themselves.

You have realized that so-and-so did a pleasing, pretty and complicated dance, but what it is called, or if it is called at all, you are unable to state. All my dances have names and are properly classified, and what these are and to what distinct type they belong is going to be spread before you here and now.

First let us consider the type that I have n a m e d American Specialty Dancing, the one that is more truly and distinctively American than any other type of dancing to be seen on any stage today.

This classification comprises every variety of tap and step dancing, and also what is commonly known as "Legmania," the latter including the high-kicking features, where the leg will execute front, back, and side kicks, and other forms of the acrobatic type of dancing. Legmania is not a possible development for every student of dancing, as nearly every other form of the art is, but is available to the few who are adapted to its exacting technique, which insures that this interesting field will never grow too many blossoms, and that supply is not likely to equal demand. I will mention Evelyn Law in "Legmania" and Ann Pennington in "Tap and Step" dancing as "sample" stars from my studios in this beautiful and lucrative type of dancing, though their dancing limitations are by no means confined to this one branch of the art.

Tap and step dances are made up of a series of steps that involve certain movements of the four parts of the foot as described in another chapter; namely, the toe, the ball of the foot, the heel, and the flat of the foot, which produce distinct rhythmic sounds or "taps" as they separately strike the floor or stage.

Under the classification of tap and step dancing, we teach the buck and wing dance, the waltz clog, the straight clog (which is like an English clog or a Lancashier clog), jigs, reels, and the old form of what we call step dancing, which was popular forty years ago in the old "variety" days. They did the jigs, reels and clogs then, and these different types of dancing modernized combine to make what we today call the American Specialty type of dancing. My course in tap dancing, for instance, includes beginners' "buck" and "soft-shoe" dances, intermediate, advanced, semi-professional and professional "buck" and "soft-shoe" dances. Of course, when you get into the

semi-professional "buck" and "soft-shoe" you will begin
to get complicated "taps," and you will get difficult triple-
taps in professional "buck" dancing.

You are no doubt familiar in a general way with the
Musical Comedy type of dancing, which is really an exaggerated form of fancy dancing. It includes the now
popular but simpler "soft-shoe" dances, dainty, soft,
pretty movements with many effective attitudes of the
body, all sorts of "kicking" and "fancy" steps. As a
matter of fact, this type of dancing is perhaps the most
difficult of all to define exactly, because often musical
comedy dances include a few tap steps and sometimes simple ballet movements, or combinations, as we term them.
Our musical comedy dances are arranged in routines, or
sequences of not less than ten steps, including an entrance,
eight steps to the dance, and an exit movement. The
entrance is a travelling step, a step which gets you onto
the stage; then comes the dance itself consisting of eight
steps; then the exit which must include a step which will
make a decided climax to the whole dance. I have already
explained the importance of making an effective exit. In
a subsequent chapter, I will describe more in detail a
musical comedy routine.

Perhaps Acrobatic Dancing is the most difficult of all
the types to master—that is, it most certainly requires a
degree of strength that the other dances do not demand;
sufficient strength in the arms to support the weight of
the body in the hand-stand and the cartwheel, flexibility
of the muscles in order to do the "limbers" and back-bends.
All of the acrobatic tricks—hand-stands, cartwheels, splits,
roll-overs, back-bends, front-overs, inside-outs, nip-ups,
"butterflies," flip-flops, Boranis, somersaults, etc., are very
difficult and require special adaptability and inexhaustible
patience, but almost any normal human being between the

ages of four and thirty can learn even the advanced tumbling tricks in time, but only by keen application and persistent practice.

The fourth of the basic types of dancing is my Modern Americanized Ballet, a most graceful type of dance which requires and developes beauty and grace of motion of the head, the hands, the arms, the feet and legs, of the whole body, in fact. This Americanized ballet is subdivided into various types of dances—toe dancing, classical dancing, character dancing, interpretive dancing, covering all kinds of National and folk dancing. These have attention elsewhere in this volume.

Exhibition dancing constitutes the fifth type, and is varied in its possibilities. It is the kind you see exhibited by a dancing team in public and private ballrooms and at social or club functions, and may take the form of the exhibition fox trot, the exhibition one-step, the tango, the exhibition waltz or the whirlwind dance. It is very pretty and very profitable work for those who are adapted to its interpretation. This type of dancing is not taught in classes in the Ned Wayburn Studios, but is given special attention under qualified private tutors, in private lessons, and has prepared some remarkable dancers in this field. Two of the popular dances which I have conceived and arranged and which have lately swept the world are the ball-room "Charleston" dance and the exhibition "Charleston."

As my pupil you will discover in the course of your advancement that you have a particular preference for one of these types of dancing, or perhaps two, or three. Each person has his or her own personality, and certain personalities are better suited to the Tap and Step style of dancing than to the Ballet, for instance. But in order to meet the competition in stage dancing in the future, you require a knowledge of the five basic types, as outlined.

I cannot emphasize too strongly the importance of *personality* in a successful stage career. Along with the actual mastering of the dancing steps and acquisition of health and a beautiful body, comes just as surely the development of personality. And since each individual has a distinct personality it is advisable for everyone to select the type of dancing best suited to that personality. It is because of this quality that the performance of stars like Evelyn Law, Marilyn Miller, Ann Pennington, Gilda Gray and Fred and Adele Astaire leaves a lasting impression. Every step, every movement is designed to drive home the characteristics of their individuality. Even more important than the actual dancing steps they do is the manner in which they execute them—the individuality which gives expression to all that they do. It is the almost indefinable factor called personality which lifts one out of the ranks of the chorus and makes the solo dancer. In this book I am trying to help you develop your personality, in the way that I have discovered and developed the personalities of so many of today's stars.

Most emphatically I want to impress upon you that it is not "chorus work" that you learn in my courses. It is professional, individual dancing, taught thoroughly and completely.

Anyone who masters the dances takes on a certain confident feeling in time, after exercising great patience in practice. With this confidence the happy pupil radiates a new magnetic personality which the audience feels. But more about this later on, when you will learn just how one's self is injected into the dances until they are vitalized and made living exponents of a beautiful art.

NED WAYBURN'S FOUNDATION
TECHNIQUE

T HE human body is the instrument of the dancer,
and must be as much under the direct command of
the dancer as the violin is at the command of the
musician. It must respond instantaneously and without
effort to every emotion and thought in the dancer's mind.
To do this it is obvious that the physical mechanism of
the entire body must be completely mastered and controlled.

The first stage of the work to achieve command of the
human frame as a dancing instrument is to bring about
flexibility in all its parts and obtain muscular guidance
and control. This demands a special technique that shall
coördinate in harmonious functioning all parts of the
body by an unconscious effort of the mind.

The foundation technique which I evolved for the Ned
Wayburn courses is a limbering and stretching process for
the body, which precedes the teaching of dancing steps, fitting all pupils properly with a basis, a foundation for the
important work to come. Without these exercises, all of
which are set to inspiring music, muscles employed in
dancing would remain taut or soft and not respond properly, the pupil would quickly tire, and the attempt to
dance become an unavailing effort. With the limbering

and stretching course, time is saved in preparing the student for the lessons to come, and the time necessary for the training and development of a dancer is much shortened from the long apprenticeship that once prevailed under the old antiquated Ballet technique. What is known as the Ned Wayburn method brings into play all the bodily muscles that are essential to the dancer's use, gives strength, suppleness and symmetry to the entire body. All forms of outdoor exercise are valuable adjuncts to bodily health and strength and beauty, but supplementing them the dancer must carry on with just the foundation technique I have devised, in order to waken and strengthen the dancing muscles, a result not brought about by even the best of romping sports or one's other usual exercising.

In connection with correct diet, which has attention in later chapters of this book, my methods of preliminary exercise will aid the over-stout to reduce pleasantly and surely, and also enable the under-developed to put on needed weight, in both cases the attendant blessings of health, strength and symmetry following in due order.

My method induces perspiration, opens the pores, eliminates unhealthy tissue, and at the same time supplies new tissue replete with health, which is placed evenly over the entire body where nature wants it.

Do not let the words "limbering and stretching" mislead you. Perhaps there may be words that describe the work better than these do. But my idea in using these words is that flexibility, suppleness, grace and freedom of movement are all covered by "limbering," while "stretching" is intended to convey the idea of a proper fitting of the body and limbs for the various forms of kicking that are absolutely essential in modern stage dancing. Some people get the idea that stretching exercises will lengthen the body or limbs. This is not so. Neither is the result of any mechanical operation whatever. You bend your body rhythmically, and by degrees acquire a proficiency that enables you to "stretch" and "limber up" yourself to an extent that may surprise you. No one was ever hurt by my exercises; you gradually limber and stretch yourself! All who have taken the exercises and have practiced them as directed have materially benefited. They bring health, graceful figures and a fitness for learning dancing as nothing else does of which I have knowledge. That is what these exercises are for, and just what they do.

And another important fact in connection with my foundation technique for dancers, it does *not* bunch the muscles into unsightly shape; it does *not* make huge, knotty muscles in the arms and legs, as has long been the case with certain Russian and Italian ballet methods. You have no doubt seen ballet dancers with distorted bodies. The American woman will not be content with any development that mars the appearance of her figure, and she is right. You have seen the Ned Wayburn trained girls on many a stage, and never yet saw one that was not pleasing in figure, to put it mildly, and that is the way we insist in developing them at the studio. Our pupils acquire agility without angularity or unsightly protuberances anywhere. We take the "raw material," child or adult, between four and forty, with or without any former experience or training, proceed with them through my foundation technique of limbering and stretching, and advance them from there to courses in any of the various forms of dancing, with the perfect assurance that they have the necessary basis of flexibility and muscle control that will support them on their way to perfect dancing success.

In conjunction with this work, all types of kicking steps are taught, front kick, side kick, back kick, hitch kick, and the others. Since strength for kicking comes from the abdominal muscles, a workout that will especially exercise these muscles around the waist line is essential, and a series of strengthening activities is given to this end.

Imagine that you are in practice costume, one of a class of students similarly dressed, standing in line on a padded rug in my Foundation Technique studio. The instructor begins with the simple exercises, and directs you through a number of them during an hour's lesson today, repeating them briefly tomorrow and adding new ones to those you learned yesterday, till soon you have progressed through the entire list. The work is done rhythmically to music, and all exercises are in eight counts. Each is repeated in measured time till the class masters it, and the student is requested to practice the lessons at home faithfully and earnestly, and the proficiency thus acquired is looked for in the class work of the day after.

Here are a dozen of the Ned Wayburn series of Limbering and Stretching exercises selected from my Foundation Technique:

EXERCISE 1.

For limbering and stretching the triceps, and loosening the waist line along the sides.

Stand erect, head up, heels together, arms down at sides, raise right arm straight up over the head. Bend body to left as far as you can, sliding left hand down the thigh. Return to erect position, then with left arm raised bend to right. Alternate left and right eight times to count of "one, lean; two, lean," etc.

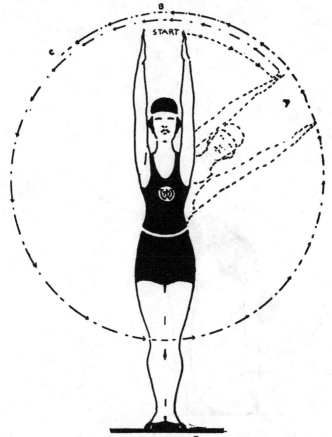

EXERCISE 2.

For loosening the dorsi and abdominal muscles, developing muscles of chest and waist line.

Stand erect, chin in, heels together, toes pointed out, raise left arm straight over head, right arm down at side. Swing right hand up over head also, and lean the body right oblique. Swing both arms down, then up and lean left oblique. Do this for eight counts of "one, lean; two, lean," etc.

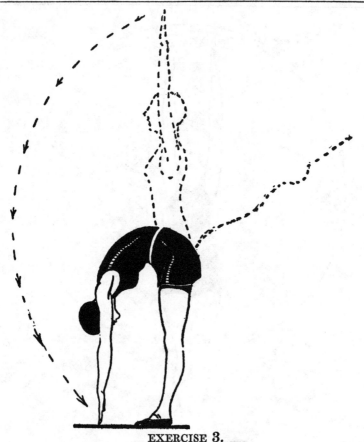

EXERCISE 3.

*For limbering muscles of the back, biceps
of the legs, developing abdominal muscles
and reducing waist line.*

(Forward bend.) Raise both arms straight over head
the width of the shoulders apart, heels together, knees
stiff. Bend forward and touch the floor with the palms of
both hands, if you can, if you cannot, then with the ends
of the fingers. Raise arms again over head and lean back
as far as you can. Count "one, touch; two, lean," etc., to a
count of eight.

EXERCISE 4.

For making the waist line flexible. It limbers the muscles of the thighs and back.

Stand erect, both hands above head, arms stiff. Keep hands in this position throughout, step left foot straight forward, bend the body back as far as you can. Then body erect and left foot returned to position. Step right foot front, bend back again. Alternate with each foot for eight counts: "left, lean, straight, in; right, lean, straight, in," etc.

To strengthen calves and ankles.

Stand erect, knees stiff, heels together, hands on hips. Rise on the toes; down, up, down, etc., for 48 counts.

EXERCISE 6.

For limbering the back and the waist line.

Kneel, knees about eight inches apart, trunk erect. Extend arms horizontally in front to count "one." On count of "two" raise the hands above the head, shoulder-width apart and lean back. Keep arms stiff. On count of "and," trunk again erect and arms extended front. On count of "three," hands over head and lean back. Repeat for eight counts.

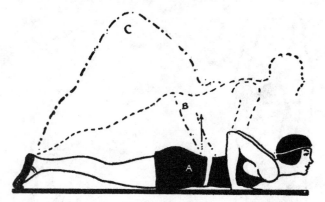

EXERCISE 7.

To strengthen the biceps and triceps of the arm.

From kneeling position of Exercise 6, lie flat on the stomach, palms on floor alongside the hips, elbows up, to count of "one." On count "two," raise the body, straightening arms, supporting body on hands and toes. Lower body to floor on count "three." Alternate raising and lowering body for sixteen counts.

EXERCISE 8.

For limbering and stretching the abdominal muscles.

Stand erect, heels together, chin in, chest out, step right foot forward, bend body front, place both hands flat on floor (footrace starting position). Jump, bringing right foot back and left foot forward at the same time. Jump, bringing left foot back and right foot forward. Right, left, right, left, for sixteen counts.

A   B

EXERCISE 9.

To develop the front of the thighs and the biceps.

Stand erect, feet fifteen inches apart. Raise arms straight above the head, shoulder-width apart. Keep toes and heels flat on the floor. Squat down, lowering arms as you do so until they are horizontally straight in front of you. Rise to erect position, raising arms at the same time above the head. Keep arms stiff. Down, up, down, up, for sixteen counts.

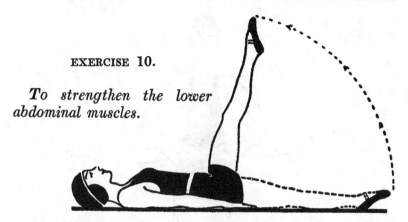

EXERCISE 10.

To strengthen the lower abdominal muscles.

Lie flat on your back, arms at sides, palms on floor. Keep knees stiff and together and toes pointed. Raise both feet so that toes point to ceiling. Count "one"; lower the feet to the floor. Count "two"; (do not hit the floor hard in lowering the feet). Count "one, down; two, down;" etc., to eight.

EXERCISE 11.

To strengthen the upper abdominal muscles and the diaphragm.

You are lying on your back. On count "one," sit up, bend forward, touch your toes with your hands and place your head against your knees. Count "touch." On count "two," bring your trunk erect, arms straight overhead. On count of "down" you are again lying in your back. Count "one, touch, two, down, three, touch, four, down," etc., to "eight, down."

EXERCISE 12.

To strengthen the thighs and biceps.

Stand erect, heels together. Raise arms horizontally to the sides. Bend the knees and assume a squatting position. Rise to erect position. Count "down, up, down, up," etc., eight times.

There are more than thirty different exercises given in the Ned Wayburn courses in this work. If you desire a complete list, address an inquiry to the Ned Wayburn Studios of Stage Dancing, Inc., 1841 Broadway (at Columbus Circle) entrance on 60th St., New York, for prospectus of the New Ned Wayburn Home Study Courses in Dancing.

THE BIRTH OF VENUS

MARION CHAMBERS.

VIRGINIA BACON

With sincere appreciation
to Ned Wayburn
whose producing
genius created
the "record breaking"
"Follies of 1922"

Gilda Gray

GILDA GRAY

MR. WAYBURN ADDRESSES THE BEGIN-NER'S CLASS IN FOUNDATION TECHNIQUE

YOU are starting on a course of not less than twenty lessons and exercises in my Foundation Technique for dancing, which is a feature exclusive to this studio, known as the Ned Wayburn Limbering and Stretching process for the human body.

This is one of the most important things that ever came into your life. It is at once a necessary foundation upon which to build the perfect dancer and an unequaled system of cultural exercises for the correction of certain physical ills in those who have no expectation of pursuing a professional career.

Primarily I originated this series of exercises to make good dancers quickly. There was nothing of the kind in existence that would do the work I wanted done, so I carefully thought it out myself, and finally developed the complete plan. Some of it will be taught you here. It has proven to be all I anticipated,—a method of preparing the muscles and ligaments to respond instantly to the dancer's call upon them for precise action. It is the object of this series of exercises to eliminate fatigue, create sturdy yet symmetrical and flexible frames and increase the health, grace and beauty of the participant. It is, therefore, no wonder that others than those who expect to enter upon a stage career have sought these exercises for their own improvement in personal appearance and physical well-being.

Now all please stand in line around the room, stand quietly and without leaning against the wall. Stand shoulder to shoulder, hands down at sides, heels together, feet flat down, toes pointing left oblique and right oblique; the weight equally distributed between the two feet. Hold your chin high and look straight ahead on a line with your eyes.

I organize the class by first arranging the pupils according to their height. There is a reason for this. If you are five feet tall and stand next to a girl who is five feet eleven, you at once become conscious of your size. It is to avoid this handicap of self-consciousness that I grade you by height.

You are now in line as to heights. Please each of you stand in front of a chair, one pupil to a chair, and number from "one" at the left end. Number thirteen will be called twelve and a half. Speak out your individual number loud and clear. This number you are given is your personal, distinctive number during the life of this class and is never changed. The number of this class is 501. As you call your number out loud please be seated in the chair back of you, and while the stenographer takes your names and the instructor collects your weekly tickets I will say a few words.

I expect you to arrive promptly in the classroom, and request that you time your arrival so as to be here in the studio at least fifteen minutes before class time, so as to be in your practice costume and ready for the call to class right on the hour set.

We have to observe discipline in all your work in the courses, otherwise nothing would be accomplished. We have printed rules posted in the office and elsewhere, and expect you to read and observe them.

Please do not talk at all during class work. It interrupts the work seriously. You have all been to school before and know that silence is one of the important rules of every school. This one is no exception.

Now, the first thing to do is to have your ticket ready. You must have your name signed on the ticket, where it says "Signature of pupil." Turn the ticket over and read it through on both sides. Remember your class number and your individual number in the class. The success of our school depends largely upon the way the classes are organized and thereafter dominated. Much of the success of the work depends upon the lectures you hear in the classes. They are in the form of inspirational talks based on different subjects. You are required to read all of our literature. Get and read the booklet entitled "Your Career." Every month we issue a school paper, "The Ned Wayburn News," which tells of the activities of pupils of the school who are now appearing in New York, or out on the road, and which has many interesting articles and information monthly for students of the dance. Please get a copy and read all of our literature—because it gives you an idea of what the school and its present and graduate pupils are accomplishing.

It is a well established rule of the studio that pupils shall weigh themselves every Monday and keep a record of their weight from week to week. For this purpose use the scales in the main office of the studio, please. They are accurate. We have them tested and adjusted at intervals to be sure that they are right. You are requested and expected to come into my private office and talk with me once a week, and when you do so I shall ask you about your weight, and you must be prepared to tell me. I know just how much you ought to weigh, and am interested in hearing whether you are gaining or losing flesh in the proportion that you should. At the end of the four weeks' period I shall ask each of you individually in the class about the variation in your weights, and I am then able to tell who is faithfully following my instructions as to practice, diet, hours of sleep and the other simple and necessary requirements of our courses. For I know that if my regime is observed as I request that it be, you will show it, and if you neglect to follow my advice you will not have made the progress you should, and will show that. You cannot disguise the real facts from me.

I do not want any of you to overexert at these limbering and stretching exercises. They are scientifically constructed to do for you what no other known cultural movements of this kind will do. At first they will tire you, leave you "all in," I have no doubt. I expect that. You see, in these exercises you are putting into play a lot of muscles that have been lying dormant, perhaps never been used in the way you will use them in this class as preparation for health, comeliness and dancing strength. You need to use these muscles. It is to stir them up and make you strong, and at the same time supple and shapely, that I have devised this series of exercises. It was not made by guess, this plan of developing and conditioning, but as the result of years of study and proof.

These exercises will make you feel perfectly wonderful after a while. Nothing else will do you as much good. But do not, please, expect the perfected results to show in a day or two. It cannot be done so quickly. You have been several years getting the way you are, and if you can improve greatly in a few months you must consider yourself fortunate.

Let me say, as a word of caution, that if you have any organic trouble, or have been weakened by a serious operation or recent illness, I wish you would report the facts to your class instructor or to me before you take on this work. In any event, don't overdo at any time, neither here nor in your home practice. If you find it necessary, stop at any time and sit down in your chair a few minutes till you get your breath. But don't stay out of class tomorrow because you find your muscles are tired. Every other student's muscles will be sore tomorrow, as well as yours. If you remain absent you will be much slower in getting those sore muscles feeling right than if you come into class and work the soreness out.

If you are absent you may miss something you will want to know. There is something new taught every day—or there may be a special lecture which you cannot afford to miss.

I hope you are going to be patient. I hope you are not going to say: "This is too much for me!" No matter how tired you are this work will do you more good than any medicines. You are not to take medicines without telling me about it. You are not to eat between meals; you are not to take any liquids with your meals. Masticate your food carefully. Don't bolt your meals in a hurry. Take time to eat properly. Don't sleep more than eight hours. Don't dance half the night away. You must look out for your health while you are training. Some of you are underweight, because you are not properly regulated so far as your meals and living is concerned. You are eating things you should not eat. Others are eating in such a hurry that the food is not properly assimilated by the body. You should drink not less than forty-five ounces of water a day. That is about nine glasses. You should drink a glass of water before and after each meal, NOT during your meals—one about eleven o'clock in the morning, another about four o'clock in the afternoon, and one just before you go to bed at night. NOT ice water. Water not only flushes the system but it induces perspiration. And you must perspire freely in all of our work because you get rid of many impurities through the pores. I reduced my own weight, by diet, exercise, and dancing, from 262 pounds to 207 pounds. But you have got to be very patient in reducing or building up. If you take off or put on a pound a week you will be doing very well. But let me regulate that, please. Sometimes pupils who are underweight when they first come here begin to lose weight, and they get worried about it. But you shouldn't worry. That means that you are losing unhealthy tissue, which will be replaced in time by healthy muscular tissue. That doesn't mean that you will get big knots of muscle on your arms and legs, such as you see in pictures in some of the magazines. The new tissue will be evenly distributed over the body. It is my business to manufacture symmetrical bodies. I have manufactured hundreds of celebrated beauties since I began my theatrical career, sometimes through facial makeup, sometimes through exercises and diet, but always with dancing as the chief feature in health and beauty culture.

There is a reason why this school has grown to its present proportions. It is because I have made a thorough study of anatomy and know how to make human bodies healthy and beautiful. I could tell you a very interesting story of Clan Calla, a little Irish princess who came to me with curvature of the spine to see if I could help her. She was very weak and hardly able to walk; they had to carry her to the studios from the subway. Now she is strong and well and dances beautifully.

Don't try to reduce too fast. I had two friends who died as a result of reducing with medicine. They took some sort of baths for reducing, and some kind of medicine to shrink themselves. That is why I became interested in reducing and began to practice on myself.

Now make up your minds to make this class a success. Don't make it necessary for your instructor to have to address any one of you personally. When your instructor gives an order execute it at once. Always get into your places promptly. Don't forget that you are going to be lame—but you must work it out.

You will begin with mild calisthenics—then, later on, you will learn several kinds of kicks—the side kick, the front kick, the hitch kick, etc. But before you can kick, you must have the strength necessary for kicking. You must practice the exercises in order to get this strength.

Now you are organized and you can accomplish real work. If there are any questions you would like to ask me, come to my private office at the end of the hall on the second floor—Broadway front. You will progress according to the way you practice. You must put in hours of faithful practice. If you take one hour of instruction a day at the studio, you should practice three hours a day at home. If you can possibly do so, always go through your Foundation Technique when you first get up in the morning. The lesson itself is not enough. Faithful practice means success, and without practice you won't succeed at all, and you won't get your weight off or you won't build up. Three times the length of a lesson is my rule for practice. Some practice from three to eight hours a day so as to gain dancing strength. You must have a lot of flexibility in order to dance in a professional manner.

Get the habit of deep breathing. Gradually you will increase your breathing capacity and deep breathing makes good blood. The oxygen you take into your lungs goes through the blood and takes off the impurities in the blood, and oxygen is necessary in properly assimilating your food.

Don't let anybody else advise you about diets. If a doctor has put you on a diet, let me know about it. My diets won't do you any good unless you are taking the limbering and stretching work along with them. You will enjoy them; you do not have to starve yourself.

Another thing let me warn you about! Don't bring or wear valuable jewelry to the studios. All of our employees are trustworthy, and besides, we investigate the pupils who come into our studios. We know all about them. If the wrong kind of person does get in, he or she doesn't stay more than an hour or two. We also have detectives in the classes. But don't take any chances. Don't bring valuable things into the place. Do not leave pocket-books in the dressing rooms; bring them into the class room.

We keep a strict record of the attendance and the progress of each individual pupil. We insist that you have the best that money can provide for you. If anything should happen at any time to which you could take exception, I hope you will report it to me. Our policy of giving you the very best to be had has appealed to a world of ambitious youth.

Be careful about giving advice to other girls. I don't want anybody in this class to presume to give advice to anybody else in the class. Many times a girl comes here to the school from clear across the continent. She comes with great hopes and aspirations, ready to work hard, and with all the enthusiasm in the world. Then, some girl in her class may tell her that she doesn't dance well—and her hopes will be shattered and she will become discouraged. Now none of you has any business to give advice or criticize other members of the class. If you can learn stage dancing anywhere, you can learn it in the Ned Wayburn Studios. Persistent practice will do wonders. Remember all I have said about this, and keep smiling.

NED WAYBURN'S MUSICAL COMEDY
DANCING

THIS is one of the most useful a s well as attractive t y p e s of stage dancing, and a p p e a l s strongly to all aspirants for theatrical h o n- ors and emoluments. I say "useful," for the reason that Musical Comedy dancing as I teach it supplies dancers with a reper- toire of fancy steps and neat dance routines that should en- able them to sell their services in the best theatrical markets of the world, which seems to me to be a pretty "useful" sort of a property for one to have in their permanent possession. If I here repeat that frequent practice on the part of the student is necessary for the correct acquirement of Musical Comedy dancing, I am merely stating what is right and necessary that all should understand who desire to make their services in this line of endeavor available for public approval and a corresponding cash return. And this applies to every other kind of dancing as well.

Now you may think that you know just what Musical Comedy Dancing is, and perhaps you do, but the name of it hardly defines it so that it would be recognized for ex- actly what it is by one not thoroughly stage-wise. You see a pleasing ensemble or solo dance at some revue or musical show and, without seeking or desiring to classify this dance as this, that or the other kind, you are satisfied to realize in your inner consciousness that it is a pretty movement and well worth seeing. So exact is the execution that it arouses your wonder how the dancers ever manage to get so many intricate steps and rapid motions and pretty flings of their heels into a united and harmonious picture; all working in perfect unison, to a pleasing tempo, smiling the while and doing it all as a mere matter of course, with seeming unconcern, just as though the steps and kicks and posing and grouping were second nature to them all.

That is a Musical Comedy dance, and instead of growing on bushes to be gathered by every careless hand, it is actually the result of studious endeavor and persistent drilling on the part of the participants, and of careful and conscientious training by competent dancing instructors. It is well done and gratifying to the spectator because it is the finished product of qualified teaching, earnest endeavor, tireless energy, practice, rehearsing. Remember this, the next time you attend a show where dancing is a feature, and accord the dancers the credit that is their due.

True Musical Comedy dancing is in reality an exaggerated form of what was formerly styled "fancy dancing." It is a cross between the ballet and the Ned Wayburn type of tap and step or American specialty dancing. It combines pretty attitudes, poses, pirouettes and the several different types of kicking steps that are now so popular. Soft-shoe steps break into it here and there in unexpected ways and places, adding a pleasing variety to the menu. The tempo enhances and harmonizes the scene and the action. There is no monotony, no tiresome sameness; yet the varying forms of action blend into a perfect continuity. The dance is full of happy surprise steps, perhaps, or unexpected climaxes and variations that arouse the interest as they quickly flash by.

Often there is featured in Musical Comedy dancing a bit of so called "character" work, which may be anything— Bowery, Spanish, Dutch, eccentric, Hawaiian, or any of the countless other characteristic types. Also there are touches of dainty ballet work interspersed among the other features, at times. Yet to accomplish the ballet effects or the character representations exacts of the dancer no special development along strictly ballet or classical lines, when she obtains her Musical Comedy training here, for these features are given the required attention as part of the regular course in fitting the student for this branch of the stage dancing art, and thus our Musical Comedy graduates are qualified for all the variations of effort that naturally come under that head.

My foundation technique is a prime factor in the successful accomplishment of any type of dancing, and the scientific limbering and stretching exercises that constitute that work are indispensable in perfecting the pupil to handle every phase of the varied demands in Musical Comedy dancing. Hence my insistence that our foundation technique precede the entrance of the pupil into the classes of this or any of the other various types of stage dancing that we teach.

Two of my most famous pupils in Musical Comedy dancing are Fred and Adele Astaire, brother and sister. They came to me to study from Omaha, Nebraska, as little tots of about six and seven years of age. Adele was always fond of coming to her classes; but Fred says that he just "followed on" through brotherly association rather than from any preconceived ambition to become a professional dancer. Then, through reverses of family fortunes, the

time came when they felt that they should be supporting
themselves. They continued to study under me, and I was
very happy to be able to place them in vaudeville in a singing and dancing act, which I had prepared for them. This
started them on their career, which has led them to Europe
and back again. They have appeared in "Over the Top,"
"The Passing Show of 1918," "Apple Blossoms," and in
"The Love Letter." They then scored a sensational success in London in "Stop Flirting" (575 performances).
Now they are starring in "Lady, Be Good," on tour after
a long run in New York.

In this chapter I shall now describe in detail 32 bars of
a simple musical comedy dance, a "soft shoe" routine, as
we call it, to give you some understanding of how modern
stage dances are developed at the Ned Wayburn Studios.

MUSICAL COMEDY ROUTINE—4/4 TEMPO

Tune: "Way Down Upon the Swanee River."

The dancer enters from stage left.

Step right foot to right oblique on count of "one." Step
left foot behind to right oblique back on count of "two";
step right foot around behind the left on count of "and";
step left foot to right oblique on count of "three"; repeat
same for "four," "five," "and," "six." Step right foot
to right oblique, count of "seven"; drag left foot in air
behind to right oblique and slap left heel with right hand
on count of "eight."

Step left foot to left on count of "one"; drag right foot
in air behind to left oblique and slap right heel with left

hand on count of "two"; step right foot to right on count
of "three" and drag left foot across in front in air on count
of "four"; step left foot to left facing left, count of "five";
right foot front small step on count "and;" step left foot
back facing back, count of "six;" right foot to left, small
step on "and." Left foot to right facing right, count of
"seven"; right foot to back, small step on "and." Left
foot to front facing front, count of "eight." Now repeat
entire movement.

These two movements should take the dancer to the centre of the stage; done in eight measures of 4/4 time.

Step right foot to right oblique count of "one"; hop on
it in same place with left foot in air behind to left oblique
back, count "two"; step down to left oblique back with
left foot on count of "three"; hop on left foot, extend right
foot in air right oblique on count "four"; step right foot
back behind left foot on count "five"; step left foot to
left oblique back, count "six"; step right foot across to
left oblique, count "seven"; hop on right foot, extend left
foot in air right oblique back, count of "eight." Now
reverse this entire movement to other side. These two
steps are done in four measures of 4/4 tempo in the centre
of the stage.

Step right foot to right, count "one"; step left foot behind to right oblique back, count "and"; step right foot
down in same place, count "two." Reverse to left for count
of "three," "and," "four"; then step right foot to right,
count "five"; step left foot in front to right, turning and
facing up stage, count "six"; step right foot around stage
front to right, turning front again, count "seven"; drag
left foot across in front of right to right, count of "eight."
Reverse this entire step to other side. These two steps are
done in four measures of 4/4 tempo in centre of the stage.

This finishes the first half of the chorus, or 16 measures.

Facing left oblique, drag right foot from left oblique to right oblique back, count of "and"; hop on left foot in same place, count of "one"; drag right foot from right oblique back to left oblique, count "and"; hop on left foot same place, count of "two"; drag right foot from left oblique to right oblique back, count "and"; hop left foot same place, count of "three"; displace left foot with right foot from right oblique back, left foot extending to left oblique, all on count of "four." Hop on right foot same place, count "and;" step left foot to left oblique, count "five"; step right foot across in front to left oblique, count "six"; hop on right foot same place, count of "and"; step left foot to left oblique, count of "seven"; hop on left foot same place, and turn, kick right foot to right oblique, count "eight."

Going up stage right oblique back facing right oblique, step right foot back to right oblique back, count "one"; step left foot to right foot, count of "and"; step right foot to right oblique back, count "two"; step left foot to right foot, count of "and"; step right foot to back, facing back, count "three"; hop on right foot turning right to face front on count "four." Step left foot to left oblique on "five"; step right foot to left foot on "and"; step left foot to left oblique on "six"; step right foot to left foot on "and"; step left foot to left oblique on "seven"; hop on left foot and kick right foot to right oblique on "eight." Reverse all of these steps. These are done in eight measures of 4/4 tempo in the centre of the stage.

Step left foot to left oblique, count "one"; step right foot behind to left, bend left knee, count "two"; hop on right foot and kick left to left oblique, count "three"; swing left foot back to right oblique back on "four"; bring right foot around behind left on count "and"; step left foot to front, count "five"; step right foot back to left on "six"; bring left foot around behind right on count "and"; step right foot to front on count of "seven"; step left foot to left oblique on count "eight."

Step right foot to right on count "one"; swing left foot up stage and step to back on "and"; right foot straight in place, facing up stage, count "two"; step left foot to stage right on count "three"; facing right swing right foot to right, count "and"; step left foot straight in place, count "four"; now facing front, having made complete left back turn. Now step right foot to right oblique back, count "five"; step left foot to right oblique back behind right foot, count "and"; straight with right foot in place, count "six"; step left to left oblique back, count "seven"; step right foot to left oblique back behind left foot, count "and"; straight with left foot in place, count "eight." Reverse these steps.

These steps are done in eight measures of 4/4 tempo, in the center of the stage.

This completes the first chorus, or 32 measures.

MR. WAYBURN ADDRESSES A CLASS IN
MUSICAL COMEDY DANCING

IN Musical Comedy dancing it is necessary that you should have control of e v e r y muscle in the body in order to do the work effectively. If you have not that control you are going to fail to get the steps. That is the reason for the limbering and stretching work of our foundation technique, a necessary preliminary for all who enter this class. Our foundation process will give you the mastery of the muscles of the feet, the upper leg, the lower leg and your whole body, without which you will never be able to learn this type of dancing. It requires concentration, patience, incessant practice, on your part, but you soon see the good results of your efforts in the strengthening and flexibility of all your muscles.

This class is organized for a period of not less than twenty lessons, during which time you will have the satisfaction of acquiring four complete routines. Each routine consists of not less than ten steps. Some have more, but the average routine consists of ten steps, one to bring you onto the stage, which is called a travelling step, eight steps in the dance proper, usually set to about 64 bars of music, or the length of two (2) choruses of a popular song, and an exit step, which is a special step designed to form a climax to the dance and provoke applause as you go off stage. Now, there may be two travelling steps to bring you onto the stage instead of one, depending upon the arrangement of the routine, but you will be taught about two steps every lesson, in the beginners' courses, so that at the end of each week, or five lessons, you will have learned one complete routine.

You must learn to throw your personality into the dances. And when you get further along in the dances you can begin to work your facial expressions into your dancing. There are many things to learn about dancing besides the steps, and you will do well to improve your opportunities in every way you can while you are preparing for a stage career. Go to see as many expert professional dancers as you can—study them—and absorb all you can about stage dancing from the "Ned Wayburn News" and other dance magazines.

This course teaches complete professional routines such as you would do on the stage, and may be used as solo dances. "Routine" is a professional term for musical comedy or any kind of a stage dance. It is a sequence of steps. Routines are arranged so that they will provoke applause. Maybe the fourth or the eighth step will be "climactic" steps, especially arranged to make a climax in the dance and win applause. In different routines, the climax you will find comes on different steps, depending upon the arrangement of the routine. In order to put over a climax you must throw your personality into it.

Exits as well as entrances are difficult of successful accomplishment. It takes a great artist to make an effective exit. The exit should always be made with the face toward the audience (unless there is some special reason why the back is turned), so that the audience gets the full effect of your facial expression.

All the dances in my courses are taught in a professional way. That does not mean, of course, that you have to go on the professional stage. Many girls and boys study with me who have no intention of ever going on the stage. They do so because they know that my limbering and stretching work and my type of dancing will make them healthy, flexible and graceful, but nevertheless they are all taught in a professional stage way, which is the only successful method.

My stage dancing is the type of dancing that gets over with an audience. The old folk dances and the old-fashioned fancy dances no longer appeal to the interest. But I teach the kind of dancing that is in demand. If you should appear in any kind of entertainment for charity or any private theatrical performances, you can make use of my really professional stage dances; and since you are properly taught, you will make a success, providing you profit by expert advice and devote ample time to practice every day.

One reason that we get such good results in our school is on account of the way in which we organize and conduct our classes. Everybody must conform to discipline. You certainly will get discipline if you go on the stage.

Everybody should get a copy of our booklet, "Your Career", if you haven't already done so, and read it through from cover to cover. (A copy will be sent free on request.) Read the call-board outside in the office. In the professional theatre the call-board is usually placed near the stage door. Anything of interest to the company is posted on the call-board. Pupils in my courses are required to read the call-board because in reading the call-board, the booklet and the other literature that we get out, you will absorb a lot in the way of showmanship and stage-craft. Any one of you, after taking my course, should make a success on the stage because you will know how to dance in a professional way. You will know how to sell your dancing. Specialized training is very necessary in order to get a foothold, and the rewards are enormous for those pupils who do get over. Make an effort to acquire an easy presence. This you must get by appearing before an audience. Now, I represent your audience. I come in to visit your class in order to make constructive criticism, and to watch your physical progress. Whenever any of our pupils are appearing in the city theatres you should go and see them, because from their work you will get inspiration, and you *must* have inspiration. Without it you can't do anything; you won't get any benefit out of the work at all. You must concentrate on the work and enjoy it. Only through patient practice will you ever make a success of it. Some girls come into the musical comedy work and are inclined to take it lightly. They don't practice enough. Or perhaps they get discouraged if they miss one step and can't seem to get it at first. You must be enthusiastic about your work if you are going to succeed.

I want to tell you about a group of my girls who recently started out on their professional work. They were in the Ned Wayburn "Symphonic Jazz Revue," which was arranged by my producing department for the Middle Western Moving Picture Theatres. These girls had all been around the Studios for about six months, practicing and working hard, and this was the first experience for most of them. They were a wonderful bunch of girls, mentally and morally. Four of the girls had their mothers with them as chaperones. One of them saved $275.00 in 24 weeks out of a salary of $50.00 per week.

Ned Wayburn's "Honeymoon Cruise" is made up of pupils from the Studio, also, and has made a great success. They are girls and boys of good breeding, personality and good minds.

I want you to come to me and advise with me about what you are going to do with yourself. Let me be the one to guide you, please. Don't listen to any girl you may meet in classes. You will learn to like some girl in the class very much and you will become great friends. All of a sudden she gets an idea about a professional engagement and she drags you along with her, and you both think you are ready to start in and do something big. But there is a right way and a wrong way to go about getting started, and you must start with the right manager for the sake of your whole future success. Remember that I am always glad to talk with you and to help you about engagements when you are ready, but you must prove your ability first.

No girl or boy can get an endorsement from me who misses a lesson without offering a plausible excuse. You must be regular in attendance and you must be punctual. If you miss a class you are obliged to telephone in before the class starts. If you are ill you must bring a doctor's certificate the next time you come to class. Your excuses must be sent to me personally. If you telephone in, be sure that it is sent through to me. I keep track of all the past pupils, and I do not recommend pupils who have not worked faithfully or who have been irregular in attendance.

There is a great incentive in class work, since you can get encouragement and inspiration from the other girls. Some girls in the class will take to the work more easily than others because they are in better physical condition, but if a girl gets along faster and better than you do, don't be discouraged by it. Just let it make you more ambitious to do as well. Your time will come if you keep at it. Do not try to practice in this room. This is a place to learn. Practice your lesson, go over the exercises, at home, several hours a day or use the practice rooms we provide. Don't be satisfied to come into class and try to perfect your routines there. It isn't possible.

When you go on the stage professionally you will be expected to be already fully informed as to certain necessary facts that concern all actors everywhere. Much information about showmanship is given in our makeup classes. You must take lessons in makeup before you go on the stage. You will do well to practice the same things here in the studio, now and all the time, in order to make you stage-wise and perfect in necessary stage deportment.

One of the things required of you on the stage is to *stand still*. Don't move about or turn your head or lop around or move your hands or feet. You will have a fixed position established at rehearsals, when you enter upon professional stage work, and if you do not hold it and observe the rules about standing still, you will not be wanted and will not last long. It seems a very simple thing to do, when you think of it, but unless you do it right *here,* while you are learning the basic facts about a stage career, you may fall down on it *there.* Heed this advice, and you will be grateful to me for it sometime.

If you are on the stage and someone is playing a scene, and your head is going from side to side, you attract the attention of the audience from the actor to yourself. When you do it here you take the attention of the class away from me, and you also take my attention away from the class, and if one or all of you do a "go as you please" about your movements, your talking and your attitudes in class, we have a pandemonium here that will drive your teacher frantic and prevent you from getting the instruction that you are paying for.

In this studio we insist upon and enforce discipline,
just as your stage director will do when you join some
company. It is good for you to get the disciplinary
practice now that you must expect to receive when you
pass from here to a regular stage. Those of you who really
mean business and are going to succeed do pay attention
to the studio discipline, always.

MAURICE.

PEARL REGAY

HELEN FABLES

MARILYN MILLER

RITA HOWARD

NED WAYBURN SHOW GIRLS, FOLLIES OF 1922.

PAULETTE DUVAL AND NED WAYBURN PUPILS, FOLLIES OF 1923

MOONLIGHT BALLET, FOLLIES OF 1923

"LITTLE OLD NEW YORK," FOLLIES OF 1923

NED WAYBURN'S TAP AND STEP DANCING

SOMETIMES CALLED CLOGGING

YOU will remember that in a preceding chapter I said that Tap and Step dances were those composed chiefly of motions of the feet which resulted in combinations of various sounds made by different parts of the foot tapping or beating the floor, these sounds or beats being called "taps." This type of dancing expresses the American syncopated rhythms. It was the most popular type of stage dancing about forty years ago, when it was most beautifully performed by the greatest American dancing stars like the late George H. Primrose, the famous American minstrel.

Buck-dancing is done to syncopated rhythms, and you must get the right accent on those syncopated beats or taps or you cannot get the knack of doing a buck dance properly. So it is most important that you practice over and over again the four kinds of "taps" and "hops" which I shall describe now. First of all, stand in an imaginary circle the diameter of your feet, with your heels together, your right toe pointed right oblique and your left toe

pointed left oblique, your weight equally distributed between the two feet, as described in
a previous chapter.

Every dancing step is in counts of eight.
Remember that all of your counts begin with
the left foot unless you are instructed to the
contrary. Remember always, when you hop,
to land with the knees bent; otherwise, the
landing of the body with stiff legs after the
hops will be a shock to the nervous system
which in time will undermine your health.

The first tap is called a "straight" tap.
Put your weight on the whole right foot. The

Straight Tap

left foot should be held about one inch from the floor. Tap
the floor with the ball of the left foot for seven counts,
working the foot on a hinge from the ankle, keeping your
feet directly opposite and inside the circle or place. On
the eighth count put the flat of the left foot down on the
floor, shifting your weight to the left foot. Now in doing
these straight taps count: 1, 2, 3, 4, 5, 6, 7, flat. And
when you say "flat" you shift your weight to the left foot
by putting it flat on the floor. Then comes the same with

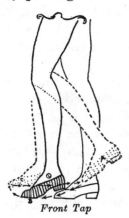

the right foot—seven taps with the
ball of the right foot and "flat" on the
eighth count. Now do the sixteen
counts, first with the left, then with
the right. Thus: (left) 1, 2, 3, 4, 5,
6, 7, flat; then (right) 1, 2, 3, 4, 5, 6,
7, flat.

The next tap is a "front" tap. The
front tap goes front—it gets its name
from the direction it takes. Swing the
lower leg (from the knee down) like
a pendulum. The tap is made with

Front Tap

Back Tap

the inside edge of the sole of the shoe, striking the floor as the foot goes front only, clearing the floor as it goes back, the back swing being made to the count of "and." Put the accent on the number as you say it out loud. "*Front*-and," "*2*-and," "*3*-and," "*4*-and," "*5*-and," "*6*-and," "*7*-and," and "*8*-flat" (weight on the left foot). Swing the lower leg from the knee back and forth, not the upper leg at all, striking or tapping the floor only on the front swing. Then execute the same taps with the ball of the right foot, stopping after the count of "8-flat" with both feet flat on the floor, the weight equally distributed between them. Now, you have had the "straight-tap" and "front-tap" with both feet.

The next is the back tap. Make the back tap like the snap of a whip, swinging the lower leg from the knee only, like a pendulum, with a sharply accented move to back, striking the floor with the ball of the foot as it goes back only to the counts, and swinging it front to the count of "and" when the foot must clear the floor each time. Snap it down— "*Back*-and," "*2*-and," "*3*-and," "*4*-and," "*5*-and," "*6*-and," "*7*-and," "*8*-flat" (with the left foot); then with the right foot, "*Back*-and," "*2*-and," "*3*-and," "*4*-and," "*5*-and," "*6*-and," "*7*-and," "*8*-flat."

Heel Tap

We now come to the heel tap, which is made and counted like this: Heel, 2, 3, 4, 5, 6, 7, flat (8 counts). The same with the right heel for the same counts (8).

Practice these four taps, the straight, the front, the back, the heel, and the hop faithfully before you try to learn the buck dance, because from these four taps and the hop are built up many combinations which form complicated steps which you will want to learn later on. And the more you practice these fundamentals the better dancer you are going to be. Be sure to review, too, over and over again, the eight stage directions—front, left oblique, left, left oblique back, back, right oblique back, right, and right oblique.

In "tap" dancing, as in the musical comedy dances, there will usually be ten steps; one "travelling" or entrance step which will bring you onto the stage (from "off stage" into the line of sight of the audience), eight dance steps, and one exit-step to take you "off," out of sight of the audience, which will always be in the nature of a *climax* to provoke applause.

But, as I have said above, in buck-dancing or in any type of tap and step dancing, the rhythm is most important, and in order to be thoroughly grounded on syncopated rhythms, I shall give you first of all a beginner's "time-step." After that you will learn a beginner's "break."

The "time-step" and "break" are the keys to tap dancing and must be mastered before the tap dance can be learned. The "time-step" and "break" must be perfectly timed to the syncopated rhythm. And it is going to take long, patient periods of practice in order to perfect them. Do not get discouraged. Apply yourself keenly to both of these fundamental steps.

THE TIME STEP

The purpose of the time step is to get the syncopation into the dancing step, and establish the "tempo" of the dance.

With the weight on the left foot, front tap with the right, back tap with the right, hop with the left, with the right foot back and raised from the floor. The count is "And a *one,*" with strong accent on "one." Now straight tap with right foot to count "two" and accent it.

Do a front tap with the left (count "and"), left foot straight front (count "three" and accent), right foot straight (count "four" and accent).

With the weight on the right foot, front tap with the left, back tap with the left, hop with the right, with the left foot back and raised from the floor. The count is "And a *one,*" with strong accent on the "one." Now straight tap with left foot to count "two" and accent it. Do a front tap with the right (count "and"), right foot straight front (count "three" and accent), left foot straight (count "four" and accent).

Repeat all six times.

THE BREAK

With the weight on the left foot, front tap with the right foot, back tap with the right, hop with the left, with the right foot back and raised from the floor. The count is "And a *one,*" with strong accent on the "one." Tap right foot straight (count "two" and accent). Tap left foot front, tap left foot back, then left foot straight, to the count of "and three and." Now right foot straight, to count of "four" accented. Hop on the right foot with the left raised from the floor in front, count "five" and accent it. Front tap with the left (count "and"), straight tap front with the left (count "six" and accent it), straight tap with the right, place the right toe even with the arch of the left foot (count "and") then left foot flat front to count of "seven" accented.

Now, first of all you had the eight different directions; after the eight different directions the four different parts of the foot and the "hop," and then the different kinds of sounds or taps that I just gave you. We begin to make all sorts of combinations of those sounds. For instance, one of the primary steps which you must know is a combination of front, back and straight tap together. Stand on the ball of each foot; the weight is off the heels, and equally distributed between the balls of the feet.

Now beginning with your left foot, do one front-tap, one back-tap, and one straight-tap, *accenting* the straight tap—counting it 1, 2, *3*. Now, begin with the right foot and do one front-tap, then one back-tap, and one straight-tap, counting it 1, 2, 3, and then alternately with each foot. On the third count your weight should rest on that foot. When perfected, that makes the first actual step in "Tap and Step" dancing.

One of my pupils of whom I am very proud is Miss Ann Pennington, another of the "Follies" stars. She became one of the leading exponents of "Tap and Step" dancing, and although she has reached this high point in her career, she still comes to me for advice and for pointers, and I am glad that she does this, because it shows that she realizes the necessity of new ideas and hard work to keep herself at the top. In dancing, as in many other professions, one must "keep everlastingly at it." The story of Miss Pennington's career is similar to that of many who have come to me for instruction. She had innate ability, good looks, a sense of rhythm and a willingness to work hard and patiently, and with these qualities has achieved success.

MR. WAYBURN ADDRESSES A CLASS IN TAP AND STEP DANCING

WHAT you are learning in this class I like to call "bread and butter" dances, for if you succeed in mastering them thoroughly, as you surely will if you give attention to your instruction here in class and then practice several hours daily at home, you will possess as your own individual property a means of livelihood that will remain at your command all your stage life.

When you know how to execute the routines of these dances and add to and develop your routines to keep them fresh and up to the hour, you have a lot of neat steps that will get over with the producers of many of the better types of modern shows. That is what I mean by "bread and butter" dances; something you can sell most easily in the present show market, and get not only food and raiment and lodging, but build up a savings bank account for the future as well. So it is well worth while to take your instruction here seriously and earnestly, as I am sure you intend to do. There is big money in this line of dancing if you practice and keep at it long enough. There are many four-figure salaries being paid every week to qualified dancers with an established name and reputation, and the way to earn these big salaries is to become qualified yourself. We teach you right and start you right—then it's practice for you; practice and more practice.

Let me tell you just how you should practice from now on in order to become a competent solo specialty dancer. Practice one step at a time. In a routine take the first step; practice that step until you are tired, then sit down and rest five or ten minutes. As soon as you feel like getting up again, take the second step and practice it until you are tired; sit down and rest again. Then do the first and second steps—no more; then sit down and rest again. Practice until you feel yourself tiring, but DO NOT overdo it. Practice faithfully and don't slight any one step. Then practice the third step the same way. When tired sit down and rest—then get up again. Put the first, second and third steps together, and so on all through the routine of eight or ten steps. No other way you can think of to practice will result as well as this particular way. It is a systematic, practical way.

I am taking a big responsibility with you, because when you finish your course you are going to appeal to me and ask if I know of an opportunity for you; where I think there is a good chance for you to begin; how you can get started. You are now getting along in advanced work. Try to get on in some charity entertainment; some place where you are employed in the day may have some benefits. Try for church entertainments. Some evenings in the neighborhood where you live there may be little entertainments. No matter how small an affair, try to go on. Get in front of an audience and feel the tension of an audience; it will give you encouragement, and on each succeeding appearance you will gain confidence and see how you "get over" with an audience. After a few appearances any feeling of stage fright will gradually disappear, and eventually you will gain confidence in yourself. Do not try to go on at first in any Broadway benefit. Be satisfied to make a very small beginning.

You have to begin now to put yourselves in the work. You can't be looking down at the floor and wondering what step comes next. That is no longer possible. You must acquire a method of executing the step; a little smile on your face; a little personality behind it; inject character into all your work.

Recently the Friars put on a Minstrel Show in New York that was a sensation. It shows that the public are gradually coming back to the old-time Minstrel Shows. The show business moves around in cycles; styles change in dances the same as in fashions. Light operas and musical comedies are coming in. Those of us who watch the theatre know that the styles are changing, and when I tell you this type of dancing is coming in you can believe it. Many prominent society women are studying this style of dancing. The Universities are taking it up, and we are gradually establishing it. Kansas City, Atlanta—the Junior League Follies, all did this type of work. There are 10,000 dancing teachers in America, and out of these, 2,350 are already teaching it, and there is every incentive for you to learn it, for it is popular and profitable, and with our foundation technique already acquired as a basis for this work you should not find it difficult to master.

This class is going to be taught four complete professional stage dances this month. If you got that outside of this school you would have to pay not less than $100 to $200 for each routine. I make it a point to give my scholars the very best there is in the line of instruction, and at the same time charge them only a reasonable fee.

We also give you the backing of every part of this establishment—publicity, advertising, and bookings when we can, but not until you have made good during your study.

Now there is one little thing I am going to talk to you about that really is a bigger thing than it seems—and that is gum—chewing gum. If you had had stage experience you would know that gum is taboo in the theatre, and the reason for this is not only that to chew in sight of an audience would be an insult and result in immediate dismissal, but also for this very important reason, that a cud of gum if dropped on the stage would destroy that stage for dancing—your own dancing and everybody else's. And it would be the same way here in the studio. We have here the finest of clear-maple dancing floors in every one of our studios. Drop a piece of gum on this floor and then try your dance and see what would happen to you. You'd step on it and you'd get a fall; you couldn't help it; and an unexpected fall like that might break your ankle, very easily. It has been done before now. Just make believe that you are under a theatrical producer on a Broadway stage, while you are with us here, and park your gum on a lamp post before you come into this building. Then you and the rest of the young ladies will not be in danger of meeting with an accident from that source.

Real flowers are not allowed on the professional stage for a similar reason. A flower petal falling on the floor acts as a banana skin would, making a slip and a bad fall possible to anyone on the stage. You'd not like to have your dance spoiled by a wad of gum or a flower petal, and perhaps get put out of commission and have to forfeit a contract because of a personal injury. So let's play we are on the professional stage here and do as real professionals do—cut out the cud and forego the posies. If you have flowers handed to you over the footlights when you get to be stars, ladies, let it be at the final curtain. Then you won't break anybody's neck.

I say often to every class, and I say it again to you—come and see me in my office and tell me how you are getting along here. And I mean this for every one of you. If I wasn't certain that I am going to be able to help you I wouldn't ask you to do this. If I didn't care I might do as some others do—take your money and let you go along in the class work as you choose to without bothering myself whether you made good or not. But that is not my way—not this studio's way at all. You must make good, for your own sake—and for the sake of this school's reputation. Now remember, there is absolutely no charge for my advice or counsel about anything that concerns you—your health, your reducing, your improvement in dancing—anything you want to know.

One day a girl came to me for the first time after she had been in the school about four months. I asked her in some surprise why she hadn't been in to see me before. "Why, Mr. Wayburn," she said, "I understood that you charge a high price for consultation, and I didn't feel that I could afford it."

Not only do I not charge anything for counseling you, I esteem it a favor to myself to be allowed to advise you. Candidly, I have never yet had a girl or boy take my courses here who has made a success of a dancing career who didn't write to me or talk things over with me first. If you don't come, you cannot get my ideas, cannot cooperate with me in matters that concern you.

Come to my office at any time. Between 11 and 1, or 4 and 6 are usually the best times. If I am busy with some important matter I may have to ask you to wait awhile or come in at some other time. I'm a pretty busy man some of the time, myself!

Weigh yourself and tell me about your weight.

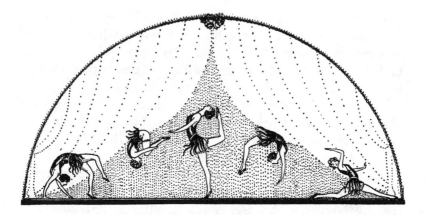

NED WAYBURN'S ACROBATIC DANCING

THERE is a very decided distinction to be drawn between acrobatics pure and simple, and acrobatic dancing, which is quite another matter. It is, of course, acrobatic dancing that you see on the stage accompanying and accentuating the more formal dancing steps in musical comedies, revues, and spectacular performances, and it is this acrobatic dancing that receives wide attention in the teaching of the dancing art in the Ned Wayburn courses.

There are properly two divisions into which acrobatic dancing is naturally separated:

(1) *Bending exercises;* including the back bend, handstand, inside-out, front over, back limber, cartwheel, tinseca, nip-up, the various splits, and several more advanced feats that should be attempted only after thorough physical preparation.

(2) *High-Kicking exercises;* including all the so-called "legmania" varieties of dancing, which are best acquired

by thorough preparation of the body in the Ned Wayburn foundation technique and studious attention to the drill in the Ned Wayburn Americanized ballet technique.

All of the acrobatic dancing tricks that are properly classified under bending exercises have for their foundation the back bend and the hand stand, as they are called, both of which must be mastered absolutely before attempting other and more complicated acrobatic exercises.

I want to go on record with the emphatic statement that acrobatic dancing must not be attempted except by those who are entirely and absolutely physically fit. The acrobatic dancer must possess unusual strength in the arms, in order that the weight of the body may be safely supported; and there must be strength and flexibility of the waist muscles and the abdominal muscles, and of all the muscles of the back and shoulders, to enable the performer to execute the front and back bends and their companion strenuous exercises. First, the pupil must have an unusual adaptability to this type of dancing, and then must prepare carefully and properly in advance of entering upon the real work of the course.

The best development comes from our limbering and stretching exercises. There is nothing else like it nor anything equally as good as a foundation for all types of dancing, and it is especially needed by the amateur entering upon an acrobatic dancing career. We have put literally thousands of pupils through this course, and every student of our acrobatic dancing classes who has taken this essential preliminary course has come through in fine shape.

You must be extremely careful if you have or ever have had any abdominal trouble. You must get the abdomen strengthened before you undertake any acrobatic work. If you have had an operation for peritonitis, appendicitis, hernia, or elsewhere in the abdominal cavity or region, you must, out of consideration for your own health, avoid any violent bending exercise. This does not imply that you should not exercise properly. You should, for it is easily possible to strengthen the tender muscles into a normal condition by suitable and systematic exercises.

Try this test: Lie flat on your back on the floor. Now, without aid of the hands or elbows or any outside assistance, bring your body to a sitting position. If you cannot do this, get your back muscles into training before you attempt any difficult exertion. If you succeed in your test, you can safely consider your abdominal muscles to be in sufficiently good condition to go ahead with acrobatic dancing.

Let me describe a few of the most common of the acrobatic tricks that all acrobatic dancers must know, and you will no doubt recognize them as being also favorite tumbling acts of boys and girls on the lawn. The most complicated and difficult acrobatic exercises are taught in full in the Ned Wayburn Studios, and are printed in detail, with simple instruction for their successful accomplishment, in the Ned Wayburn Home Study Course in Stage Dancing. The few we give you here are not difficult, and can be mastered at home by anyone who persistently practices and follows the descriptions with care.

BACK BEND

Stand erect. Spread the feet about fifteen inches apart. Have the toes pointed well out, at about a sixty degree angle. Raise the arms directly overhead, the hands shoulder-width apart. Put your head back, pushing forward with your knees. Lean back, bending the arms as far back as you can, till the palms of the hands rest on the floor. In doing the back bend, relax the lower jaw and keep the mouth slightly open to breathe. Throw the strain of the bend in the small of the back. To come up, acquire a little rocking motion forward and back, lean forward, and you will come up easily.

How to do a back bend while standing near a wall.

Stand about 3 feet from the wall, with your back to the wall, feet about two feet apart. Bend back, touch the wall with the palms and walk down the wall with your hands until you touch the floor. Then walk up with your hands until you are erect.

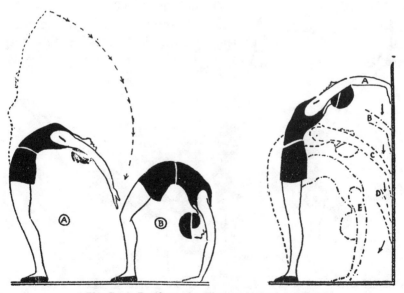

The Back Bend on the Flat, and Near a Wall

HAND STAND

Take a wide step forward with the left foot, place both hands flat on the floor at least eighteen inches apart in front of the left toe, fingers open and pointed directly front, right leg perfectly straight, extended straight back. Swing the right leg up and over and follow it with the left leg, and when you come down bring down the left leg first, then the right leg, bringing the left knee close up to the chest. Do not kick hard or you will go over.

How to do a hand stand while standing near a wall.

Advance whichever foot comes natural to you to do this act (people are right and left footed as well as right and left handed) ; let us say your right foot. Stand facing the wall with the right foot advanced to within about two feet of it. Place both hands on the floor, about eighteen inches apart, in front of left foot, fingers open and pointed front, right leg extended back and straight. Kick up with the left foot over your back so as to bring the soles of both feet against the wall, the left foot reaching the wall first; knees straight, heels together.

The Hand Stand on the Flat (A, B), and Near a Wall

CARTWHEEL

The cartwheel is the hand stand done sidewise. Instead of kicking up, as in the hand stand, put one hand down and then the other, going sidewise, kicking your feet up. Keep your head back, so as to retain your sense of direction.

One of my star pupils in acrobatic dancing is Miss Evelyn Law, a principal dancer of the "Follies," and in "Louie the Fourteenth." She came to me four years ago, a little girl fifteen years old. There are few girls who have worked so hard to succeed as has Evelyn, and there are certainly few who have achieved the top line in their profession as quickly as she has. In every respect, Miss Law is a credit to the American stage. She started in her first appearance in an engagement which I got for her at a salary of $75.00 a week. Then her salary jumped to $125.00 a week, in "Two Little Girls in Blue," plus her mother's fare; later, as a featured member of the

The Cartwheel

"Follies," which engagement I was also very happy to secure for her, her weekly salary reached the $750.00 mark. But Evelyn deserves her good fortune, because she has worked hard. Indeed, no girl could do the remarkable work which she is doing were she to live anything but a life of rigorous attention to every detail pertaining to health and physical fitness. She not only has ability, but she has the capacity for putting her heart into her job. She writes: "The encouragement which I have received urges me on to greater effort; and I am constantly trying to improve myself. I realize that only by constantly striving can I hope to win the recognition of producers and at the same time please the public." She writes of her present work that it is "a privilege which must be honored by my unflagging effort to put forth my best."

There's inspiration for all my dancing pupils in Evelyn Law's success.

ONE SCENE FROM NED WAYBURN'S "DEMI-TASSE REVUE."

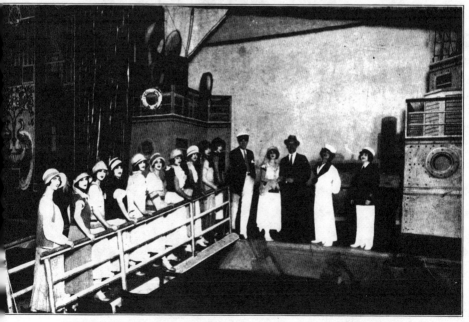

SCENE FROM NED WAYBURN'S "HONEYMOON CRUISE"

WILL ROGERS

EDDIE CANTOR

LACE BALLET, FOLLIES OF 1922

GILDA GRAY AND NED WAYBURN PUPILS IN "IT'S GETTING DARKER ON BROADWAY," FOLLIES OF 1922

MR. WAYBURN ADDRESSES A CLASS IN
ACROBATIC DANCING

I HAVE watched this class with a great deal of interest. You really are getting a physical foundation here for wonderful dancing; you are beginning to handle yourselves in a scientific way. I congratulate you.

To make a success at acrobatic or any other dancing you must not strain yourselves. Train, but don't strain. Be patient and keep practicing, and you will go far.

You are very wise to develop your ability along the line of acrobatic dancing rather than as an acrobat. There is a vast difference. As a mere acrobat one has to be a top-liner and wonderfully expert to get any kind of a salary at all, but as an acrobatic dancer you can command a place in the very best stage productions, high class musical comedies, musical revues, vaudeville, etc., and also in the better grade motion pictures and presentations, and get a very good salary. But if you let the acrobatic tricks dominate your dance, you will be classed as an acrobat, and not as an acrobatic dancer; so look out—keep your dancing up to grade and throw in these acrobatic tricks as a surprise and a climax, and you've got something the public and the producers want and will pay for.

After you have acquired these wonderful tricks and gotten hold of your bodies, and succeeded in bringing out in a physical way all the grace that nature gave you, then you can be taken and schooled in the soft, beautiful Americanized ballet work, and you will find that after this training you are now getting, our ballet technique will delight you and be comparatively easy for you. You know, of course, that in this course the ballet is not taught in the old, antiquated way, taking years of your time before you are permitted to do solo work. We teach you our own modern, scientific way, giving you first our foundation technique, then letting you learn how to use your arms, head, the upper part of your body and your legs gracefully and prettily, and making you as good ballet dancers as the old long-drawn-out practice ever made, enabling you to qualify for a paying engagement without a discouraging wait of years and years. Pavlowa, you know, was kept subordinate twelve years before she was permitted to attempt a solo dance in public. Imagine our American girls submitting to such apprenticeship! Not one of you would consider such a thing. And fortunately you do not have to, for we have revolutionized all that.

Now you are getting a wonderful dancing repertoire, with acrobatic dancing, musical comedy work and the tap and step dancing. When you add our ballet course to that, then you are ready for any call that may come to you in your lifetime. This is my aspiration for you. We are trying to realize ideals. When you have finished here you will be accomplished dancers, not mere machines going through a bunch of set exercises. Add the spiritual touch to your work now as you start on the home stretch. Finish here going strong, and your speed will carry you far.

Don't be satisfied to qualify merely as acrobats. When you come to me for a letter of recommendation to some first-class theatrical manager, I don't want to have to say to him: "Enclosed you will please find one acrobat." I have better hopes of the graduate pupils of my courses than that.

I want to say a word here to any who feel that they are slow and not keeping up with the pace set by the rest of the class, and that word of advice is, take the same class for another four weeks' period. Don't have any false pride about it. You want to fit yourself perfectly for your profession. If the four weeks you have already had here are not time enough to do that, go in for another month. Really, two months is a very short time for completing a training of so much value to you.

I tell pupils in the courses in the other branches of dancing we teach, that if they feel stiff or have difficulty in performing their steps, they would do well to go into this class, the acrobatic dancing class, for a month, because here the students get all sorts of primary acrobatic tricks and gain in strength and flexibility. All dancing is easier to those who take this work. And besides, if you go out and accept an engagement you will be proficient in cartwheels, splits, and many other neat tricks that will be of great service to you. These are stunts that you cannot learn in a theatre; no one has time to teach them to you, nor the necessary equipment or facilities, and you want to be ready when the stage director calls for those who are capable of doing something unusual, to show him on the spot. And you cannot afford to try to learn things from another girl. You may injure yourself severely if you do. These difficult feats should only be attempted under the best instruction. Do not allow any girl or boy who is inexperienced to try to teach you anything in the line of acrobatic work.

Fresh air in your lungs, correct diet, and nine glasses of water a day will do wonders for you in many ways. You have heard me say this before. Well, I shall say it a good many times more, just as long as I have students under my charge who want to be "healthy, wealthy and wise"—and good looking and good dancers. And please do not treat this advice lightly. I can only ask you to observe these simple rules. I have no way of enforcing them, and possibly because they are simple you do not give them the consideration they deserve. Now let me tell you some facts, and then you decide whether or not you think it wise to neglect yourself.

Surely none of you will object to taking a glass of water nine times a day. Do not drink ice water, nor take water with meals. Liquids taken while eating will bloat you, make you fat, or make it impossible to assimilate your food properly, and that will keep you underweight. Take a glass on arising, one after breakfast, one before and after dinner and luncheon, one at about eleven in the morning and another at four, and one just before getting into bed. Water taken into the system this way induces a healthful perspiration which eliminates the bodily impurities. Your skin must be ventilated, which means that the pores must be opened, and water-drinking as I have directed will do this. If you drink milk, sip it slowly; don't pour it down. Don't eat between meals. Have a meal an hour and a half before class or before a performance, then the digestive process will have had time to complete its work and leave you in the best condition for mental and physical exertion.

After exercising here in your class, do not dress and hurry out into the street until your pores are closed. You have free shower baths at your disposal in your dressing rooms here in the studios, put there for just the purpose of enabling you to get into perfect condition before you go outdoors. Use them, with my compliments, please, and keep fit; then take a good rub down.

It is important to you to have a good clear skin and complexion. Some of you have it, and you want to keep it; some will be glad to know how to get it. I am going to tell you just how to acquire it and keep it, and clear up any little blemishes on your skin,—but it is so simple I am afraid you won't think it worth doing. To have clear skins you must have pure blood and good circulation of the blood, and to obtain these you must breathe deeply and correctly and so get fresh air, full of oxygen, into your lungs. That's all there is to it. And now, here is the correct way to breathe to accomplish all this, and I wish you would practice it now here in the class as I tell you about it:

Breathe in through your nostrils, with the mouth closed. Inhale slowly and way down deep, filling your lungs as full as you can; then exhale slowly through your mouth. Do this as an exercise, and do it ten times before you stop. Then do it again whenever you think of it, not less than three times a day. You cannot do it too often, no danger of that! It won't hurt you or cost you a cent. The air drawn into your lungs this way expands your chest and increases your lung capacity. This makes good wind for dancing, and all dancers need lots of wind; you have to have it, you have to call for lots of breath when you dance rapidly or long. Start in right now, and by the time you have a stage engagement you will be prepared with a bellows that will furnish all the air you call for—and meanwhile watch your skin and your complexion put on the clear, healthy, beautiful appearance that every woman envies. The air in this room, as in any room, is not entirely free of impurities; it is not the best air for your breathing exercises. Outdoors—say, over in Central Park, only a block from here—is where you find the beautifying, pure oxygen that will start your blood tingling, expand your chest, and give you the real beauty of skin and complexion that nature meant all women should have. Walk. Exercise. While you're out walking, take your beauty-breathing exercise as you go.

In my office I have a list of foods, with sixteen rules for good health. The word "diet" suggests starvation and going hungry and a lot of disagreeable things like that, I suppose, and so you would much rather not hear about it. Well, it isn't as bad as you think, and a proper diet is a health insurance, and should be carefully observed. Do you know that I have made a study of diets and dieting, and of anatomy—the structure of the human body? My interest in dancing and in my pupils here— and in my own health—has prompted me to study that subject thoroughly. I could tell you a great deal about getting and keeping healthy, if you cared to hear it and if I had time to go into the subject.

My best dancers, and all good dancers, diet. That is, they are careful to eat what is best for them, and not everything that may tickle the palate yet raise a rumpus inside one and upset the whole system, and make them cross and cranky and homely and bad actors generally.

Good food, pure air, plenty of water, internally and externally, the right amount of sleep, not more than eight hours, and not less than seven, proper exercise and practice—all of these are essential to make good dancers—to make *you* good dancers.

Come in to my office tonight after class. Weigh yourselves before you come in. Then talk to me about yourself and get my diet list to take home, please.

NED WAYBURN'S MODERN AMERICANIZED BALLET TECHNIQUE

I HAVE invented a method of teaching the ballet that eliminates the long and tedious training formerly considered necessary, and fits the pupil for a stage appearance in the briefest possible length of time. That my method is a perfect success is evidenced in the best theatres everywhere. I have taken amateurs who never did a ballet step in their lives, put them in training by my personally devised method, and made perfect solo dancers of them in a few months' time, secured them engagements, and their fame as ballet dancers par excellence is today worldwide. Elsewhere in this book I shall name several of these whom you know best, and you will admit that I am right in what I have just said when you peruse their names.

I am assuming that you are aware of the fact that in all foreign countries the ballet student is taught for years before she is allowed to attempt a public appearance or permitted to consider a professional engagement. This ultra-conservative custom has been brought across the water, and the idea has always held here in America that the four, six, ten year apprenticeship was a necessity; that no dancer could qualify for a professional appearance in a shorter period. It was taken for granted that there was no short cut to this trade, and up to the recent present there has been none. But our American girls who are gifted with a talent for this superb form of graceful dancing will not consent to devote the best years of their lives to unproductive labor. The idea of signing away several years of their happy lives in order to become entitled merely to a critical teacher's approval, and all this time without compensation of a financial nature, does not appeal to any, and least of all to that very person, the young person who would make the best dancer.

Yet there was an increasing demand for capable ballet dancers, and the supply was limited and dwindling. So, in order to make a world happy, I put my wits to work and evolved a plan that has revolutionized the entire industry. And I have called it Ned Wayburn's Modern Americanized Ballet Technique; and it is a Ballet Technique at its very best. If I had done nothing else in the years of my theatrical experience, I should still feel that I had accomplished much that is worth while.

And, really, it is all very simple. The wonder is that others did not figure it out before I did. And it is no secret. I am going to tell you all about it, and what the results have been, and then you can see for yourself why it is no longer best or necessary to go to foreign lands and take lessons the old way, for years and years.

There is what is called the Universal Ballet Technique. It is the standard of the dancing world, recognized and observed everywhere that the ballet is taught or danced. My method follows this Universal Technique closely, and is identical in many of the essentials. The chief difference between the old way and my new method is in the preparatory work. Now, this will never become a world full of ballet dancers, because not everyone could learn this graceful undulation if they wanted to. (All the more reason, I say, why those who have the talent should profit by it.) Not all of my pupils, nor all of my best pupils in other forms of the art, can hope to become solo artistes in ballet work. I can glance over a class at work in any of my studios, and select the few who may hope to perfect themselves in the ballet. I have had to discourage and no doubt disappoint some of my ambitious ones who have aspired to master the great art of ballet dancing; but I know I did what was best for them in advising them as I did. These same girls will be topnotchers in other fields of stage dancing, and I would rather direct their pathway to sure success than to let them wander into byways where their feet might stumble. So first of all, the candidate for ballet dancing must have my approval, she must be qualified according to my high standards, and when I say "Yes," and the student enters faithfully upon the work as I lay it out, she is going to make good.

And the first instruction she will receive in my courses is in the nature of a muscle culture, a foundation technique that consists of exercises, on the felt floorpad, in limbering and stretching. It is very beneficial to everyone in every way, and unqualifiedly essential to the beginner in stage dancing in any of its forms. The prospective ballet dancer, by going through these exercises in the studio for a series of twenty lessons or so, and practicing three hours or more at home daily during the same period, develops strength in the muscles of the back, legs, ankles and feet that fits her for the ballet technique; and it is this foundation work that enables her to eliminate the antiquated exercises and some combinations of steps, and the unduly long, tedious and once necessary trials that fell to the lot of the old-country ballerina. So the secret is out; it is our special foundation work in limbering and stretching combined with my Americanized Ballet Technique that builds our American pupil into a strong, healthy, flexible, graceful person, well prepared for advancement into the beautiful art of the ballet.

This does not mean that the entrant for ballet honors has nothing to do but go at once upon the stage, a completed artiste. If this statement of my easier plan suggests such a thing, let me hasten to correct so erroneous an impression. There is work, and hard work, too, and lots of it, before our pupil becomes a ballet dancer, even under our less strenuous and much shortened course of training.

Grace of the entire body is sought and taught, graceful movements of the head, arms, legs and torso. In addition to grace and poise, there is need of great muscular strength, and this we are able to develop in our pupils without bunching the muscles of their calves, thighs or arms into unsightly knots. And this fact is not one of the least of the recommendations of our system. We insist upon symmetry and beauty of figure. This is really more important to the professional dancer than beauty of face. To possess both, a beautiful face and form, is the ideal condition, of course, but the figure is susceptible of being made attractive by our development technique, and any imperfections of the facial contour or features, and any defects in the complexion, are easily disguised or corrected by my method of teaching stage-makeup.

It must be considered that in the ballet the movement of the arms is very important, and to perform it properly requires long study and extreme accuracy. Just as the art of painting blends and composes colors, and by the composition of scenes and figures makes a whole that is pleasant to the eye, so the movements of the arms in dancing add many and diverse forms of grace to the body, guiding and regulating its movements so as to result in a harmonious whole. One authority has styled dancing "the music of the eye." The dancer who neglects the difficult study which the arms require because she believes that the only necessity is brilliant execution in the legs, will be an imperfect artist. It is not enough to know how to dance with one's legs; the ballet must also be executed with the trunk of the body and the arms. Their movements must be graceful and in harmony with those of the legs, since they constitute a weight for the equilibrium of the body when it rests on one leg. The arms must accompany the trunk, making a frame for it.

The movements of the head, of the eyes, the expression of the face, all are of tremendous importance in perfecting the ballet. It is because of the necessity of bearing constantly in mind the various attitudes of head, torso, arms and legs that I believe that the ballet contributes more than any other type of dancing to the general development of grace and poise of the whole body.

In addition to teaching what we call the legitimate American Ballet, we add to the students' repertoire what are known as "tricks," which earn applause for the dancer. Many of our pupils go directly from our courses to the professional stage, since it would be difficult for them to earn a supporting salary in the musical comedy field doing straight ballet work alone. We teach straight toe dances, and also eccentric toe dances, as will be demonstrated in another chapter.

You are now a student in our beginner's ballet class. First, you must provide yourself with soft ballet slippers, as without them it would be impossible to do this type of work. As you enter our ballet room you note full length mirrors on the walls, to enable you to watch yourself as you dance—the original "watch your step" propaganda. Also you will see a wooden rod, technically known as a "bar," running around the walls of the studio. This is about three and a half feet above the floor, and is easily grasped by the hand for support in practicing.

In your practice at home, in the absence of such a bar, substitute an ordinary chairback or other firm object as a support, being careful that its height is correct.

Now the first thing to acquire is a knowledge of the fundamental rules of the dance, since everything depends upon them, and no one may hope to attain proficiency without this knowledge.

The fundamental positions of the ballet are five, and their complete mastery has been the prime factor in the success of every ballet dancer since the dance was invented. You will be constantly referred to "first position," "third position," and the others throughout your instruction, and you must know instantly and intuitively what each reference means as you hear it or read it, and to do this you must have the five position thoroughly absorbed into your inner consciousness. That means, practice the five positions over and over, day after day. No ballet dancer ever was entitled to this name without she knew these five rules of the dance.

The five positions for practice at the bar are here given, and the primary exercise at each position described and pictured.

First Position: Stand erect, with the head up, the legs straight, the heels together, the toes pointed out, the weight of the body evenly distributed between the two feet. Ex-

First Ballet Position

tend one arm to lightly grasp the bar, and carry the other arm straight out from the shoulder, in a slightly relaxed position, as shown in the diagram. The thumb should rest on the tip of the first finger, the middle and ring fingers slightly bent, the little finger extended so that it is slightly separated from the others, the wrist bent slightly downward. The whole attitude should be flexible and graceful.

Now lower the body by bending the knees. The feet should be kept flat on the floor, the heels raised from the floor as little as possible when bending the legs. The knees should be extended to the sides, as shown in the diagram. The free arm should follow the attitude of the legs—that is, it should be lowered to the waist when the knees are bent. This bending should be repeated four times.

Second Position:
From the first position, keeping both legs straight, slide the right foot sideways until leg and foot are fully extended without moving the torso. Then p l a c e the weight of the body on both feet with heels on the floor. The head should be in a straight line above the center of the space between the heels. Now bend and rise slowly four times, without raising the heels from the floor.

Second Ballet Position

Third Position: From the second position, shift the weight to one leg, fully extending the foot and toes of the other leg. Then glide the extended leg slowly in front of the other, the heel leading, until the ankle of the leg behind is covered by the front leg. Bend and rise slowly four times; keeping the head in a straight line above the heel that is in front.

Third Ballet Position

Fourth Position: From the third position, slide the front leg forward as far as possible without moving the body, until foot and toes are fully extended; then put the heel on the floor, the foot turned outward. Place the weight of the trunk on both legs, the head being vertically above the heel of the front foot. B e n d and rise s l o w l y four times.

Fifth Posi- tion: F r o m the f o u r t h position, shift the weight to the back leg,

Fourth Ballet Position

fully extending the front leg and foot. Slide the front leg slowly back to the other leg with heel well turned out, until the feet are on a parallel line, with the heel of the front leg in front of the toes of the back leg. The weight of the body

Fifth Ballet Position

should rest on both legs, and the throat should be virtually above the ankle of the front leg. Bend and rise four times.

TERMS USED IN NED WAYBURN'S MODERN AMERICANIZED BALLET TECHNIQUE

Arabesque—A posture executed with one foot on the floor.

Assemblé — To bring the feet together.

Attitude — A posture executed with both feet on the floor.

Balance — A combined s l i d e (glissé), closing of the feet, rising on the toes and lowering of the heels.

Changement de Pied—Changing the position of the feet.

Chassé—A chasing step in three movements: Slide (glissé), cut (coupé), slide (glissé).

Ciseaux—The scissors step: A point and swing with one foot while hopping twice on the other.

Coupé—To cut.

Dégager—To sway; to transfer.

Démi Pas de Basque—A half or incomplete pas de basque.

Ecarté—To jump from a closed position, open the feet in the air, and land in a closed position.

Échappée—(Escaped.) Any changement done on the toes.

Elever—To rise on the toes.

Entrechat—To spring into the air and change the position of the feet as often as possible before landing.

Fouetté—A swinging of the leg.

Frappé—To stamp the foot.

Glissé—To slide.

Glissade—Three movements combined: Elever (to rise on the toes), glissé (to slide), assemblé (to close the feet).

Grand Battement—High beating.

Jeté—To leap or throw the weight from one foot to the other.

Movement—An activity of the body from a resting position; also a change from one activity to another.

The nine standard dancing Movements are:

    (1) *Droit*—to swing the foot forward and backward;

    (2) *Overt*—to swing the foot from right to left;

(3) *Glissé*—to slide;
(4) *Tourné*—to turn;
(5) *Tortiller*—to twist;
(6) *Battu*—to beat;
(7) *Sauté*—to hop;
(8) *Jeté*—to leap;
(9) *Coupé*—to cut.

Pas.—A step.

Pas Ballonne—A combination of hop, step, hop.

Pas Boiteaux—A limping step in three movements: Hop on right foot and raise left leg forward with the knee straight; step forward on left foot; step forward on right foot.

Pas de Basque—A step of three movements: Demi rond de jambe, jeté (describe half circle in air with leg, leap); glissé (slide); coupé (cut).

Pas de Bourrée—(Stuffing step.) Three little steps on ball of the foot.

Pas de Chat—(Cat step.) Four sideward movements: Leap, slide, step, step.

Pas Marché—(Marching step.) Four movements: step, swing, step, close.

Pas Sissonne—Imitation of opening or closing of a pair of scissors, done by bending in fifth position, hopping to one side, at the same time lifting opposite leg in second position; then leg down in front and assemblé in front with the leg that did the hop.

Petit Battement—Low beating.

Petit Battement avec Port de Bras—Low bending with arm movements.

Petit Battement sur le Cou de Pied—Small beatings around the ankle.

Petite Rond de Jambe—Small foot circles described on the floor.

Plier—To bend the knees.

Pirouette—An artistic turn executed on one foot.

Pointe—The toe.

Port de Bras—Carriage of the arms. The five arm movements are: Bending, stretching, raising, lowering, turning.

Rond de Jambe—Circles in the air executed by the leg.

Sauté—To hop.

Step—A placing of the foot in any direction and transfering the weight onto it.

Terre á Terre—A series of pas de bourrées of four or more steps.

Three-step Turn—A complete turn, right or left, in three steps.

Tortiller—To turn or twist the leg.

Tour de Basque—A basque turn; pirouette de basque.

Tour Jeté—Jeté with a turn; one step sideward to right, one leap and complete turn; one step sideward onto right foot.

Tour Sauté—One step, one hop, turning completely around in direction of the step.

MR. WAYBURN ADDRESSES THE BEGIN-
NERS' CLASS IN BALLET TECHNIQUE

YOU have now advanced in your studies to where it becomes necessary to train yourselves for the stage mentally as well as physically. You have acquired the flexibility, strength of body and symmetry of form that was promised in my earlier courses to those who faithfully attended class and persistently practiced at home.

You have progressed through the hard foundation technique to a point where you are physically fitted to undertake the beautiful work of our ballet technique.

But now that you are entering on a new phase of your life work, it is no time to let down and by carelessness lose what you have already acquired by your obedience to your studio instruction. I am sure you will not disappoint me by doing this.

Please bear in mind you have still some hard work before you, both mental and physical hard work, before you are ready to capitalize your efforts, to get the substantial rewards that come to the graduate pupils of these courses. You can by looking back a few weeks see your own improvement. You are able today to do many things of value in a stage career that when you entered here you found impossible of accomplishment. But you are still in the formative period as to the finished product, as represented by the solo ballet, the stage work par excellence, to which you all aspire, and in which you will realize your fondest hopes when you possess its full technique as we teach it.

You are more fortunate than you may realize in having available the benefit of our ballet technique instead of having to go through the long years of excessive labor that would have been your lot if you lived abroad and wished to become a premier danseuse. Long training, at least four years' daily instruction and practice, is required of ballet students in England, France, Italy, Russia, or anywhere else in the world. The foreign methods tend to bunch the muscles. You have seen dancers with knotted calves, bunchy knees, huge thighs, all the result of the old technique. As you know, we insist upon your preparing for the ballet course by taking our limbering and stretching exercises, and today you know why. You have a genuine foundation to build upon. Your bodies are lithe and supple, your muscles hard yet not misshapen, and you have advanced by easy stages through the foundation work to where you are today, ready for the finishing touches.

In your ballet work you must be careful how you land when you jump into the air. My system lands the body with the knees bent, otherwise you might undermine your health. To come down full weight on your heels repeatedly would prove very injurious.

Keep your muscles exercised. There is no better exercise for the dancer than walking, and three miles a day is none too much. Take long deep breaths out of doors. Horseback riding, golf, tennis, all are good for you. Dancing itself is the best exercise you can have, but when you have a one-hour lesson or more, and then practice at home three or more hours daily you will find walking a rest, a relaxation, because it is a change of work.

Occasionally we have a Pupils' Frolic in our own Demi-Tasse Theatre, to give you a chance to do a turn before a friendly audience. This is good experience and encourages talent.

Some of you sing. Some are accomplished in other forms of dancing. I like to hear your voices and see your dances. They may be valuable aids to you in your stage work, even if not just of a stage character. I can tell about that when you sing or dance for me. Anyway, they indicate that you have talent and are accomplished and able to improve yourself, and that suggests that you possess a personality of your own, one of the great essentials of your future success. Sometimes we arrange special exhibitions for charity affairs and call upon our best talent to appear in these. Such an opportunity is very valuable experience for you and I am glad for your sake always when I can get you a chance to appear in public or social affairs, to give you self-confidence and inspiration.

Now one more very important lesson you must learn before you finish here, and that is in the art of makeup. For it is an art, and one that every actress must be fully posted upon. If you don't know how much depends upon correct makeup, come and ask me about it and I will tell you. We hold classes in makeup in our Demi-Tasse Theatre on occasional Saturday afternoons. I advise you to secure a place in this class soon. You will find it very interesting and valuable. Your application should be made at the counter in the main business office. The charge is $2.00 for a class lesson, and we teach our own methods, dry, cream, and grease-paint makeups.

Usually we take three girls, a blonde, a brunette and a red-head, and make them up in class, explaining the work as we do so. For private instruction in makeup our charge is $5.00 a lesson.

It is very practical instruction and you will obtain much positive benefit from it. It is not always the girl who is most beautiful on the street or in the parlor who makes up best. Often the contrary is the case, and the girl with the ordinary street appearance becomes very attractive looking on the stage with the proper makeup. In any event, my makeup directions will make a vast improvement in your appearance for stage effect, as well as for street.

There is no doubt but that you are obtaining in my courses the most valuable ballet instruction in America, if not in the entire world. The instructors I am supplying you with have had years of professional ballet training and experience both abroad and in this country, as I am sure you all know. Furthermore, they are not only remarkable dancers, but also very competent as teachers. So if you give attention to their instruction and watch them as they illustrate the various elements that constitute the complete ballet technique, and learn the several basic positions and the graceful movements and attitudes and kicks that go to make up the complete whole, you may expect to become expert in this beautiful art yourselves. But you must practice, practice at home, every day, many hours a day, and keep it up right along. There is no other way to succeed in any dancing, and especially in ballet work.

You have been told in your former classes in this studio about keeping yourselves fit and healthy and charming by consuming nine glasses of water daily, aided by deep breathing, correct and careful diet and eight hours' sleep.

Continue to observe these simple laws of health and beauty, if you value your present opportunities and your future success, as I am certain you do. Form regular habits now, treat your bodies well. The recompense is so great if you do, you cannot afford to be careless in any respect.

Feel free to come to my private office any time, or write me, and discuss with me personally any matters that concern yourself in relation to your health or prospects for the future. We are both, you and I, interested in and working steadily for your future. This is a forward-looking establishment where futures are made to order. Your future, and that of the hundreds of young pupils who favor us here with their presence, may depend in large measure upon your energy and studiousness while you are with us and under our tutelage. Let us help you. Let me help you. It is my mission in life to direct folks straight along the pleasant paths of health, beauty and financial independence, and I feel sure I can be of aid to you and your future if you will give me the opportunity to do so.

MARION DAVIES

ANN CONSTANCE.
(Before she entered the Ned Wayburn Studios.)

ANN CONSTANCE.
(After she entered the Ned Wayburn Studios.)

MARY EATON

NED WAYBURN'S TOE DANCING

ALL forms of modern toe dancing — and there are several — are based upon the ballet technique, of which a synopsis of my own Americanized form appears in a preceding chapter.

There is toe dancing of the really classical school in the perfected ballet. That is the kind with which we are most familiar. When a mother says, "I want my child to be taught toe dancing," she usually expects to be understood as referring to the ballet in its entirety, of which dancing on the toes seems symbolical.

But of later years there has developed in the terpsichorean art other forms and combinations of toe dancing besides the strictly classical, as for instance, the eccentric toe dance and the acrobatic toe dance.

As to the classical form, reference to the ballet chapter will find its present development duly set forth.

The eccentric toe dance and its fellow, the acrobatic toe dance, both have their beginnings in the fundamental ballet technique, in which one must be well and properly schooled before expecting to succeed in the more advanced work of these laterday favorites.

For they are favorites, as an hour at any modern playhouse where the newer dances are featured, will demonstrate.

It is at the behest of the great American audience that these newer toe dances are with us. You and the rest of the public that constitute our audiences demand action, tricks—or at least tricky and novel touches here and there —in your dancing entertainment. The old stuff doesn't "get over" with you any more. So we invent new things that present what you are bound to like, and the eccentric and acrobatic toe dances are the result.

It may be jumping down a flight of steps on the toes, or a continued hopping on one toe for 16 counts to music, or a swinging of one leg back and forth, like a pendulum, in an acrobatic way while the dancer hops on one toe— such stunts as these are the applause-getters nowadays, and they are well worth applauding, too, for they are pleasing demonstrations of real skill, and are acquired by the dancer only after long and continued effort and practice. Few if any, I am sure, fully appreciate the time and labor it takes to make a modern toe dancer, one who shall be able to perform something new and catchy in a clever way,—a real feat nowadays, and one that theatrical producers are quick to see and seize when it appears.

The fact is, the tricks I have spoken of must never dominate the dancing, but must be entirely secondary and incidental, as it were. Otherwise the dancer becomes an acrobat. You don't care for straight acrobatics, Mr. Public, but acrobatic dancing, or dancing with a neat acrobatic stunt thrown in incidentally as a bit of seasoning, is really very palatable and pleasing to you. It must remain a beautiful dance, aided and added to by a pretty surprise in the form of a bit of unexpected toe work—then you like to see it, so we are careful in my courses to promote in this kind of work only that form for which there is a demand,—and this is equally true with every other kind of dancing that we teach.

Before any toe dancing is undertaken by the ambitious student there must be a foundation laid to build upon that shall be lasting and efficient. The body must be under perfect control; every muscle immediately responsive and ready, strength placed where it is essential. Our students who have passed through the limbering and stretching course (foundation technique) and have advanced to the ballet work and through that, are ready for the advanced features in modern toe dancing. We work this way with such of our more promising pupils as desire it, and then teach them the "tricks," as we call it, that are so effective when properly done. Every toe dancer should have one-hour lessons five days each week till perfected, and at least three hours daily practice six days in the week at home.

I have already stated and now say it once more in this connection, that children should not go on their toes in the dance until they have taken what I know to be a necessary foundation course, to fit them to do so without danger of permanent distortion of feet and legs, enlarged ankles, and other ill effects. It is the parents' fault, of course, when children are forced into toe dancing at too early an age or without proper preparation. I simply will not consent to do it. I have seen children of sixteen who ought to be at their best at that age in this work, yet because of the forcing process in early years were incapable of sustaining themselves on their deformed feet.

Many of my well-known graduate pupils have been seen in the Follies and other first class productions. Their work is an inspiration to all who love exquisite dancing of this kind. They secured the right foundations on the start, and now have strength, speed, grace, and ability to do what their dances call for. There are lots and lots of toe dancers graduated from my courses, and I cannot think of one who has failed to make good.

That, I think, is because their personality plus practice plus honest and capable instruction and a knowledge of showmanship and stage-craft absorbed from my "inspirational talks" has brought forth the natural result.

NED WAYBURN'S
SPECIALTY DANCING

THERE is a wonderful field for the dancer who can create an appealing dance of his or her own, or who can take some type of dance and by sheer personality so develop it as to be identified with it as the representative of that form of dancing.

Not everyone can be a specialty dancer of this sort, but to be one is well worth the effort of every ambitious exponent of the dancing art.

Any kind of stage dancing may become a specialty dance. But it really takes a person with good mental capacity as well as expert dancing ability to develop what others may do well, make of it an outstanding and triumphant success, and identify it with one's self before the public as one's very own.

But the rewards are great for those who accomplish this, and I am always glad to see an effort made along these lines, since it means so much in the way of fame and fortune to those who make the grade.

And one may become a specialty dancer in more than one line. Gilda Gray, for instance, in the Follies of 1922 did three separate and distinct specialties in her work at

141

every performance: A musical comedy specialty, an Hawaiian dance, and her "Come Along" character dance, which she built up under my direction into a pronounced hit.

So with these facts before us, that any dance may be made into a specialty, taken out of the ordinary and individualized, and that no dancer is limited to a single line in this work, but can spread out over the entire field if competent to do so, there is surely ample encouragement to the dancing pupil to make an effort to profit by the opportunity my studio instruction affords, and become not only a good dancer but also a good, better, best specialty dancer—something quite worth while on every stage, European as well as American.

Almost any pupil will naturally specialize in some one form of dancing in the learning process. Thus one may show a preference for the musical comedy work, or tap and step, clogging, acrobatic dancing, whatever it may be. It is preferred because one takes to it easiest, or is most proficient in it, or has a personal liking for it. That is the dance for you to specialize in. Perfect yourself in it. Do a little better than anyone else does, and you are on the boulevard headed toward becoming a specialty dancer.

Legmania is a form of specialty dancing. The Charleston, at present so popular with the multitude, is another. The Hula Hula and all other kinds of character dancing are specialties. Clogging, the ballet, interpretive and toe dances—why enumerate them. Let it go at this: Any form of dancing that you like best and are most efficient in can be made *your* specialty dance if you give it personality, atmosphere,—if you vitalize it so that it stands out alive and distinctive—your very own.

It takes brains as well as legs to become a specialty dancer of real quality, capable of controlling the public's interest. Yes, and it takes competent instruction to guide you right, and it takes practice on your part after you get the instruction, too. But it is quite worth while. The rewards are sure if you merit them.

NED WAYBURN'S EXHIBITION DANCING

WHAT is technically known as Exhibition Dancing is an exaggerated form of the usual social or ballroom dancing. It is "team" work, performed by two, a man and a woman, and is never given as a solo dance, by a single artist.

There is no end to the styles of dances that may be employed in exhibition work. The public is thoroughly familiar with those most often presented to view in public and private ballroom, at social or other functions, which are either the Exhibition Fox Trot, the Exhibition One Step, the Tango, the Exhibition Waltz or the Whirlwind dance.

This by no means covers the possible field. Its limitations are measured only by the ability of the "team," and the popularity that demands this or that style of dance, as the fickle public fluctuates in its preference.

An exhibition dance of whatever nature must have an element of the spectacular and theatrical in its presentation in order to appeal. The dancers must inject some surprise steps in an effective place, throw in a little "tricky" stuff that is new or startling—do something neat and out of the ordinary to make the dance qualify as "Exhibition" and not just the usual every-day type of some well-known form of the dance.

Among the best-known exponents of exhibition dancing one naturally recalls Vernon and Irene Castle, Maurice and his several partners, Florence Walton, Leonora Hughes and Barbara Bennett, as well as the "teams" of

Clifton Webb and Mary Hay, and Basil Durant and Kay Durban. All these and many other professional exhibition dancers have amply succeeded in their efforts to please the public, and have found the financial returns to be most satisfactory. It is a very profitable line of work for dancers of the right qualifications.

Exceptional personality is essential, as well as great skill in the art of dancing, and less than a commanding supremacy will not suffice to carry the work through to a successful issue. Yet there is a large field here, open to many who may not as yet even dream of their adaptability to such a career as this suggests.

It has been my pleasure to assist in the direction of every exhibition dancer whose name I have quoted above. Some of them received their first impetus along this line from me, followed my advice and instruction, and in consequence became internationally famous and successful. I am still taking those well adapted to this line and putting them in the way they should go. I know the type of person best qualified to make a success in exhibition dancing, and if those I select will be guided by my experience and knowledge there is no reason why they should not reap the rewards their merit earns, as well as those I have named have done.

There is a knack in acquiring the necessary ability as a dancer of this type that not every instructor is able to impart. I do not teach exhibition dancing in classes in my studios. Individual private lessons is the only successful way, and that is my way. Most other forms of dancing are learned as well or even better in classwork.

I doubt if exhibition dancing will ever be overdone. It is popular, and good dancers for this line of work are not too numerous. So it seems likely to be in continued demand indefinitely.

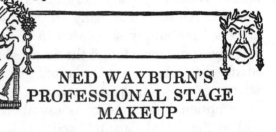

NED WAYBURN'S PROFESSIONAL STAGE MAKEUP

THE Ned Wayburn Courses teach every form of stage makeup, for men as well as for women, and for every known character part as well as the "straight" makeup for youth. To put all the expert professional makeup knowledge into this book would be to practically crowd out everything else or so enlarge the volume as to make it cumbersome. To avoid this and at the same time meet a strong public demand, I have in contemplation a book devoted exclusively to this important subject, that shall post a world of waiting aspirants for stage honors in every detail of the art of correct makeup. Meanwhile, the subject has an important bearing on the art of stage dancing and so demands a prominent place in this present work.

I have, therefore, chosen for demonstration here the one most popular stage makeup, which is that adapted to the use of the professional stage woman in every modern theatre, opera house and music hall, and am here giving it a complete and thorough exposition. In presenting this form of makeup thus prominently, I do not wish in any degree to convey the idea that men and male youth are ignored in our studio teaching of makeup, and that our sole concern is to make the young woman presentable on the stage. This is not the fact. We teach makeup to men as well as to women, and every correct form of the art.

Do not confuse a stage makeup with the customary society makeup that milady applies in her boudoir. They are two entirely different problems.

To makeup correctly for the modern stage, with its multiple lights of great intensity and all the colors of the rainbow, requires special study of yourself individually and a knowledge of what effects the various lighting schemes will produce on the human countenance.

Three ladies standing side by side on the same stage may require three different makeups, depending upon their types, in order to appear at their best to the audience. The brunette, the blonde, the auburn-haired, each needs a different treatment, and if through ignorance or indifference any omits proper attention to a single item of the very important detail of her facial makeup, the result will be disastrous. All of which emphasizes the need of one's being properly taught on the start just how to makeup in a manner to bring out one's personality, to enhance one's beauty, and create the most pleasing appearance before her audience. We are now speaking, of course, of the woman who is to appear in a youthful part; character makeup is an entirely different proposition, with which we are not concerned here.

It is impossible to go on the stage today without makeup. Should any actress try to do so, the appearance of her features would be almost deathlike. She would be repulsive to the eyes of the audience, a condition that neither she nor the producer of the show would tolerate. The very lights that render superbly beautiful the person with proper makeup cause the bare flesh to lose its natural tints, cast shadows under the brows and above the face, create hollows where they do not exist and are not wanted, and utterly destroy the pleasing picture.

Makeup, then, is one of the first essentials to stage success, and it makes no difference how truly beautiful you may be in features and natural coloring off the stage, the fact persists—you must makeup, and makeup right.

But the uninstructed amateur, whose sole knowledge of makeup is confined to the boudoir, is very prone to overdo in her maiden attempts at stage makeup, and so disastrously decorate her face that under the unaccustomed and little understood lights of the theatre she appears hideous to the folks out in front. And this is especially true of the most beautiful type of women, who think they know, and don't.

Anyone with regular features can learn to apply makeup so that on the stage she will be as prepossessing as her naturally more favored sister-woman. A beauty unadorned by facial makeup, or a beauty not properly made-up, will be far outclassed in apparent beauty on the stage by the plainer woman who has mastered the art of makeup and knows how to apply it judiciously and correctly. It is all in knowing how, and the learning is not difficult. The professional actress will not fail to obtain personal instruction in this art from expert teachers, which is decidedly the best way. Pupils in our studios avail themselves of our classes and private lessons in makeup and in doing this lay a foundation of invaluable knowledge that will continue with them through life. The aspirant or amateur who for personal reasons cannot come to our studios for this instruction will absorb much of value by a perusal and study of this chapter. For, while it is not possible to advise an unseen person, whose type you do not know, with the same exactness as you could if she stood before you, there is much here that is general in its application to all types, and the care we are taking to make our information broad enough to cover all these greatly simplifies matters for the absent students.

There are two steps to a correct knowledge of your personal needs in the makeup art: First, what to use; and second, how to use it.

I am going to start you right on both of these steps.

Any actress of experience will tell you that her most valuable stage possession is her Makeup Box. It contains the necessary tools of her trade, without which she would be helpless to carry on. It is to her what the brush and colors and palette are to the painter; the needle and thread to the seamstress; the hammer and saw and plane to the carpenter. Before you enter upon a stage career supply yourself with a complete makeup box equipped with all the needed tools and ingredients for making up for the part you are to assume. This is a necessary purchase, and will prove one of the best paying investments you ever made.

Ordinarily a makeup box stocked with the best materials will cost about $12.00 and is not extravagantly expensive at that price. So many of our students sought our advice as to their purchases in this line, as they left our studios for the professional stage, that we fitted out a line of makeup boxes, completely stocked, for each complexion type, which we are selling to them over the counter at $9.50. The actual cost to us of each set is about eight cents more than we sell it for; plainly indicating an absence of grasping commercialism in our nature, for which we hope and expect due commendation.

Buying expertly and in quantities has enabled us to get together this *Ned Wayburn Professional Makeup Box* of the best stuff in the world for its purpose, some of the ingredients being made in America, others in Paris, and still others in Berlin,—all standard goods and used every day in the year in every theatre of the civilized world,—and at the same time keep the cost to our students down below a ten dollar bill. (Applause.) We thank you.

Now we are getting orders for our professional makeup box to be sent by mail and express to professionals and amateurs throughout this continent, and while we are glad to accommodate all who honor our own profession by their presence in it, please do not expect us to do so at cost. It is one thing to hand a box over the counter, and quite another to pack that box for shipment so as to conform to established requirements by the government post office or the express companies, prepay postage, insure it, and deliver it to the New York postal authorities. So we have put a price of $10.95 on this makeup outfit for parties who do not call for it in person at our studio, with postage extra, according to the zone in which you reside, if it goes by mail. We would rather send it by express and let you pay the charges for carriage at your end, if it is all the same to you. The weight of this outfit packed for shipment is about seven pounds. We insure it in transit at $10, which adds a few cents to its cost to you.

It will save correspondence and the disappointment of delay if when you order you tell us your age, sex, color of hair, color of eyes, color of complexion, for what character you wish the makeup (youth, maturity, old age, advanced old age, or any of the possible character parts known to the stage); the nature of the play; whether for a large theatre or the more intimate small theatre or hall; if for moving pictures (which calls for a decidedly different makeup from all other stage work), and everything else bearing on this matter that you can think of. Always bear in mind when you order, that each box is fitted for one type of person only, and cannot be used indiscriminately by a brunette and a blonde and someone else who ranks between the two in coloring and type, and that in consequence each must have a personal makeup box of her own.

The Ned Wayburn Professional Makeup Box for a "straight" stage makeup for a blonde youth, suited to the use of a young woman with light hair, blue eyes and light complexion, in musical comedy, light opera or any dancing or speaking part in the usual stage performance, for presentation in a hall or theatre, with modern stage lighting facilities, is as follows:

The Box. Art steel, about 6⅜ in. wide by 9½ in. long, 5 in, high, with handle and lock and key. Strongly made on purpose to stand the wear and tear of travel and dressing room handling, and should last a lifetime. Have your name painted on it as soon as you get it, to make it your very own. It may be your frequent companion for many years.

One-half Pound Tin of Cold Cream. Usually Stein's, to which we give the preference, since it is slightly less hard and contains a little more oil than most of the others. This cold cream is the same for all types, blonde, brunette and the others.

One-half Pound Tin of Face Powder. Stein's No. 2. (Brunettes would use Stein's No. 2½ face powder.)

One Glass Jar Moist Rouge. Stein's medium. This medium lip rouge is suitable for blonde and brunette types. It is standard, can be bought anywhere, is always uniform and the colors run true. If you are ever in Chicago, visit Warnesson's. He specializes in lip rouge and makes a very good kind.

One Stick Foundation Grease Paint, Flesh. Stein's No. 2. (For brunettes, Stein's No. 3.) This is the large stick.

One Stick Grease Paint, Special Blue Lining Color. Stein's No. 11. For lining the eyes.

One Stick Grease Paint, Carmine. Stein's No. 18. Red foundation, for both blondes and brunettes.

One Box Mascaro, Black. Leichner's No. 60. For darkening the eyebrows.

One Package Cosmetique, Black. Roger and Gallet. For beading the eyelashes.

One Box Dry Rouge. Dorin, No. 18.

One Pink Velour Powder Pad. Gainsborough No. 350. This is about the finest procurable; is of large size, so it will not fall in the powder box and scatter the contents.

One Black Crayon Pencil. 6B Venus, American Pencil Co. For putting shadows under the eyes.

One Dark Blue Pencil. Faber No. 6625. For shading around the eyes.

One Orange Wood Stick. For applying beading to the eyelashes.

One Rabbit's Foot. Also called rouge paw.

One Baby Brush, with handle. For blending. Very necessary tool.

Paper Felt Liners, one package. To outline lips and to place red dots in corners of the eyes.

Cosmetic Stove, Lockwood's. For heating cosmetique to bead the eyelashes. This stove is approved by Fire Insurance Underwriters. It encloses a candle in a safe way and avoids the use of dangerous fuels in the dressing rooms.

One Mirror. 6x8 inches, in wood frame, with metal support. Will stand alone or serve as hand mirror. Strong, clear glass. The best to be had for its purpose.

This completes the list of contents in the Ned Wayburn Professional Makeup Box, for a "straight" stage makeup, for young ladies. For other types and different characterizations the ingredients are changed to suit each case, while the price remains uniform.

There is but one necessity for completing the makeup that is not included in the outfit as given, and that is Liquid White, which comes in white or flesh. This is to be applied as a wash to exposed flesh not otherwise made up. It comes in liquid form only, and can be purchased locally in any first-class drug store. We know Suratt's make of liquid white to be good, and there may be others.

A towel, a cake of soap, a basin of water and a few yards of cheese cloth should be assembled before commencing makeup operations.

A makeup is easiest applied while seated at a table with your materials spread out conveniently before you. If possible, elevate your mirror so that you can see the reflection of your features without the necessity of bending over. Always make up in incandescent light, never in daylight.

When making-up is a matter of daily routine the clothing will become badly soiled in a short time if worn during the process. To save your costume, either wear a washable kimono over it, or better, don the kimono over undergarments and put on the costume after the makeup is applied.

In private lessons at our studios we teach all the required forms of stage makeup, taking every type of person that comes to us and developing each individually along such lines as the character or part demands. Men, women, and youth come to us here for development of their correct makeup in private lessons.

In our class instruction in this line of work only the "straight" makeup for youth is presented, that being the one our young lady pupils find especially adapted to their stage needs. These special classes are held as occasion requires to meet the students' demands, and are given in our own Demi-Tasse Theatre, connected with the studios. Usually a demonstration is made with a blonde, a brunette and a red-head, to show the class the different requirements of the different types. Following this demonstration, each member of the class puts on a makeup under the advice and constructive criticism of the teachers, until thoroughly versed in the art, as it applies to his or her own individual type.

Since the reader of this may not be coming to us for either private or class lessons, we will describe the correct manner of applying makeup in simple language that will enable the distant aspirant to learn all that may be learned by reading without the presence of a personal teacher.

You are now seated at your dressing table, your mirror at a convenient elevation in front of you and between two good lights, your lay-out of tools and materials spread on a towel on the table top, a kimono or other garment spread over your person. Now take a strip of cheesecloth three or four inches wide and tie around the forehead, back of the ears, and behind the neck; or one may use a close-fitting skull cap. Tuck in all straying locks. The idea is, of course, to keep powder, grease paint and cold cream from getting into and soiling the hair. Now you are going to apply makeup.

First stage. Cold cream. Apply this liberally all over the face from the hair line to the upper part of the throat, but not on the neck. Rub it in thoroughly to fill all the pores of the skin. Be careful to cover all the space around the eyes, also rub in on the eyelashes, using care to keep it out of the eyes, for it will cause stinging. Greasing the eyelashes this way makes the removal of the makeup much easier. Now rub your face with a piece of cheesecloth until all the superfluous cold cream has disappeared. If the face shines too much, you have not removed enough of the cream. The surface should give the appearance of being well oiled, but not have a sticky, pasty or greasy surface.

Second stage. Foundation Grease Paint. The quality of your makeup depends upon this. It will be smooth or rough according to the way you develop it. Rub the end of the grease paint stick several times on each cheek, once across the chin, once or twice on the forehead and once down the nose. Use the ends of the fingers and pat this into place rather than rub it, till it is thoroughly worked into all the surface you have just covered with the cold cream. Every pore must be filled with the grease paint. Do not apply it too thick, which would give the face a pasty, unnatural look. Do not forget underneath the chin. Do not apply it to the ears or behind them. Leave no streaks or neglected spots. Have it uniform all over. Blend the paint till the face has an even tone. Watch your mirror carefully. It is better to have the grease paint a little too thin on the face than too thick, but you will soon learn to get it just right, which is what you are aiming at.

Third stage. Under rouge; foundation red; Stein's No. 18 carmine. Make a few dots with the carmine grease paint stick on each cheek and on the end of the chin. Use but little, and blend it by patting with the first and second fingers of both hands, rather than by rubbing. Begin well up against the nose, go under and around the eyes, and toward the temples, working it down below the ear and off the jaw in case there is a hollow in the lower part of the cheek. The color should extend down on the cheek, over on the temple and well up to the eye, patted and blended till no one can see where the red fades into the foundation. The chin is then blended in the same way, to leave no line between foundation color and under rouge. If your chin is pointed, blend in front, not below, or it draws the chin way down. Put on a lighter makeup for a small, intimate theatre, and a heavier one for the large auditorium.

Fourth stage. Enlarging and beautifying the eyes. This is a very important detail of correct makeup, and is indispensable on every well-lighted stage, where even the most soulful orbs with long, thick lashes will dwindle to half their size and have a faded, dull appearance if not properly made up. It is essential that the two eyes match in every detail, and to secure this result will require the taking of considerable pains and close study of your mirror. Stein's No. 11 blue lining stick is for use by the blue-eyed, regardless of the color of the hair or complexion. Stein's No. 17, for the dark-eyed. Titian-haired folks use Stein's No. 21 purple for the same purpose. With this grease paint stick of the color suited to you, draw a line across the upper eyelid between the eyebrow and the eyelashes, as close as possible to the lashes. With the fingers blend this line into a shadow, making it dark close to the upper lashes. Either pencil can be used for this purpose also. Do not get the shadow up to the eyebrows, but cover all the upper eyelid, and a little beyond the eye at the outer corner. Use the Faber No. 6625 blue pencil or Venus 6B black for shading under the eye. Draw a line with it directly under the eyelashes, and with the fingers blend this into a shadow. Carried too far down this blue suggests illness, so be careful. The shadows thus placed above and below the eyes serve to outline them to the spectators in the theatre, where otherwise the eyes would practically disappear and not be seen at all owing to the strong footlights.

Fifth stage. "Fixing" the makeup. Powder No. 2 for blondes; No. 2½ for brunettes. The creamy tints are for the dark skins, the flesh and delicate pinks for the fair ones. Press the powder first on the chin. It is feminine instinct to start on the nose, but let your start in this case begin with the jaw or chin. Don't rub it in. Pat it on thick till the underlying paint is fully covered up. The powder absorbs the grease. From the chin work upward, reaching the nose after the pad has lost some of its original load, and the nose will not stare out so white on your face as it would if you began there first. Raise the eye and powder underneath; look down, and powder the space beneath eyebrow and eyelid.

Sixth stage. Smoothing off and blending. Use the baby brush for this; there is nothing else so good. It is surprising in its results. Do not press the brush too hard on the face; dust the surplus powder off carefully with a light touch, to leave no streaks or patches anywhere. If now the face has a greasy look, you have not used sufficient powder.

Seventh stage. High lighting. Take some of your No. 18 Dorin's dry rouge on the rabbit's foot and dust a very little on your cheeks. Do not press it down, just tickle about the edges of the rouge to be sure it blends perfectly with the foundation. If there is too much white about the nose, dust it lightly with the rabbit's foot. You can turn the paw around and blend with the end that is free of paint. Never show a white ear to the audience. If ears come into style again, as they will, the lobe and rim should be made a healthy pink, but not a strong red, with the rabbit's foot.

Eighth stage. Darkening the eyelashes and eyebrows. Use Leichner's No. 60 black mascaro; dark brown for light blondes. The lower lashes are better left without the treatment, since they are almost certain to smear the face if treated, and the shadow you have already placed there takes care of the lower lashes all that is necessary. Apply the mascaro to the upper lashes with the brush that comes with the mascaro, or any fine brush will do. Start a delicate line on the edge of the eyelid at the outer corner of the eye, let it curve slightly downward at the start. This line should not exceed half an inch in length and is never carried beyond the eye socket. Do not make the line heavy nor longer. A very little mascaro must be brushed lightly on to the eyebrows, following the curve of the upper eyelid. Fix the eyebrows carefully about three-quarters the size of the mouth, using black or brown mascaro according to whether your type is dark or light.

In this place we are going to tell you how to bead the eyelashes, but unless you are a professional actress and your part will be decidedly enhanced by having the eyes very much in evidence, we advise against your undertaking it. It is not a necessary stage in the makeup process, but it comes into the story of makeup naturally and we give it here for the benefit of those who may wish to make use of it. Beading the lashes consists in placing a small bead of cosmetique on the extreme tip of each lash. This is best done on the upper lashes only, leaving the lower ones free. The Lockwood Cosmetic Stove is a small affair that holds a piece of candle and a baby-size frying-pan, or skillet, and is one device for its purpose that has the approval of fire insurance companies and so will not be objected to by the theatre fireman. There are some heating devices that you are not permitted to use in any theatre, and persistence in their use after being once cautioned has caused arrest more than once.

In this connection many interesting true tales might be told of principal actors being taken bodily from the stage in the midst of a play and landed in the local jail, causing the curtain to be lowered and the audience dismissed. The stage fireman, assigned to every first class theatre during a performance, has authority to enforce all ordinances intended to prevent fire and eliminate fire risk in play-houses, even to go to the extremity of arresting offenders against the public's safety. So be careful to use only a Lockwood Cosmetic Stove or some equally safe affair in your dressing room.

You light the candle, place a small amount of Roger and Gallet black cosmetique in the little pan and heat it over the candle flame till melted. Take up some of this molten cosmetique on the flat end of your orange wood stick and apply it with a deft quick stroke to the upper lashes, paint-ing each one separately and without clotting, so that a little bead hangs to the tip of each upper lash. Use care not to drop any of the black on your makeup. The effect of this beading is to beautify the appearance of the actress by bringing out her eyes in a wonderful manner under the strongest of spot lights.

Ninth stage. Red dots in the inner corners of the eye. Dip the paper felt liner in the moist lip rouge and with it make a tiny red dot in the extreme inner corner of each eye, but on the lid—not in the eye—to space the eyes and make them look to be the distance of one eye apart. Keep these dots well away from the nose, or they will tend to make you look crosseyed from the front.

Tenth stage. Rouging the lips. Stein's moist lip rouge, medium. If the lips are left their natural color the footlights bleach them white and colorless. Shape the upper lip into a cupid's bow and round out the lower lip. Dip the little finger into the rouge and press it tightly against the lips, being careful not to smear it; open the mouth and draw the upper lip tight over the teeth. When necessary the upper lip can be shortened in appearance by blending and putting the cupid's bow a little higher. Do not put color on the lips beyond the angle of the nose, otherwise it will make your mouth appear very large. A blonde should not apply the rouge full strength, as it is too dark for her. The lips should not be heavily painted, and the line about the edges should be soft and smooth.

Eleventh stage. Finish with a little powder, dusting the face very gently, using a swan's-down puff. Put a very little powder on the lines about the eyes, but not enough to dull them.

Now look in your mirror with critical eyes. Your handiwork should have resulted in a velvety, soft yet rich complexion that will stand the strong lights of the modern theatre.

What you have just put on is known as a grease-paint makeup. There is also a cream makeup, so called, but it is less desirable for the modern professional stage. It fails to give the right effect for a real musical show with powerful lights. I have used both and do not hesitate to give this opinion based on my own experience.

There is also a dry makeup, with powder, known in theatrical parlance as a "lazy" makeup, suitable only for a "dumb" chorus girl who has no interest in her work, who comes in late and does not care whether she appears to advantage or not.

To complete any makeup, apply liquid white with a soft sponge to the neck, chest, arms and other exposed flesh that is not already made up. If, as in some of the modern revues, the legs are not covered with stockings or tights, they too must have an application of liquid white. To look right, any flesh that is exposed must be made up, because the lights bleach the exposed flesh, making it appear bloodless and giving one a gruesome, corpse-like color.

You are wise if in the matter of makeup you study your own face. Experiment, and note the results. When you are certain you have acquired the best for your own purposes, practice it often, till you can put it on properly and always with the same result. Don't seek to look madeup, ever, but to look your best for the part you are playing, always. If the makeup ingredients are in evidence to the audience you have not created the proper illusion and must practice making up until you acquire skill. It usually takes about one-half hour to put a good makeup on after you have perfected the process with your own features.

Removing Makeup. First remove the beads of cosmetic from the lashes. Then get rid of the little red spot in the inner corner of the eye. Work this toward the nose with cold cream. Then take plenty of cold cream on the fingers of both hands and massage the face thoroughly, to soften the makeup all over. Wipe it off with cheesecloth or an old towel, that you can throw away. Now wash the face with warm water and soap, dry thoroughly, apply a bit of powder, and you are all ready to dress.

SOME MAKEUP NOTES

You makeup for the lights of the theatre, which nowadays are very strong, and may come from many directions and in various colors. The switchboard controlling all the lights is in the first entrance of the stage, and the electrician in charge has his plots and cues all carefully planned for each act. He does not throw lights on or off for the fun of it or at his pleasure, but exactly as carefully designed and mapped by the show's producing director.

The front lights are those in the body of the house as distinguished from the stage. On the stage we have the footlights in red, white and blue, a row of each, and overhead are the border lights in the same three colors. There is the first border, second, third—sometimes even seven border lights, according to the size of the theatre stage. The spotlight is an arc light. It has usually a color wheel that revolves so that either red, blue, straw, light straw, or pink or any other color may be projected onto the "spot" on the stage that it is to illuminate and emphasize. There are dimmers for the footlights and the border lights. With these you can go from daylight effects to sunset, to moonlight, dawn, etc., with gentle gradation. There are two kinds of moonlights on the stage. Number 29 blue in the spotlight gives a summer moonlight; number 35 is best for a winter moonlight scene. Good gelatines, or "mediums" as they are called, are made by the Gelatine Products Company, in Brooklyn, or may be had from Kliegl Bros., the New York Calcium Light Co., the Display Stage Lighting Co., all first-class concerns in New York City.

Under strong blue lights the under-rouge in the makeup will come to the surface, which is not desirable, so get to your dressing room and powder your makeup down if you are going to be under a blue light. The makeup will stand a white spotlight or a pale yellow, but will not look well under too much blue and never well under green.

* * * *

Put liquid white on with a soft sponge. Put this on only exposed flesh that is not otherwise made up, as the arms. Never put powder on the arms. It comes off on everything it touches. Liquid white is far preferable in every way.

The baby brush for blending facial makeup is one of the most important tools in the makeup box. If you try to buy one in a small town they will insist upon your buying a tray and comb, and everything else that goes with the baby set—everything, practically, but the baby. Better buy the outfit than try to go without the brush, but it is still wiser to supply yourself with the brush in time. You can buy it separately in the large cities.

* * * *

Never put your mirror in your makeup box, for powder and grease will ruin the best mirror made. The mirror furnished with the Ned Wayburn professional makeup box is almost non-breakable; it is clear as well as strong, and in every way one of the best for its purpose. It will stand up where you want it.

* * * *

Never makeup while in your street clothes or in stage costume. A drop of cosmetique on satin slippers or silk stockings will never come out. A washable kimono or bath-robe is the best garment to wear. Long fingernails will cut and ruin thin stockings. Don't ever wear the fingernails pointed.

* * * *

In using the 6B Venus pencil to darken the upper eyelid, use the side and not the point of the pencil. Do not use a pencil sharpener, for it leaves too sharp a point. Keep your pencil free from grease. Wipe it often.

* * * *

Rouge will fade under bright lights. Much depends upon the condition of one's health as to how long rouge will keep its color on the face. There will be certain times when rouge will disappear rapidly and you will have to renew the outer rouge, perhaps before the act is over.

Do not throw powder at your face, nor rub it in or smear it. Pat it on gently with the pad and use the blending brush.

* * * *

The tiny dot of rouge placed in the inner corner of each eye is to fix the distance of the eyes apart. When the eyes are finished they should appear to be about the distance of one eye apart.

* * * *

Rarely is makeup used in the nostrils. A big nose will look very wide if made up, but a small and very straight nose can stand a very little number 18 rouge in the nostril —not lip rouge, which would be too dark. But it is very seldom that the nostrils are made up.

* * * *

Unless very careful in removing makeup, your face will feel raw and chafed when you go out in the wind. Take time and plenty of cold cream in the removal of makeup, and dry and powder your face before exposing it to outdoor weather.

* * * *

If you wish to you can leave the mascaro on the eyelids, working over and under it in removing the rest of the makeup, and so use the mascaro on the street. On matinee days you will see shadowy eyes on Broadway, as some of the ladies of the cast keep the mascaro on till the evening performance.

W. C. FIELDS

RAY DOOLEY

FRANCES WHITE

DOROTHY DICKSON AND CARL HYSON

STAGE COSTUMES

O N THE stage, as on the street, effective costuming is a matter of good taste. The dancer must be particular always to appear in a costume in keeping with the idea and character of the dance. The producer will be certain to adhere to this rule in all cases where the company supplies the stage costumes, as is customary. In vaudeville, or in a home-talent show, where the dancer furnishes the outfit, the same rule of fitness and appropriateness must be observed, or the resulting incongruity will greatly mar the presentation. Have your stage costumes prepared with the idea of creating proper atmosphere for the dance you are giving or the scene in which the dance appears.

There are special designers of stage costumes in all the large cities, here and abroad. Bakst, the Russian artist, is a name all have come to know because of the bizarre effects he creates for the stage. In London, Comelli was an outstanding name as costume designer for the Drury Lane productions; Erte, in Paris, and there are many others abroad. New York has several concerns of the first grade whose work along these lines is in evidence in the best theatres throughout the country and overseas.

The first step in costume making for the stage is made when the costume designer and the scenic artist are brought together under the producing director to arrange and settle upon a definite color scheme for each act and scene, so that colors of costumes and stage settings shall be in full harmony throughout. This is most important for the pictorial effects and is given careful study. With the color schemes effectively planned, there follows a further conference between producer and costume designer, in which plot, locale, atmosphere, characters, lyrics, music, and everything else with a bearing on the dance or play in contemplation is fully gone over and considered. The personality of the principals is given attention, and the various possible effects of the ensemble or chorus groupings, evolution and pictures are carefully planned, with regard to lights and color effects.

The designer thus consulted submits pencil sketches of his ideas. The next step is a water color design in the actual colors to be employed. The accepted costume plate in color becomes now the working basis for the actual process of manufacturing the garments. The cost of these color plates for each design is at least five dollars, but usually more, as high as $25.00 sometimes, before a garment is cut or a stitch taken, the price for a costume plate or design depending a good deal upon the standing or reputation of the designers.

Materials as well as colors are given careful thought. Sometimes the artist's design is made around a sample of the actual materials, though usually the color idea is developed first and the goods to be used in the garments considered later. The quality of the material for stage costumes should be the very best to be had regardless of cost. It is unquestionably true that the best is the cheapest in every way. Not only do costumes of cheap fabrics not hold together, and the colors fade out when exposed to the strong modern stage lights, and repairs and renewals become a frequent necessity, but the very people on the stage who are compelled to wear the inferior costumes are literally let down to a lower level in morale as a consequence.

It is human nature for a well-groomed man or woman, on the stage or off, to be in better spirits and a better mental attitude for the very reason that they are correctly attired. Cheap garments and inferior costumes detract from the dancer's ability to do the best work, however unconscious of this fact the dancer may be. So I contend that it pays to use the best material and employ the best workmanship, if only to keep the performers up to pitch and put the show over in a way that spells success.

Then, too, there is the audience to be considered. They know the difference between silk and cotton, and are quick to judge the show by the appearance of the costumes that greet them on the stage. It is little less than an insult to modern American audiences to expect them to pay modern prices for seats in the theatre and then parade a lot of second-rate costumes before them as your idea of something that will "get by" without detection or adverse comment.

The cost of costumes varies, of course, and the range is wide. Professional costumes worn in Broadway productions under my direction have been made for as little as $23.00 and as high as $1500.00 for an individual costume. Chorus costumes have been shown on Broadway costing $50.00 to $400.00 for each girl in the ensemble. However, a satisfactory chorus costume can be produced today for around $75.00 and that for a principal about $100.00.

There are large and satisfactory rental establishments in New York, Chicago, Philadelphia, Boston, and others of our prominent cities where costumes can be rented for almost any character of show, in single garments or for a complete production. In the east, among the best are Brooks or Eaves, of New York, and Van Horn of Philadelphia.

In the wardrobe department of the Ned Wayburn Studios there is carried a varied line of up-to-date costumes well over a hundred thousand dollars in actual cash value. There is one set of twelve dancing costumes there alone worth $4800.00, or approximately $400.00 per costume. Any of my stock of costumes is available on a rental basis for amateur shows when my organization is employed to stage the productions, and an expert wardrobe mistress goes along with the outfit to insure proper adjustment and fitting of all the costumes to their wearers.

The complete costume when rented from any concern includes headdress, bloomers and parasols (if the character calls for them), besides the gown or costume proper, but never includes wigs, shoes, stockings or tights, which must be purchased outright.

In our studio work and during the rehearsal period on the stage we recommend the Ned Wayburn rompers as a form of practice dress best suited for ladies' use, except in our foundation technique and acrobatic dancing classes, in both of which the bathing suit is given the preference.

DANCING TEMPOS

ONE must possess an inherent sense of rhythm in order to become a successful stage dancer. To be able to walk or dance to music in perfect time, and find enjoyment in doing it, is one of the first essentials. I can tell by the way a person walks across the floor when an orchestra or any musical instrument is rendering a sprightly bit of dance music, whether or not the walker has the dancing sense that is so necessary to perfection in the art.

In dancing, the term "rhythm" refers to the coincidence of movement and music, and is the symmetrical regulation of time and the periodical repetition of the same arrangement. The measure of speed in music and dancing is designated as "tempo." It is the "time" in which a musical composition is written, and is shown upon the "staff" by figures. Of the many kinds of dance measures, the most common are what are known as 2-4, 3-4, 4-4, and 6-8.

Among the 2-4 rhythms, the principal ones are the March, which is indicated either in "Alla Breve" (C), as "The Stars and Stripes Forever," or in 2-4, as the more rollicking "Over There," or the well known Cake Walk, "Georgia Camp Meeting." By increasing the tempo of the 2-4 March it becomes the One Step dance.

Marches are also written in 6-8. Then they are called Two Steps, as "The Handicap March," and Sousa's "Washington Post" March.

Among the other 2-4 rhythms are the Polka, suitable
for Ballet work. The "Pizzicato Polka" is a very good
example of this type. The Gallop and Can Can are in a
very fast 2-4 tempo.

Waltzes are in 3-4, played sometimes in a lively tempo,
one in a bar, or slow, 3 in a bar. "Three o'Clock in the
Morning," a ballroom waltz is in the slow tempo, while

"In the Good Old Summertime" is more rapid, adapted
for fast movements and waltz clogs. "Valse Coppelia,"
played one in a bar, is the type for dainty Ballet work.
The stately Minuet is in 3-4 time.

The Gavotte, played 4 in a bar, is principally suitable
for Ballet, while the Song and Dance ("Narcissus"), on
account of its rhythm, is mainly adapted for the soft shoe
and its kindred dances. It is also in 4-4. The Fox Trot
is written "Alla Breve," 2 in a bar in moderate tempo.
It has a somewhat strict rhythm, while the "Charleston,"
played usually in the same tempo, is rhythmically different. As one can notice, it has an anticipated second beat.

Perhaps the most popular music for the Charleston dance is the Charleston number from "Runnin' Wild."

There are a great many varieties of national dances, all having a peculiar rhythm of their own, portraying the

Copyright by Leo Feist, Inc., Used by Special Permission

Copyright MCMXXIII by Harms, Inc., N. Y.

character of their people. Among these are the "American" characteristic dances, as "The Rube Dance" and the peculiar rhythm of the Stop Buck, the "Essence" played in moderate 6-8 tempo, as in "Comin' Through the Rye."

Among the Irish Dances, the most popular are the Jig, a fast 2-4; and the Reel, a fast 6-8. The Scotch have their "Highland Fling," a fast 4-4, and there is the Hornpipe.

The Spanish dancers are particularly fond of the **Waltz,** played lively, and when still more increased in tempo it becomes the "Fandango," a wild and merry dance. The **Tango** is in 2-4, played in moderately slow tempo; its rhythm is also adapted for the Habanera.

("Rosita" Tango Fox Trot)

The Italians have their "Tarantella." It is played very fast. It is supposed to cure the bite of the tarantula, hence the furious tempo. The Egyptian (Oriental) Dance is of a more sensuous type, either moderately fast in 2-4 or slow (in 6-8).

The Soft Shoe Dance is played 4 in a bar in Schottisch tempo.

Most any 2-4 March movement is suitable for "buck" dances, but they must be in syncopated rhythm with characteristic melodies and accompaniments and not what is called straight marches, but must have the right atmosphere musically in order to inspire the dancer.

Egyptian Ballet (slow Movement). A. LUIGINI

There are a number of very good dance albums published annually with popular dance melodies and piano arrangements. Among the best are those published by Leo Feist, Inc., Jerome H. Remick & Company, Shapiro, Bernstein & Company, Harms, Inc., and M. Witmark & Sons, all of New York.

DIET AND DANCING

THERE are three kinds of people who should use care in all that they put into their bodies in the way of food and drink: The thin, the just right, and the stouts. That seems to cover about everybody on earth, doesn't it?

Well, that is just the idea. It is my way of saying that everyone, everywhere—you and I and the other folks, will be better looking and in better health and better spirits, more capable every way, if we pay attention to our diet.

This treatise is intended for men as well as for women and is equally applicable to both. It is addressed to the ladies, for reasons that surely are obvious, but the rebuilding of the figure is accomplished by the same methods in both sexes. Remember this, and substitute "man" for "woman" in your reading and application of this chapter if you are a male.

Incidentally, it is not stage dancers alone who need to be told what is best for them, but as our professional dealings here in the studios are with dancers, we are directing our advice to them. For really the need is greater in the case of the lady whose "job" and salary depend upon her bodily appearance and health and mental condition, than it is in the case of any other of her sex. The lady of society wishes to look at her best, and usually succeeds in doing so, but her "job" doesn't depend upon it, as yours does.

So believe me when I say that what I am about to put down here in black and white is not said for the fun of it nor for any other purpose but to enable every woman to increase her capital stock and secure the largest possible dividends in the beauty market.

The thin, slight, under-nourished woman will heed my words on this subject with satisfaction. Her procedure is pleasant and easy, comparatively. She can and will improve rapidly if she is determined to do so and will stick to what I tell her.

The "just right" woman wants to remain in her perfect form, and the words here printed will serve as a sign-post to direct her in the way that is best for the accomplishment of that desirable end. Her task is easiest of all.

The stout woman who would regain the more pleasing figure that nature intended she should have can do so if she will, but her inclination to indolence and indulgence must be overcome—by herself, not by anything anyone else can do for her—and she must make up her mind that she has a real task before her, and one that calls for all her will power and stern determination. And she must be patient, for in her case results are apt to be slow. But let her be encouraged: Some of the most admired women of the stage have experienced her same difficulty with too abundant flesh and have perfected themselves by this identical plan set forth here. So it has been done, and can be done in your case; but it all depends upon you, your zeal and your stick-to-it-iveness.

To see how your present weight conforms to the proper standard, I present here a table of average weights based on heights and age. **In** this table the weights are taken in scant costume, a single garment and no shoes. Any table of this kind can be only approximate, however, for the frame and general build vary in different people and the bone structure must be considered in fixing the weight.

STANDARD TABLE OF AVERAGE HEIGHTS AND WEIGHTS OF MEN AND WOMEN OF VARIOUS AGES

WOMEN

Heights		*Weights*								
		15-19 yrs.	20-24 yrs.	25-29 yrs.	30-34 yrs.	35-39 yrs.	40-44 yrs.	45-49 yrs.	50-54 yrs.	55-59 yrs.
Ft.	In.									
4	11	110	113	116	119	122	126	129	131	132
5	0	112	115	118	121	124	128	131	133	134
5	1	114	117	120	123	126	130	133	135	137
5	2	117	120	122	125	129	133	136	138	140
5	3	120	123	125	128	132	136	139	141	143
5	4	123	126	129	132	136	139	142	144	146
5	5	126	129	132	136	140	143	146	148	150
5	6	130	133	136	140	144	147	151	152	153
5	7	134	137	140	144	148	151	155	157	158
5	8	138	141	144	148	152	155	159	162	163
5	9	141	145	148	152	156	159	163	166	167
5	10	145	149	152	155	159	162	166	170	173
5	11	150	153	155	158	162	166	170	174	177
6	0	155	157	159	162	165	169	173	177	182

MEN

Heights		*Weights*								
		15-19 yrs.	20-24 yrs.	25-29 yrs.	30-34 yrs.	35-39 yrs.	40-44 yrs.	45-49 yrs.	50-54 yrs.	55-59 yrs.
Ft.	In.									
4	11	111	117	122	125	127	130	132	133	134
5	0	113	119	124	127	129	132	134	135	136
5	1	115	121	126	129	131	134	136	137	138
5	2	118	124	128	131	133	136	138	139	140
5	3	121	127	131	134	136	139	141	142	143
5	4	124	131	134	137	140	142	144	145	146
5	5	128	135	138	141	144	146	148	149	150
5	6	132	139	142	145	148	150	152	153	154
5	7	136	142	146	149	152	154	156	157	158
5	8	140	146	150	154	157	159	161	162	163
5	9	144	150	154	158	162	164	166	167	168
5	10	148	154	158	163	167	169	171	172	173
5	11	153	158	163	168	172	175	177	178	179
6	0	158	163	169	174	178	181	183	184	185
6	1	163	168	175	180	184	187	190	191	192
6	2	168	173	181	186	191	194	197	198	199
6	3	173	178	187	192	197	201	204	205	206

Now first of all, weigh yourself and see how near you come to the standard, and take note how many pounds you have to add or subtract to reach the perfect mark. Weigh yourself at regular intervals, every Sunday or Monday, but weekly, if possible, and keep a record of your weights and the dates they are taken.

First I am going to direct the too thin as to the best method for them to put on flesh, fill out hollows, become symmetrical and graceful and pleasing to the eye.

HOW TO GAIN WEIGHT

1. If you are thin, have an examination by a competent physician to be sure you have no organic trouble, before you try to put on flesh.

2. Calm yourself. "Learn to accept the trivial annoyances and the small misfits of life as a matter of course. To give them attention beyond their deserts is to wear the web of your life to the warp."—Hubbard.

3. Exercise and air. Take at least 10 minutes of Ned Wayburn exercises every morning as soon as you get up. Begin with a small number of movements and increase gradually. Be in the open air as much as possible.

4. Sleep. Resistance is markedly lowered by a lack of sufficient sleep. Have a rest period during the day if possible. Do not sleep longer than eight hours. For every hour you are in bed over that time the fat piles on or else you are losing flesh.

5. Avoid unnecessary exertion. Don't talk too much. Delete the details. Never talk about your ailments except to your physician. You pay him to listen (or should).

6. Avoid tea, coffee and nicotine and other stimulants.

7. Masticate your food thoroughly and leave your troubles behind when you go to the table.

8. EAT. Stretch your stomach and train it to take care of more food. You must eat three meals each day at regular intervals. They must consist of what your system requires and not just what tastes good on your palate. Never eat between meals. Give your digestive apparatus a chance to function as it should, three times daily, at the same time each day, always giving it an opportunity to rest as well.

9. EAT. Eat whether you enjoy it or not. You will enjoy it later. Don't heed the advice that you should not eat as a matter of duty. You should.

10. EAT. But no second helpings.

I have seen printed advice never to eat unless you enjoy your food and to avoid eating as a mere duty. I tell you to discard that advice. Do eat whether you enjoy it or not, and do eat as a matter of duty.

Once the food is in your system, whether you like it or not, a large part of it will be assimilated. Perhaps not so well nor so readily, for we know that the enjoyment of food adds to the efficiency of the digestive juices.

There is a small bird called the ortolan, which is highly esteemed by the Italian gormands. When it is fat it is very delicious, but as it feeds normally only once a day, when the sun rises, it naturally has no fat on it. So the Italians confine these birds in a darkened room and succeed in getting them to eat four or five times a day in the following manner:

They put a lantern at a little window in the room. The ortolans, thinking the sun has risen, hop around and eat. The lantern is withdrawn and they are left in darkness four or five hours. Now the lantern is again put in place. The ortolans, evidently an unsuspicious, guileless type of bird, thinking the sun has risen again to perform its duty by telling them it is time to eat, hop down from their perches and busy themselves very seriously and dutifully with their breakfast.

Apparently they do not keep track of time and do not suspect that only four hours of the 24 have elapsed. This same sun rises for them four or five times during the day and each time they obey its summons and gallantly eat. The result is that they are converted into little balls of delicious fat.

You can get a lesson from these birds.

DIET TO INCREASE WEIGHT

Thick soups. Thick gravies. Plenty of butter and sugar.

Fruits. The best fruit to fatten is bananas, eaten slowly with cream and sugar. Any kind of stewed fruits, cooked with sugar. Orange juice, with plenty of sugar. Grapefruit, with plenty of sugar. Any kinds of berries, with plenty of cream and sugar.

Cereals. Oatmeal, Cream of Wheat, Corn Flakes. Avoid bran foods.

Meats. Anything fried is good. Roast beef, roast veal, roast pork, roast ham, veal chops, pork chops. No lamb. Must have steaks rare. Ham and eggs.

Vegetables. White potatoes, creamed, hashed, any kind of fried potatoes, sweet potatoes fried, mashed potatoes with butter. Beets are fattening boiled—not pickled. Spaghetti, macaroni, boiled onions, spinach, creamed, creamed carrots, lima beans, peas.

Bread. White bread, fresh bread, hot tea biscuits, plenty of butter.

Pastries. Pies, cakes, puddings, bread puddings, any sort of French pastry, and candy (in moderation).

Beverages. Sweet milk, cocoa, chocolate, malted milk. Perhaps one cup of coffee a day, not too strong, with plenty of cream. Weak tea with cream and sugar.

Keep your system well flushed. Drink plenty of water, about 45 ounces a day, say nine tumblerfuls. A glass of water before and after each meal, one in the middle of the morning, one in the afternoon, and another just before going to bed, are essential. This induces perspiration, which opens the pores and lets out the impurities, the worn out tissues, and keeps the system healthy, incidentally relieving the kidneys. Never take any liquids during a meal. This interferes with the work of the digestive juices and prevents the proper assimilation of the food.

There is no hardship involved in selecting one's meals from this extensive and comprehensive menu, and if proper eating were all that is necessary to perfect your figure the process would be a joy indeed. But we are seeking to make you not only pleasant to look upon, but also physically adapted to a stage career, which means that vigor, strength, endurance, "wind" and flexibility are demanded as well, so, in order to accomplish both, we unite exercise to diet, and the combination of the right food and habits and the Ned Wayburn Foundation Technique brings about the direct result; you become shapely, graceful, strong, and accomplished in a great art, all as the result of the same instruction, and simultaneously.

NED WAYBURN'S DAILY MENUS FOR THE UNDERWEIGHT

MONDAY

BREAKFAST

Shredded wheat with sliced banana, ½ cup thin cream or top milk and 1 rounding teaspoon sugar; poached egg; 2 slices toast, 2 squares butter; coffee with ½ cup hot milk or cream and sugar as desired.

LUNCHEON

Cream of tomato soup; 3 saltines; Swiss cheese and rye bread sandwich; 1 square butter; prune whip, soft custard sauce; 1 glass milk.

DINNER

Vegetable soup; roast beef with gravy; baked potato; lima beans; French roll; 2 squares butter; hearts of lettuce, French dressing; ice cream, chocolate sauce; coffee if desired.

TUESDAY

BREAKFAST

Baked apple (large) with 1 tablespoon cream; scrambled eggs with 2 slices bacon; 1 cornmeal or graham muffin; 1 square butter; coffee as above.

LUNCHEON

Club sandwich with mayonnaise; lemon meringue pie; coffee with half cup hot milk.

DINNER

Fillet of sole, Tartar sauce; boiled potato; lettuce and tomato salad, French dressing; 2 slices bread; 2 squares butter; ice cream; glass of milk.

WEDNESDAY

BREAKFAST

Grapefruit with sugar; $\frac{1}{2}$ cup oatmeal with $\frac{1}{4}$ cup cream and 1 rounding teaspoon sugar; 2 boiled eggs; 1 slice toast; 1 square butter; cocoa.

LUNCHEON

Lamb chops (2); creamed asparagus on toast; tomato and lettuce salad, mayonnaise; 2 rolls; 2 squares butter; $\frac{1}{2}$ cantaloupe.

DINNER

Broiled steak with gravy; scalloped or mashed potatoes; buttered beets; 2 slices whole wheat bread; 2 squares butter; ice cream; glass of milk.

THURSDAY

BREAKFAST

1 orange; 3 griddle cakes with 2 squares butter and 3 tablespoons syrup; coffee as in breakfast (1).

LUNCHEON

Fruit salad, mayonnaise; raisin bread and cream cheese sandwich; doughnut; glass of milk.

DINNER

Substantial soup such as minestrome, chowder, petite marmite or pot au feu; roast chicken or duck with stuffing and gravy; candied sweet potatoes; green peas; 2 rolls or bread; 1 square butter; raw fruit, honey-dew melon or ½ cantaloupe; coffee.

FRIDAY

BREAKFAST

6 stewed prunes and juice; cornflakes with ½ cup top milk or cream and 1 teaspoon sugar; 2 slices hot buttered toast and marmalade or jam; 1 glass milk.

LUNCHEON

Cream of pea soup; ham omelette; French fried potatoes; 2 slices buttered toast or bread; strawberry ice cream; tea as desired.

DINNER

Breaded veal cutlet or roast leg of veal; spaghetti with tomato sauce; string beans; celery; French roll; 1 square butter; apple brown Betty, hard sauce; glass milk or coffee with hot milk.

SATURDAY

BREAKFAST

1 serving strawberries, raspberries or sliced peaches with 2 tablespoons cream and 1 teaspoon sugar; ½ cup wheatena with 4 tablespoons cream and 1 teaspoon sugar; 3 slices bacon; 1 French roll; 1 square butter; cocoa.

LUNCHEON

Chicken or egg salad with mayonnaise; 2 rolls; 2 squares butter; baked apple with cream; glass of milk.

DINNER

Cream of asparagus soup; baked ham; potato salad; mayonnaise; fresh green or red cabbage, cooked; 2 slices rye bread; 1 square butter; raspberry sherbet or peach ice cream. Coffee.

SUNDAY

BREAKFAST

1 glass orange juice; 3 tablespoons grapenuts with 4 tablespoons cream; cocoa; creamed eggs on toast.

LUNCHEON

Macaroni and cheese; spinach with oil and vinegar; 2 slices whole wheat bread; 2 squares butter; chocolate cornstarch pudding with cream.

DINNER

Beef stew with vegetables; red beet or cabbage salad, French dressing; 2 rolls; 2 squares butter; strawberry short cake; glass of milk or coffee with hot milk.

Note: If underweight is marked, it may be advantageous to take additional nourishment at 10 A. M. and 4 P. M., such as a glass of milk or cocoa with 2 graham crackers and a glass of hot milk and crackers at bedtime. This will add 750 to 1000 calories to the day's total.

Any one of the above breakfasts contains 800 calories. Any one of the above luncheons contains 1000 calories. Any one of the above dinners contains 1200 calories. This gives a day's total of approximately 3000 calories of heat or energy.

HOW TO LOSE WEIGHT

To get rid of superfluous avoirdupois is one of the necessary steps to beauty. A ponderous actress has a limited field. Certain character parts, a few vaudeville acts, a singing turn, or a burlesquing of her own abnormality (if she has the personality to carry it off with), and there her availability for stage purposes ends. But you cannot dance and waddle at the same time. "It isn't done." If you aspire to be the kind of stage dancer that the public demands and that we produce in our courses, you will have to submit to diet and exercise, the only coin of the realm that will buy physical beauty and perfect development. There is no other way. Medicines for this purpose are dangerous, because they contain poisons, like arsenic and mercury. Make up your mind to either abandon all hope of a dancing career, or to faithfully follow the prescribed routine of proper exercise and non-fattening foods. If you continue to take into your body the foods that build fatty tissue, no exercise alone will dispose of the excess fat that is sure to result. While our exercises in the studio do help greatly, they cannot entirely correct a basically wrong condition unless supplemented by proper diet. And diet alone is not sufficient, either; you must have the exercises along with it.

DIET TO DECREASE WEIGHT

You must partake of no soups, nothing that is fried, no gravies. The only meats that you will be permitted to eat are roast lamb, lamb chops, broiled or boiled white fish, or white meat of chicken or turkey; no other meats of any kind, no other fish of any kind.

Vegetables. You may have any green vegetables, especially plain spinach, carrots, string beans, lettuce, celery, onions, sliced tomatoes, never any stewed tomatoes or beets. But you can have beet tops. Radishes are hard to digest.

You are not permitted to have any pastry, and by that is meant pie, cakes or cookies; no candies of any kind; no ice cream or ice cream sodas, no sarsaparilla or ginger ale, no liquor, no smoking, no cigarettes. *You are not to take any liquids while having your meals.*

You are not to partake of whole milk, cream, or white bread. Use *little* or *no* sugar or butter. The only kind of bread that you are permitted to eat is the whole-wheat bread, gluten bread, or whole rye bread. You may take stale bread toasted. Gluten bread is good when toasted.

You are prohibited from taking coffee. You may take very weak tea—very weak—but there should be no sugar in the tea, nor should there be any cream in it. You may have a slice of lemon in your tea. Lemon juice can be squeezed on the lettuce instead of using sugar or rich dressing. Vinegar on the lettuce or spinach, and plenty of it, is permissable.

Buttermilk is excellent, and so is postum, but the postum should be taken without sugar and used with hot skimmed milk, not cream.

For fruits: take baked apple, applesauce, grapefruit, orange juice, raspberries, blueberries, huckleberries, a few strawberries—not many—occasionally.

About potatoes: no potatoes except a baked white potato, occasionally—no sweet potatoes, no French fried, home fried, hashed or creamed potatoes—no mashed potatoes; the only kind you are permitted to partake of being the *well-baked* white potato, and you may eat the skins if you like, but do not butter the potato.

For cereals: take bran, bran flakes or hominy—but the hominy must be cooked for one hour and a half. That is the best cereal for your diet. The hominy should be flavored with about one-half teaspoonful of currant jelly, put into the hominy and stirred up, just to give it a little taste. Do not use any cream, milk or sugar on your hominy, which is really the most nutritious cereal when cooked this length of time

I am reproducing here the Ned Wayburn daily menu for a reducing diet. It is one I have worked out carefully and studiously and used successfully on many of my pupils and myself. By means of this diet and my studio exercise I reduced myself from 262 pounds to 207 pounds in twelve weeks—a loss of 55 pounds, and felt better when I got through than I did when I began, but, I do not advise anyone taking off weight too fast. With my method of reducing all of the unhealthy fatty tissue will be gotten rid of before the remaining firm muscular tissue will be distributed about the body. You may get thinner in the face first, and about the thighs last. Be patient; it may take you six months or longer. Unless you have gland trouble or some other serious disorder it will go in time, provided you will work to get rid of it and stick to the diet for not less than three months. Those taking the conditioning work lose an average of about one pound per week, while those who are trying to build up gain about one-half pound each week after they have gotten rid of all the unhealthy unnecessary tissue, those underweight frequently losing five pounds before they begin to show any gain. It will surely bring back youthful buoyancy and insure your health and figure for the future. After you have succeeded in getting down to the right poundage you can go on my balanced diet for those who have reduced, but you will still have to do about ten minutes of my exercises every morning, and you must never over-eat again.

NED WAYBURN'S DAILY REDUCING MENUS

MONDAY
BREAKFAST
Orange (without sugar) 1 medium; 1 poached egg on thin slice toast; 1 small pat butter; coffee with 1 teaspoon sugar and ½ tablespoon cream or coffee with ¼ cup hot skimmed milk.

LUNCHEON
Lettuce, tomato and cream cheese salad, with ½ tablespoon French dressing; 2 thin slices whole wheat bread; 1 small pat butter; 1 glass skimmed milk.

DINNER
Bouillon, clear; lean roast beef; 1 medium baked potato; spinach; 1 small pat butter; pear or apple.

TUESDAY
BREAKFAST
½ grapefruit (without sugar); 1 egg and 1 thin slice crisp bacon; 1 thin slice toast; 1 small pat butter; coffee with hot skimmed milk.

LUNCHEON
Cheese sandwich; asparagus salad with ½ tablespoon mayonnaise; tea with lemon.

DINNER

Roast or broiled chicken (no stuffing or gravy); green peas; lettuce and cucumber salad with ½ tablespoon French dressing; baked apple (no cream).

WEDNESDAY
BREAKFAST

¾ cup strawberries with rounding teaspoon powdered sugar; ½ cup oatmeal with ¼ cup skimmed milk and 1 level teaspoon sugar; glass of skimmed milk.

LUNCHEON

Cream of tomato soup; medium serving cold meat; 2 thin slices rye bread; 1 small pat butter; ½ small cantaloupe.

DINNER

Broiled sirloin steak, moderate serving; 1 ear corn on cob; tomato and lettuce salad, with ½ tablespoon French dressing; 1 small pat butter; cup custard (small).

THURSDAY
BREAKFAST

1 apple; 1 egg omelet; 1 bran muffin; small pat butter; coffee with hot skimmed milk.

LUNCHEON

Macaroni and cheese; lettuce with French dressing; fruit gelatine pudding (clear).

DINNER

Beef or lamb stew with vegetables; 2 thin slices whole wheat bread; small pat butter; tapioca cream pudding; black coffee.

FRIDAY
BREAKFAST

1 peach, with 1 rounding teaspoon powdered sugar; shredded wheat with ½ cup milk; 2 thin crisp slices bacon; thin slice dry toast.

LUNCHEON

1 French lamb chop; 1 medium baked potato; lettuce with ½ tablespoon French dressing; lemon ice.

DINNER

Vegetable soup; broiled halibut or other white fish with lemon; 1 medium baked potato; 1 slice bread; 1 small pat butter; French ice cream (small serving).

SATURDAY
BREAKFAST
½ orange; 1 French roll; small pat butter; glass of skimmed milk.

LUNCHEON
Clam or corn chowder; 3 saltines; moderate serving peach or strawberry ice cream, or apple, cream, or custard pie.

DINNER
2 small lamb chops or 1 large one; tomato salad with French dressing; mashed turnips; 1 thin slice whole wheat bread; 1 small pat butter; raw peach.

SUNDAY
BREAKFAST
1 banana; ¾ cup cornflakes; ½ cup skimmed milk; 1 slice toast; 1 small pat butter.

LUNCHEON
Egg or chicken salad; 1 slice bread; 1 small pat butter; 1 small piece loaf cake, or 2 plain cookies; tea with lemon, no sugar.

DINNER
Hamburger steak with tomato sauce (2 cakes); string beans or asparagus; 1 thin slice rye bread; 1 small pat butter; glass of skimmed milk or coffee with skimmed milk; raw apple, orange or pear.

Note: If overweight is *excessive* omit all desserts given in menus except raw unsweetend fruits.

Any one of the above breakfasts contains 350 calories of heat or energy. Any one of the above luncheons contains 500 calories. Any one of the above dinners contains 650 calories. The day's total will be 1500 calories.

You will no doubt be interested in hearing the story of a young lady, Miss Ann Constance, who came to me a little over a year ago to be reduced. She was sixteen years old, was five feet five inches in height and weighed one hundred and seventy-nine pounds. At the end of nine months, under the treatment I am recommending for those who are over-weight, she tipped the scales at one hundred and nineteen pounds. Her photographs, in this book, taken "before and after," will tell the story better than I can in words. Miss Constance is in better health today than she has ever been before in her life; and she has become an exceedingly good dancer—recently with the Greenwich Village Follies and at this writing just beginning a career in the movies with the Famous Players at their Long Island Studios. She is, however, only one of many girls whom my diets and exercises have helped.

We have never failed in reducing any of our pupils who came to us for that purpose, but we have to have their coöperation, of course. Quite recently we had a very puzzling case that challenged the Sherlock Holmes in us, and I think it will interest you to know how we solved it.

A young lady of really huge proportions, resident of another city, called on me at the studio accompanied by her mother, and placed herself in my charge for reducing. I studied her, arranged a special diet for her and she entered the class in limbering and stretching. I watch the progress of all my pupils, and expect them to record the change in their weights every week. I watched this young lady with especial care, and was dumbfounded to notice that she was steadily gaining in weight. She never lost a pound but kept on adding fat to more fat all the time, notwithstanding that she was working her head off in the classroom—when she came to class. She skipped seven lessons of the twenty in the first month's course, reporting for only thirteen, finally insisting that the lessons were not doing her any good.

I felt that there must be something wrong and wrote the mother of the girl about it, as she had requested me to do. She told me that the girl had a charge account at a certain hotel where she took her meals. I asked the mother if it would be possible for me to get the meal checks signed by her daughter, which would show just what she had eaten. The meal checks were turned over to me. I found that the girl had been eating the prohibited things; that about once in two weeks she had followed my diet, and at every other time she had eaten everything she liked—enormous meals, consisting of starchy foods and all sorts of desserts—mostly sweets. I also found out that she had been taking some of the other girls at the studio along with her, fattening them up. The mother was inclined to be easy with the girl. I called her father's attention to the matter, because the girl paid no attention at all to me, and as far as I could see was hurting the school. Of course she was only fooling herself.

I insisted that we were not going to fail with her, and her father came to New York to see me. About this time the girl was taken ill, suffering with acute indigestion and finally the mumps. On my advice her father took her home. Lately I have heard from the young lady, and she wants to re-enter the school. If I decide to take her back, she will have to keep strictly to her diet and attend regularly, which I believe she is now ready to do, as she has gained much weight since leaving here.

Lillian Russell was a beautiful woman, with a personality and a stage presence. She was fond of the good things in life, and was obliged to watch carefully a tendency to embonpoint. She has gone on record as saying that lots of walking, lots of dancing, and two meals a day was all the reducing exercise she ever employed. She advised a light breakfast, no luncheon, and a good dinner, with no between-meals, no "piecing," no candy. The chief trouble with this plan is, that one is apt to become ravenous by dinnertime and over eat at that meal, and thus undo what you are attempting. The best way is to follow the Ned Wayburn diet faithfully, and take three meals each day, just as I have suggested.

CONDITIONING CLASS AT THE NED WAYBURN STUDIOS.

ONE OF OVER TWENTY DAILY DANCING CLASSES
AT THE NED WAYBURN STUDIOS.

TOE SHOE WITH PADDED
BOX TOE, USED FOR
TOE DANCING.

SOFT BALLET SHOE, FOR
BALLET, LIMBERING AND
STRETCHING AND ACRO-
BATIC LESSONS.

STAGE SHOE WITH EXTRA
FLEXIBLE SHANK, USED
FOR HIGH KICK, ETC.

CUT-OUT SANDAL, FOR
ORIENTAL CHARACTER
AND BALLET WORK.

"MARY JANE" TYPE OF
SHOE FOR TAP AND
STEP DANCING.

LACED TYPE OF SHOE
FOR TAP AND STEP
DANCING.

A SPLIT CLOG SHOE WITH
FIBER HALF SOLE AT-
TACHED, FOR ADVANCED
"TAP" WORK.

TYPE OF SHOE SUGGEST-
ED FOR GIRLS DOING
ACROBATIC DANCING.

"GREEK CHARACTER"
LOW BALLET SHOE.

RUSSIAN BOOT.

"GREEK CHARACTER"
HIGH BALLET SHOE.

TYPE OF MAN'S SHOE
SOMETIMES USED FOR
ACROBATIC DANCING.

TYPES OF DANCING SHOES

THE NED WAYBURN PROFESSIONAL STAGE MAKEUP BOX AND OUTFIT

A—BLACK COSMETIQUE. B—BLACK MASCARO. C—BABY BRUSH. D—BLACK CRAYON PENCIL. E—DARK BLUE PENCIL. F—CARMINE GREASE PAINT. G—BLUE LINING GREASE PAINT. H—FOUNDATION GREASE PAINT. I—ORANGEWOOD STICK. J—PAPER FELT LINERS. K—COSMETIC STOVE. L—PINK VELOUR POWDER PAD. M—FACE POWDER. N—COLD CREAM. O—DRY ROUGE. P—RABBIT'S FOOT. Q—MOIST LIP ROUGE. R—ART STEEL BOX. S—SPECIAL MIRROR.

A PRIVATE LESSON WITH MUSIC, BEING SUPERVISED BY MR. WAYBURN
(AT WINDOW)

MILDRED LEISY WEARING TYPE OF PRACTICE COSTUME
WORN FOR BALLET DANCING.

POLLY ARCHER WEARING COS-
TUME (BATHING SUIT) FOR
LIMBERING AND STRETCHING,
AND ACROBATIC DANCING.

OLIVE BRADY WEARING PRAC-
TICE ROMPER SUGGESTED FOR
USE IN ALL CLASSES EXCEPT
THOSE IN BALLET DANCING.

DANCING AND GOOD HEALTH

THE dance is its own justification. It needs no excuse, nor do the many millions who share its delights need to be told how beneficial it is to them. They know that they are healthier and happier men and women, and therefore get more out of life and give more to others, because they dance. If the purpose of life is, in the words of an immortal document, the pursuit of happiness, surely those who train their bodies to move in harmony with natural laws are fitting themselves for capacity to enjoy all that life brings. To live well requires good physical health, for which a prime requisite is an abundance of pleasant exercise. Not alone to those who are free from the necessity of the various forms of exertion that are termed "work," but to every human being, exercise is as necessary as food. To those whose daily callings involve substantial physical labor, the need for exercise is just as great as for those of lighter employments. And nowhere can there be found so satisfactory a bodily exercise as in the dance. Sports, outdoor games, horseback riding, etc., have their place, but are available to a comparatively small percentage of all the people. Now that the introduction of the automobile has turned America into a nation of riders on soft cushions, the need for proper exercise has become more important than ever.

To live well, breathe well, sleep well, the body demands
activities that will develop and strengthen it. The most
delightful form in which this want can be supplied is in
the dance.

The universal desire of mankind is for enjoyment; the
qualification of physical, mental and aesthetic needs. To
enjoy requires the possession of the Roman prime essential; a sound mind in a sound body. So closely are physical and mental health related, so complex the reactions
of a disordered nervous system on bodily health, or the
effect on the mind of physical weakness, that the wisest
doctors do not pretend to say this illness is either wholly
mental or physical. They do know that some violation of
the laws of right living, some neglect to follow natural
impulses, is chiefly responsible for the long list of ills that
afflict mankind. And they are unanimously agreed that
proper diets and an abundance of exercise are far better
than cures; they prevent disease.

It is not necessary to go into physiological details to
explain why the well-nourished body demands suitable
exercise. That it does is an admitted fact. The question
that confronts the millions who know that their bodily condition is not what it should be is: "What must I do to
make myself stronger, and capable of enjoying life better?" The obvious answer is: "Dance."

In dancing there is found a form of exercise that stimulates circulation of the blood to the remotest finger tip;
that develops, under proper training, every muscle; that
aids digestion to perform its functions of supplying nourishment to every tissue of the body, and brings to the
dancers the glow of vigor and animation. These effects
of the dance have long been proved by the experience of
millions of men and women. Other millions who have not

yet tried it will sooner or later make the experiment. They will find that life takes on a new outlook, that instead of listless indifference they are actively interested in many things that they formerly ignored; that with restored bodily vigor they have quickened minds and better appreciation of all their daily contacts with their fellows, and that they are enjoying each day's existence with a zest never known before.

The dance is a physical, mental and moral upbuilding. It brings a greater capacity for success in the daily tasks and duties. It stimulates and restores. It shows the door to the glooms and welcomes gladness. It brings self-confidence in undertaking new enterprises, and banishes the mental depressions that result from bodily ills. It forms new circles of agreeable companions, and affords opportunities for congenial friendships. It avoids wasted expenditures for nauseous drugs and doctor's bills. It puts humanity in harmony with fundamental natural laws, and makes of all who resort to it healthier, happier and better men and women.

SHOWMANSHIP

DO YOU know what "repeaters" are in the language of the stage?

They are people who like a show well enough to patronize it more than once—well enough to spend their money to see it a second or a third time, perhaps many times, and bring their friends to enjoy it with them. There are many more "repeaters" on occasions when attractions have real merit of one kind or another than the casual public dreams of. The show manager watches for them and spots them, and rejoices greatly when he finds them abundantly in evidence, night after night, for he knows then that he has displayed real showmanship in his selection of a cast, a play, and in its rendition. The frequent return of a pleased patron accompanied by his companions attests the success of a show in stronger terms than any other one thing could possibly do. I go on record as saying that no show was ever a real financial success without it produced "repeaters." It is a real test of genuine showmanship, recognized as such the world over by every shrewd theatrical manager.

Good showmanship consists of the ability to anticipate the verdict of the playgoing public. The successful showman must have his fingers on the public pulse in matters that concern entertainment. He cannot afford to guess. It is too expensive. He must correctly diagnose the case in advance of prescribing for its needs if he expects to be successful.

The wise showman always plans his play to have the very widest possible appeal, for the public is many sided, and a single narrow idea will fail to touch it at all points, as it must do if it is to have a popular acceptance. He knows, being a wise showman, that people come to his playhouse for entertainment, pleasure, laughter and relaxation, and not for a learned discourse on some abstract or wearisome theme. There are proper places for the lecture and the "big wind," but that place is not in the theatre of the wise showman. It is his business to create his proffered entertainment into a valuable piece of property that shall declare actual cash dividends at the box office. That is being a successful showman, and he who does this exhibits real showmanship.

The successful stage dancer must possess showmanship. That is why the subject is brought into this book on stage dancing—that dancers may be made to realize a need of which they may be wholly uninformed.

It takes showmanship on the part of the dancer to get fully in touch with the audience, get down to their level, if you like to say it that way, and never go over their heads. Successful dancers always use good judgment in their offerings. The same kind of dance does not do for vaudeville, musical comedy, revue and opera. Each requires its own kind of dance. The revue has its own audience, the musical comedy one of another character, vaudeville still a third kind, and opera still another. Here is where the dancer's showmanship comes in—to recognize this difference and adapt the offering to the audience before whom he or she appears.

Dancers who would profit to the fullest extent in their profession must learn how to absorb this essential element known as showmanship, in the various ways in which it may be done.

Reading along right lines is very important. Read the dramatic reviews and criticisms in the daily press, and read regularly the leading theatrical weeklies. Identify yourself with your profession in this way; read "shop" and talk "shop." Make it a point to see and study other dancers, in vaudeville, musical comedy, opera and revue. Meet your fellow dancers in their own habitat, behind the scenes. The actual experiences that you are recommended to undertake in your own behalf in the chapter I have called "Making a Name" will be invaluable aids to you in harvesting a lot of the best grade of showmanship.

Travel will help you learn a lot. The traveled and successful theatrical person is always alert, quick, bright, posted in all important matters that concern the profession and all who are connected with it.

Those who take my courses as students of dancing are given a wide mental as well as physical training, to prepare them to cultivate showmanship that shall complement their skill as dancers when they become professionals. I call my lectures "inspirational talks," for I do want what I say about their future careers to be inspiring to them, and encouraging and beneficial. I speak to my pupils from many years of stage experience, and I know if what I say is heeded and given full consideration they will be better dancers and secure better engagements, and do so in less time, as a result.

Good showmanship in dancing consists also in being able to "sell" one's own personality in a dance. Select your offerings to suit your public. Put in the effective "tricks" in your exits that are so important in inviting applause. And learn to leave your audience "hungry" for more of you. Let them go away with a wish that they might see more of your dancing. That is your cue in successful showmanship, my dancers. Let the audience come back to see the same show again in order to once more enjoy your pretty work. That means "repeaters," and repeaters, as I told you, mean successful showmanship, and both artistic and financial success.

It is never good showmanship on the part of the dancer, or of an actor or actress in any part, to let the audience know that you know they are out there. The way you handle an audience will have much to do with the opinion of your work that will be held by the big men in the theatrical world, who may be among those present at any performance, you never can tell when—and they, remember, are hiring good dancers now and then. Their judgment of how you handle an audience is worth consideration.

And bear in mind, too, that the most important part of your dance is the very end of it, the finish, upon which always depends the applause and the recall. You like to earn your bow, and that is right. Take your bow in front of the audience gracefully and quickly. Don't milk the audience dry by your bows. Never do that. Get general applause, but don't work up a lot of bows. Come right back, bow modestly and do a short dance, to acknowledge the applause. Such good work as that will stand the inspection and secure the approval of every theatrical manager whose approbation you value. An audience does not want to see you take bows. Bows simply gratify the vanity of the artist.

So, you see, there is quite a bit of showmanship for the dancer to study and acquire, and it is very much worth while for all stage dancers to put it into practice, early in their career.

There are entertainment values that the showman himself must be able to create from his available material, which he will find and develop in dialogue, lyrics, tuneful music, voice, singing, dancing, characterization, costumes, settings, scenery, properties, lighting, and everything else connected in any way with the stage picture or the presentation of his offering. The publicity and exploitation of the show will tax his showmanship from another angle and is of great importance to the success of the play or the artist. The selection of proper music also has much to do with the appeal to the auditors. No musical show can ever be made a success without beautiful, appealing melodies, or "song hits," as we call them.

And now one final word of advice to my dancers: Three minutes is long enough for your solo dance. Concentrate your efforts. Do not present a long-drawn-out and padded dance that will weary everyone. Brevity is the soul of good dancing as well as of wit, and you will be wise to heed this from the very start of your professional stage career. Never show a dance to any prospective employer unless your dance has been thoroughly set and properly rehearsed with whoever is to play the music, pianist or orchestra. Never offer any excuses at such a time. Be sure of yourself, and only do one dance, your very best one.

CALL BOARD.

REHEARSALS.

Chorus. Mon - Wed. Fri.
9:30 AM — 12:00 —
until further notice

ACT I.—

ACT II.—

ACT III.—

NED WAYBURN

LOST

"WHO'S WHO" IN THE SHOW

TO THE members of an audience attending a theatrical performance it may appear as though the actors were the entire show and the only principals concerned with the carrying on of the affair. Of course the man in the box office, the ticket taker, and the ushers have been in evidence, and there is the orchestra and its leader. Others than these have not been seen or heard, and so perhaps are given no consideration. Who the "others" may be, or if there are any others, and of what their services to and interests in the show may consist, would puzzle many theatre-goers to determine with any degree of accuracy.

Let me take you "behind the scenes," as you may call it, but "back-stage," as we say in the theatre-world, in this matter and disclose the forces that move the puppets on the stage; the powerhouse that generates the current that moves the whole machinery of production. The intricacies of theatre management may come as a surprise to you.

Chief of all comes the owner, the promoter, known to the profession as the Theatrical Manager. He it is who selects the author of his contemplated production, and also the writer of the lyrics and the composer of the musical score. He engages the producer, the creative genius who realizes the possibilities of the production and directs and rehearses it, and the principal actors and singers, and some of the members of the chorus as well, but the producing director usually recruits his own chorus and dancers. A most important step is the choice the manager is to make of a producer, or production director, on whom is to devolve the entire handling of all matters back of the curtain line from the day of his selection to the rising of the curtain on the initial public performance. He is well aware of the importance of this choice, and places his reliance only on a man known to be thoroughly experienced and competent in this line of work. Having selected him, the theatrical manager steps out of the picture and the producing director assumes control. And this control is absolute in his domain. Not even the power behind the throne, the man who placed him in his position, is allowed to interfere in any way whatsoever with his orders or plans. The wise theatrical manager possesses full knowledge of this and keeps hands off. Should he venture to countermand a single order of his producer, the latter would be certain to say "Take your show and direct it yourself," and walk out.

And the reason why no producer of the first magnitude will brook interference, opposition or disobedience from any source is, that he is held strictly responsible to the owner for the form that the show takes and for the manner in which it is performed. His own reputation is always at stake in every production of which he accepts control. He makes the show a success, if he is that kind of a producer, and is entitled to the credit of successful accomplishment. If, on the other hand, he gains a reputation of "breaking" rather than of "making" the show, his career is abbreviated in short order. His job depends upon making good; he is the "realizer," the dominating and master-mind of the show.

Let us name some of the duties that devolve upon the ubiquitous producer:

He must know by heart the book, lyrics and music of the entire play, and bring out to the full, in all of the actors, principals and chorus, every possibility that their parts, acts, songs, dances and groupings permit or demand. All the comedy must be developed and emphasized, and the personality of the cast studied and properly brought to the fore. The principal artists engaged for the production are under his sole direction. He creates all solo and ensemble dances; gives all readings of the dialogue, sets the dialogue syllable by syllable, devises nearly all the entrances and exits for everyone on the stage, indicates the tempo for all songs and dances.

He must be capable of inspiring the lyric writer and composer, the costume designer and the scenic artist. He must possess imagination, suggest the locale, color and architecture—the atmosphere—of all scenes, select the color schemes for all costumes and scenery. He makes up all orders for scenery, costumes and properties, and must, to that end, know both qualities and costs; prices per yard of silks, satins, and every kind of material required in the production, whether for wardrobe or in the scenic effects. He must order the correct number and size of shoes, stockings, tights, wigs—everything, in short, that the company supplies to the players, which is usually all save the street clothes which they wear into the theatre. The orders for properties include all furniture, rugs, bric-a-brac, draperies, and everything else that serves to dress the stage or the performers. If period furniture is called for, the producer must be competent to say what is correct for the locale and the period.

He must furthermore make out a plot for the switchboard, to control every lighting "cue." There will be a front light plot for the "floods" and "spot-lights" as well as separate plots for side-lights, overhead lights, and all the rest, to be thrown on or off at a certain cue. This necessitates his knowing how many and what colors he requires in front of each lamp for his many different lighting effects.

For each act the location on the stage of all scenery and furniture must be definitely determined, as well as the exact place for each performance, and the producer determines the location of the same, and the different heads of the mechanical staff mark the stage ground-cloth in colored crayons or water-colors for the guidance of the stage carpenter, property man, and electricians, upon whom devolves the duty of setting the stage, props and electrical equipment. The producer is absolute monarch behind the curtain line, his dominion extending not only over the actors, singers and dancers—the entire company—but also over all members of the mechanical staff and the orchestra. He alone is responsible to the owner for the successful presentation of the performance. His is a man's size job.

How many American producers of the supreme type, capable of the bigger things, are there in the United States?

I know five. And I know them all. Five out of 110,000,000 people. How many do you know of?

The Stage Manager takes the show from the Producer after the opening performance and is thereafter responsible for everything connected with the show back of the curtain line. He it is who presses the buttons that run the curtain up and down, and gets the performance under way and keeps it moving, changing the scenery and lights exactly as arranged by the Producer. He is accountable to the Company Manager for the way every performance is given, and maintains a close supervision over the principal artists and the chorus, sees to it that they stick to their script and do not interpolate matter of their own or "guy" each other or the audience. Actors or actresses who are insincere in the parts assigned to them should be barred from the professional stage. There is evidence of "guying" an audience at times in some of the best companies on the part of some players of established reputations who should be ashamed of themselves, and who certainly should be punished for such offenses. I have known some star comedians to go on the stage intoxicated, which is an unpardonable offense, and for which such persons should be driven out of the show business. If an actor would dare do such a thing in a company directed by me, I would go before the curtain and denounce him to the audience and refund the price of admission. An actor who would do a thing like that is called a "ham," which means a common person with no mentality or breeding,—a type that is practically extinct now in the theatre.

The Stage Manager is responsible for every facial makeup, and will personally pass upon each individual's appearance. He is usually an actor of long experience, and knows makeup thoroughly, but not the straight makeup for youth as taught in the Ned Wayburn Studios which is the makeup I perfected when glorifying the celebrated "Follies" beauties. He is capable of maintaining discipline, and is the watch dog behind the curtain. He commands respect by reason of his knowledge, experience and good judgment. He has presence of mind and is able to handle any emergency that comes up. He must thoroughly know his business. He is versatile. Like the several instructors in my studios, who have had long stage experiences and specialized training for their jobs, the Stage Manager is able to answer any question that can come up concerning stage matters, and he is able to understudy and play most any part in an emergency.

The Assistant Stage Manager is under the Stage Manager. In the larger productions there are often two assistants. He has charge of the chorus, male and female, and is required to make all calls, to get the principals and chorus to the stage. He calls "half hour," thirty minutes before the overture time, "fifteen minutes," fifteen minutes before the overture time, and "overture," and when the overture is called everybody in the opening of the first act must come to the stage. He does the clerical work for his department and keeps the record of attendance, etc.

The Musical Director, who is the leader of the orchestra, is responsible to the Stage Manager for the way in which all music is played at every performance, as well as for the correct rendition of all vocal numbers on the stage. Every tempo throughout the play is his personal responsibility, and the composer exacts of him the most careful and effective execution of the score as written. It is he, too, who conducts all music rehearsals. He and his entire orchestra are members in good standing of the American Federation of Musicians, and the amount and time of their service in the theatre are definitely agreed upon and duly set forth in a signed contract in established legal form and binding upon both parties.

All shows carrying scenery require the services of a Stage Carpenter, who is the custodian of all scenery and scenic effects, drops, solid drops, cut drops, leg drops, gauze drops, borders, exteriors, interiors, ceilings—all flat stuff and set stuff. (I am using the usual stage nomenclature for these, assuming that you will know the meanings of most of them, can guess at others, and won't care especially if one or two are not in your vocabulary. Stage jargon has crept pretty well into the understanding of the general public, till now most theatrical terms are matters of common knowledge.) The scenery is set for each scene on the exact floor marking indicated by the producer. Stage-hands, known as "Grips" in stage parlance, set the scenes.

There is usually a second stage carpenter, or second-hand assigned to work at the side of the stage opposite the stage carpenter, and a boss flyman, whose station is up above in the fly-gallery. He gives the "fly-men" the cues to lower and raise the scenery as required, upon receiving signals by "buzzer" or "light-flashes" from the stage.

The property man, known as "Props," has charge of the furniture, rugs, pianos, telephones, everything of this nature, as well as of all handprops, such as bric-a-brac, books, flowers, fruit, food for stage banquets, table silver and china, everything in fact that the play requires—even to a prop baby or any animals required. It is his duty to see that all props are in place for each act, ready to the hand of each player as the action calls for them.

There is also an Assistant Property Man, who has charge of the clearers, the men who set the "props" and clear off the trappings after each act, preparatory to setting the scene for the act following. At the close of the last act of the play the stage is again cleared, both of props and scenery, to permit unobstructed passageway. This is a state requirement, enacted as a fire-prevention measure.

The Chief Electrician operates the switch-board and is the custodian of all lights on the stage; that is, of all portable lamps, of all that actually light. A lamp that is merely a prop or a decoration and not used to yield light is under the control of props and no electrician will touch it. The Assistant Electrician has the responsiblity of all lamps in the theatre other than those on the stage.

Nobody ever touches a light in the theatre. A call goes out for the electrician if anything goes wrong with a light anywhere. Nobody ever shifts or moves any part of the scenery except the stage carpenter or the crew under him. None but props ever places a piece of furniture on the stage. If you want a chair moved half an inch you must call the property man to do it, otherwise the several unions involved will immediately and without any question stage a drama of their own that is not down on the bills; one that may really turn out to be next door to a tragedy, since the penalty for failing to observe union requirements would undoubtedly be to stop the performance, walk off the stage and fine the stage-hand who was guilty of over-stepping the bounds $100.00 and ban him from the union.

Every musical production has its wardrobe mistress, and sometimes, if large enough, her assistant, both good seamstresses. The dressing room assigned to them is called the wardrobe. All costumes are in the care and charge of the wardrobe mistress. She alters and keeps them in repair, and sends out to be pressed or cleaned when occasion demands. The wardrobe women also have a union.

The Company Manager represents the owner of the show and controls the "front of the house." He has nothing whatever to do with matters back of the curtain line, which are strictly within the province of the producer or stage manager. He has enough cares and important duties of his own without going back stage to find more to add to them. Moreover, any effort on his part to dictate to the producing end would cause an immediate rupture. He knows that, and attends strictly to his own affairs. Probably in no other craft, trade or profession is the line so carefully drawn between the business end and the producing end as in the show business. It is the Company Manager who is the custodian of the funds, handles all the finances and acts as paymaster. He maintains a close supervision over the sale of tickets sold at each performance and with the aid of the resident house manager and house treasurer "counts up" the tickets directly after the sale has stopped for each performance, usually after the curtain goes up on the second act. He makes up the payroll at the end of every week and pays the company on Saturdays during either the matinee or evening performance, as is required by the standard theatrical contracts.

The Company Manager is the watch dog of the show from "front." The box office receipts tell him a story that he must heed, and he is quick to catch its warning. There comes a time when even the most successful play must be withdrawn from the stage or continue at a financial loss. He is a wise company manager who can correctly determine the exact point to call a halt and terminate a run for the best interests of the owner and all others concerned. And it is because he can do this that he holds the important position that he does. He is almost invariably an experienced showman. Furthermore, his multiple duties require him to be a diplomat if he would maintain his standing for preeminence.

When the company travels, he arranges the transportation, provides rail or other transportation, supervises and controls everything connected with the entire trip. He is held financially responsible, and signs many contracts. The Company Manager handles everything connected with money and transportation and is an important cog in the wheels of things theatrical.

There is a press representative connected with the show who finds plenty to do in attending to all newspaper advertising and advance writeups, publicity, photographs, billboard posters, photograph lobby frames and other display matter, as well as all other printing, including the newspaper ads and the distribution of printed matter. The fixing of the prices for tickets, which is most important, is usually his duty, provided he is a shrewd showman. The Press Representative, or Director of Publicity, or "Agent" as he is known professionally, is generally found about two weeks in advance of the company arranging every detail to anticipate a successful opening or presentation in each city, or "stand," as it is called.

So much for the personnel of the show's management and working crew.

Now we will say our company has just arrived in town and taken over the theatre in which it is to appear for an engagement.

It finds at the theatre a resident house manager, a resident house treasurer, in charge of the local box office, and his assistant treasurer, who acts at times as relief for his chief, opens the box office in the morning, and sells the gallery tickets at show time. There is a house music director, a permanent chief usher and the other ushers, front ticket takers, an advertising agent, bill poster, a day and night stage door tender, who are usually watchmen, who are custodians of the building, besides the janitor and cleaners.

There is no conflicting of authority by reason of the arrival of our show upon the scene. It is understood by all hands that the show staff takes precedence of the house staff, and all work together for the general good, to put over a perfect and complete performance and get the public's patronage and approval.

One thing you will do well to remember if you ever become a member of any theatrical business or mechanical staff:

If you have occasion to purchase anything for the show or theatre at any time, be sure to get the company's stage manager's OK, or order or voucher of some kind in advance. It is an invariable rule of the craft that any purchase of over five cents made without this formal sanction will not be paid by the management, but will be considered as a donation—however involuntary—on your part.

There is one very important man behind the curtain at every performance on every stage, whose rule is arbitrary and absolute, and who is not on the company payroll. This is the house fireman, a city officer, with the power of the city and state behind him. The fire regulations are posted in plain sight on every stage. "No smoking" is one peremptory order that admits of no violation. Woe unto the actor or actress, principal or chorus girl, who tries to sneak a smoke in a dressing room, if found out! The fireman is using his nose as well as his eyes, and the familiar odor of a surreptitious cigarette will lead him straight to the culprit. Mr. Fireman is authorized by law to enter any dressing room under such circumstances, and no matter what the state of your toilet, he will exercise his authority, enter your room—and remove you forthwith. Fine or imprisonment, or both, are the legal penalties for violation of the no smoking law, and for using a flame or canned fuel, in most theatres. Principals have before now been taken off the stage in the midst of a performance and landed in jail, necessitating the dismissal of the audience. It is a mighty important man who can do a thing like that, and consequently the fireman commands the profoundest respect of every member of every company, from the chief all the way down the line.

No man is ever employed back of the curtain line in any first class theatre who is not known to be of good character. Those who are old in the theatrical business know this fact. If you harbor any other idea of these men, get it right out of your mind. Every theatre manager today demands that his employees be qualified in respect to character as well as in ability.

Now that I have taken you back of the curtain line and out into the front office and shown you just how the wheels go 'round that make the show go, you have become aware that there is something more in the theatre business than a mere group of good actors and singers and dancers doing their best to please you up on the stage. The more the machinery of the stage is kept out of sight, the better the management and the greater the satisfaction, both to the folks behind the curtain and the audience out front. Your attention should not be distracted from the play, the opera, the spectacle, by the intrusion of any noise or the appearance of anything or anyone not concerned with the actual presentation. The drop curtain or the tableau curtain should move silently and without revealing the human agents that manipulate them.

Scenes and sets should be made in silence and out of view of the spectators. No person should ever be in evidence on the stage, not even momentarily, save only the actors, whose presence you expect and welcome. Otherwise the illusion is interrupted, perhaps destroyed—and ours is an art where illusion holds a major place in imparting pleasure. Such an extraneous element would also break the continuity. It is not tolerated in the best houses.

So you see there is a definite reason why the "men behind the guns" in the battery of the stage are out of sight and so, often, out of mind. The hard work of the producer and his faithful subordinates is shown only in the superior attainments of his troupe and the ensemble as presented to your vision. They, themselves, the men who finance, prepare, rehearse and drill the show into shape, are seldom in evidence—never on the stage.

PROFESSIONAL COACHING AND PRODUC-
ING FOR AMATEUR ENTERTAINMENTS

I AM often called upon to "put on" an amateur show, and the call is not confined to New York alone, but extends to many far distant cities. These are usually community or social affairs, charity organizations, college shows, or entertainments by the employees of some large establishment. Once I have put a show across for these lovers of theatrical activities, the habit of continuing the plan of giving a show seems to have become established, for with many cities and clubs and associations the call continues year after year, an annual or periodical production under my direction being demanded. This indicates that I have been successful in directing the non-professional in a theatrical way, and I am sure it is so, for I have handled the whole situation and the "company" just as I would if they were going on the professional stage, taken personal charge of everything, coached principals and subordinates, put the show across, and been on hand to see the results.

Spread here before you is the story of just how I organize, coach, develop and handle an amateur company in a musical comedy or revue performance to occupy a full evening's time on a theatre stage; from the first "call" of an untrained troupe of inexperienced actors to the final curtain of the actual, completed performance.

First of all, I make a call for anyone and everyone who would like to take part in the entertainment. This call is usually made in a hall, sometimes in the ballroom of a hotel, but usually in a large hall where there is a good floor and a piano. I always have a pianist in attendance.

I take the people who are going to take part in the ensemble first and arrange them according to their height, always having the shortest person to my left. Sometimes a great many people will try out for a thing of this kind. I have had as many as three and four hundred at many of the calls, and possibly more than that. I have always arranged them, as I say, from my left according to their height.

Then I get them to stand in a huge semi-circle before me, as large a semi-circle as the hall will permit, and if I have too many for that one semi-circle, I put the others behind them into other semi-circles. I begin by placing my first semi-circle shoulder to shoulder. I watch their shoulder heights and their head-lines all the way along the semi-circle. The semi-circle will begin at my left, cover the whole side of the hall—whichever is the longest side—and the end of the semi-circle will be at my extreme right. I have my table and chair in the center, but near the wall opposite this semi-circle. The pianist I usually have on my left-hand side, if it is convenient. He must have his piano turned in such a position that by looking slightly over his shoulder he can see me as well as the group.

I number the entire group, beginning with number one and running consecutively from my left as far as they will go. Then they are required to sit down in the same order. Each person must have a seat and they occupy the same

seat at each call, after the elimination process. Before I
do anything else I have their names taken, with addresses
and telephone numbers; the first and last names directly
opposite the number that I have given them. Then they
stand up and I arrange them in straight lines across.
Sometimes I will have eight in a line across, and I may
have six lines of eight to begin with; sometimes eight lines
of ten, and perhaps as many as twelve in a line, all depending on the shape and size of the hall.

After they have been arranged in perfectly straight
lines one directly behind the other, the next thing I do is
to teach them the eight different directions, which are so
important. Let me recall them to you: (1) left oblique,
(2) left, (3) left oblique back, (4) back, (5) right oblique
back, (6) right, (7) right oblique, and (8) front. They
are taken through these directions until I am sure they
understand them thoroughly. Then I divide the foot into
four different parts, just as I do in my courses: the
toe (the end of the shoe), the ball (the halfsole), the heel,
and the flat. I always make them stand with their knees
together, their heels together, the left toe pointed to left
oblique, the right toe pointed to right oblique, hands down
at their sides, the weight equally distributed between the
two feet, heads up, and looking straight front on a line
with their eyes. I insist upon their standing this way.
Every time they come to their places on the floor during
rehearsal, I remind them of it.

Now, I begin to show them simple movements in order
to get them to shift their weight easily and to give them
confidence. First the hopping step. When they do this
I can immediately tell just how far they can go in my
dancing—by giving them what I call the hopping test.
They hop on the ball of the left foot eight times and they
repeat that eight more times, on the ball of the right foot

to a 4/4 tempo. Then they hop on the ball of the left foot
for eight counts, and alternately for eight on the right
foot, through a number of refrains or popular choruses.
I caution them to be careful about bending the knee when
they land the weight of the body on the floor, because
many of them have never danced before in their lives.
They know nothing about it, but by bending their knee
they make a cushion for their weight, and they must land
on the ball of the foot, not on the heels.

After I try them out doing that, I put them in a circular formation, where everybody can see me, for I stand
in the middle of the ring. I turn them toward the left
hand, and I start them around in a circle on the hopping
steps; left hop, right hop, left, 2, 3, 4; right hop, left hop,
right 2, 3, 4; alternately through, in time with the music
of a popular 4/4 tune. This test has never failed with
me. I can immediately find the clumsy, awkward ones
and select the apt ones. This, of course, I do in my mind,
making mental notes of their numbers. After I get them
back in a straight line at the end of the hall I call out the
numbers of those who have qualified, but I do not hurry
to do this because many times they are nervous at a first
try-out. So I encourage them as much as I dare to. One
has to be tactful at such times. But right away you can
find your awkward people and also those who have a
natural grace. I can pick them out immediately.

They move around in a circle. Many times I will stop
them and divide them into smaller groups, all the time
noting the ones that get it and the ones that don't. I will
get to know number 1. I will watch her or him, and I will
say to myself, 1, 3, 5, 8, 9, 14, 16 and 18 have it; the rest
haven't. Then I ask them to sit down. I can find out just
about the way they are going to do my work from this
little try-out. I never individualize my criticism.

The main idea is to find out the ones who are interested. There are always some people who come to these calls who are out for a lark, and they must be eliminated at the first call. After the hopping test I am able to pretty well decide just which ones are going to get the ensemble work—and very often you will find some splendid natural dancer in a group like this.

Then I have another little test that I use in a 2-4 movement. Two hops on the left, two hops on the right, two on the left and two on the right. Get them to do that to a 2-4 tempo.

After I determine in my own mind those who are most apt, I ask the members present if they have ever done anything in the way of any individual stunt, either a dance or a song, or if they ever played a part in amateur theatricals. Usually a few will stand up, and I bring them around my table one at a time to get an idea of what they have done. I get them to write down their names and addresses and exactly what they have done or what they think they can do, gradually getting the whole thing on paper. In this way I am getting all of the available talent organized.

In the meantime I am watching the members of the ensemble. I am trying them out in some of the simple routines. I gradually work them into it before they realize it. I get them all enthused about it, and through long experience I am able to tell which group is going to be what I call my dancing girls or boys. They will be the smallest ones, five foot one, five foot two, three and four. Then I pick out those who are a little slow in picking up the steps, and they will be the "mediums," the sort of "in between" ones. Then I pick out the very best type of show girl, usually the taller girls, who can't move as fast as the smaller girls, but who have grace and good figures, and who are good looking. Until I have the three final groups, of course, I make all the members of the ensemble dance. The show-girl will be more dignified perhaps, with a stately bearing. Naturally I pick out the girls who have natural aptitude to do my work properly and make them the real dancers. I have eight, twelve or sixteen of these in a set, never any more. Then the others who don't dance quite so well will be the mediums, and then the show-girls who can stand in the back of the stage, or at the corners, and dress the stage or do "parade numbers," or walking numbers. After I get these sets worked out I give them their next call and take the principals in hand.

Then I have copies of the manuscript, and usually carry along three sets of the parts. If it is a play, I have the play completely read. If it is a revue, I have all of the skits and numbers with me.

I have the principals come in and sit down in a semi-circle before me while I seat myself behind the table on which I keep my papers and the brief case in which I carry the "scripts," parts, etc., and we have a meeting similar to the meeting that was held with the ensemble. The pianist is there, and they bring along their songs. Whoever is going to be the stage manager of the company is also there. He is usually one of my coaches that I carry with me. The local casting director and usually the president or chairman, also sit at the table at the left side of me, with my own assistant (the "coach") at my right.

Now, those who want to read parts for me are put at one side into one group; that is, those who wish to try to handle important parts in the dialogue. Then I place another group together which expects to do solo dancing— at the other side. They are called principal dancers. Then I make a separate group of those who expect to sing, or to do any sort of a musical specialty, or any kind of a

"stunt" that might be included in the show. I have had
the greatest variety of specialties in a show. I have had
them do magic, burlesque magic, play ukuleles, and all
sorts of stunts which I have placed effectively in a show.
We had a man in the Princeton show who did a little trick
with a cigarette that was a scream. I saw him standing
around, and I asked him if he could do a specialty. "I
don't think so," he said. He was smoking a cigarette
at the time, and he said "This is the only thing I can do."
He took the cigarette from his mouth, broke it in two,
lit both ends of it, and he was smoking with both ends of
the cigarette sticking out of his mouth. Then he put another cigarette in his mouth and did the same, and finally
he lit the third cigarette without using his fingers but from
the other butts in his mouth. Well, I had him do this
stunt in the second act, in a proper spot, and it stopped
the show every performance. Some of those connected
with the show told me before the show that they didn't
think what he was doing was going to get over, but I told
them in as nice a way as I could to mind their own business, as I always do, and I put this "bit" in. I put a 50-am-
pere spotlight (very strong) on his face, and he did just
this little trick beautifully. Well, there was more talk about
that than anything else in the whole show. It had commer-
cial value and it helped the box office. People went especially to see him do it. We had stunts there that had been
planned for a year, and they didn't get as much favorable
comment as this one little trick did. Of course, it was
properly fitted in, cued in, as we call it, just as everything
else has to be in the right spot.

I only point this out to you to tell you that sometimes
in arranging your recitals or shows—whatever you may
call them—you will find a lot of talent which you would
otherwise overlook unless you go about it the thorough

way that I do. I do the same with a professional organization, because after all I am a builder of entertainments and I must know entertainment values in order to make a success of my business. I must be able to recognize and fully realize talent when it is present. You must have a lot of patience to do this work. Some people are able to do lots of things that will prove entertaining. After all, what you are concocting is an entertainment. You should always aim to present something different, something original or novel that will surprise and amuse your audience, not the hackneyed old stunts that everyone has seen time and again.

After I get them divided into groups and get their names down, I go through the tests for principals. I will always hear the songs first; but before you hear them sing they have to put down on paper what they have ever done before, how much training they have had, and so on. Then they go over to the piano and sing. But I usually try to be tactful and let amateur singers try-out for me with no one listening, to spare them embarrassment. From the piano they come up to the table and sit down before me. As they are sitting before me, I note their appearance. I engage them in conversation. I note their teeth, mannerisms and personalities, incidentally classifying them in my mind and casting them in my mind's eye. If they are in any way possible and I feel that they should be given a chance, I make a note of it and the songs I want them to try.

Then I grade them, number 1, number 2, 3, 4 and so on. All of those who are trying for the leading parts are graded as they should be, but always on paper so that I will not forget or overlook anyone.

After I am through with them I go through the solo dancers the same way and mark them and what they can do. I get them down on paper. As I see them dance I find out which is the best dancer, with the idea of placing her or him in the show to good advantage. That's the important thing in planning your show. They all have to be placed in a certain sequence in the show. If the best numbers are all in the first act, you kill the act or acts that follow. The success of any show is in the way it is laid out. It is the placement of the personalities, and what they are given to do—when they do it—that makes or mars the entertainment. One with a great deal of personality can go into your show, and if not cast properly he or she will kill the rest of the show. Casting must be done with good judgment and common sense.

After I have my list of singers and dancers worked out, then I pick the people who are capable of playing the parts. Some of them may have had previous experience, but never perhaps professional coaching. Now the reason why these amateur shows are usually so rotten is on account of the incompetent coaches who put them on. It is always the fault of the stager if the show doesn't go over. Some of them are terrible. They don't know anything about the show business. They don't know how to lay out a show. They don't know how to put on the dancing. They don't know a comedy scene when they see one. They do not understand how to rehearse dialogue or how to set the inflections of the voices which make the lines get over as they should. These coaches are usually people without any actual staging experience, consequently they are not competent to rehearse anybody. Amateur organizations all over the country are beginning to realize the necessity for professional stage direction in order to register success, both artistically and financially. It is not nearly so costly to employ my organization as it is to have some other which is only giving a very poor imitation of us, which means a thoroughly competent staff of real producing directors, who are up to the minute with their dance routines and everything else required. If you will take the trouble to investigate you will no doubt discover that the coach you have employed has been to my school for a very short time, just in order to get our latest dances and ideas in staging. Why get this service at second hand? It will cost no more to get it from me direct.

Before you let them read a part for you, you should first hand them a copy of their part and tell them to go to one side and sit down and read it through thoroughly. Some of them don't know anything about a part. A copy of a part is typewritten, and the dialogue that they are to speak begins at the margin. The cue that they speak on begins about an inch away and there is a dotted line in front of the cue, but always what they are to say starts at the margin when parts are properly typewritten. Parts are made up of what we call speeches. It may be four lines or four words or two words or even one word. "Yes" is a speech. What they should know is what their speeches are. What they have to say is called a "speech," and in parenthesis must always be the "stage business" or what they are to do. Stage directions should always be in parenthesis. They are sometimes typed in red ink on the first copies of the parts.

When they study the dialogue, they should try to fathom the speech; that is, they should form a mind's eye picture of what the line conveys to the audience. That is how I teach them to study. They read a sentence. A sentence is supposed to express a complete thought. They must get the proper inflection by reading it out loud. No method of expression is brought into play yet. By that I mean no pantomimic by-play or facial expression. They are only reading at first. In most of the amateur shows, the players never do anything else but read the parts. They read, crossing back and forth whenever the coach thinks they ought to cross, and it doesn't mean a thing. I watched that very thing in an amateur show not so long ago, and it was inane. Nobody should move from one place on the stage to another without a reason for moving. There is a reason for every inflection of the voice. A person with common sense will read a part intelligently, but only a person with a dramatic spark inside of the body will be able to act a part naturally. If the dramatic spark is not there, no human being will put it there. If it is there, a real director will discover it and awaken it and make much of it.

After this first reading rehearsal, where the parts should be cast, more than one person can be tried out for the different parts. I make a call for the dialogue rehearsal where I walk them through the action, holding the parts in their hands as they walk through the physical action of the play. You will find that each one has his or her own idea as to how it should be done. I have them speak their lines distinctly and slowly at first. While this is going on I do not allow any visitors. Not one word is spoken except by the person who is reading the lines, or myself. I make notes as to who reads the parts best. Many times you will find that the local folks will have ideas about who is to play this part or that part. I pay no attention to them at all. I always use my own judgment about such things; in fact, about everything concerning the production. I don't allow anybody else to dominate the show or arrange anything for me. But you must know your business before you can assume such an attitude.

After the dialogue rehearsal is over, all the participants are carefully marked, noting the ones who are most natural and apt at the dialogue; those who have resonant voices that will dominate the auditorium as well as those who have positive personalities. You know there are a great many negative people on the stage; they never get anything over. I always have tried to pick personalities that will go over. I can take a crowd of professionals or amateurs and place them before me in a semi-circle, seated; get them to read a play for me and immediately pick those who will score a success. This, of course, is the result of years of experience, yet if you try this you will have some with strong personalities dominating your little semicircles. They will usually dominate your show. There is always one personality that dominates everybody. It might be a comedian, it might be a singer, it might be a dancer, but there is always some personality that sticks out, and after all, such a personality must be reckoned with and properly cast, otherwise it may even dominate the play. It usually does. If properly cast it may carry the play to success.

A rehearsal usually lasts about three hours. Accomplish something every minute of the time. Get on with the business of rehearsal—no discussions or arguments. When rehearsal is over make your next call for these people, at a definite time and do not change it. After dividing all of your people into groups as I have said, make separate calls for principals and the ensemble. For instance, take your dialogue and principals' songs Monday, Wednesday and Friday evenings, from 7:30 until 10:30, or thereabouts; and the chorus or ensemble sets Tuesday, Thursday and Saturday at about the same time. I think you will find that you can accomplish a great deal on Sundays. I usually call the principals and members of the chorus the first Sunday at 2 o'clock, and keep them

until six, unless there are religious scruples against rehearsing on Sunday, which is really not considered sacre-
ligious. (I was brought up in the Episcopal Church and
sang in the choir as a boy.) Then I run right through the
play as fast as I can, to teach them the sequence of it.
Then I usually call the principal singers back Sunday
evening and give them a good rehearsal on the "business"
of the numbers.

At the first rehearsal for the chorus I have the musical
coach teach them the music and lyrics by ear, one phrase
at a time. Provide a complete copy of the lyrics for every
member of the chorus; we usually collect them at the end
of each rehearsal. Do not allow any talking, laughing
or playing at any of your rehearsals; make everybody concerned take everything seriously from the very beginning.
They will welcome it, since it saves time for everybody.
Put them under the strictest discipline; get rid of those
who do not want to take you seriously; do not be annoyed
by them, as they jeopardize your chances of success.

Sometimes I carry my own musical coach, and I have
found out that when I don't carry my own pianist I always
have trouble with my work. I have never found anybody
who can play the piano for my rehearsals to suit me unless
they have played professional rehearsals before. They
must have a certain touch to inspire me, so a good pianist
means a lot. Insist upon one who reads easily and who
can play by ear as well. If you have a rotten piano
player the numbers will usually turn out to be terrible.
There must be something in the way the number is played
to make the members of the chorus want to dance.

After we get the numbers taught—that is, the songs—
then I start to teach the ensembles to dance the different
routines. I pick out what I would say would be the "hit"
number of the show, the best popular tune, something that

appeals to me, that has a production idea in the lyric. It is usually in 4-4 tempo, what I call the song-hit tempo. I pick out this one song and we try a simple soft-shoe movement to the chorus of it. Our routines fit any 32-bar chorus. I work with the song for a while, then give them a 5-minute rest. Then I may pick out a waltz number and try a few steps to that 3/4 tempo. But first of all they are in a ring in a circle around me, and they first are required to walk in time to each tune in the show.

I show them how to walk in time to the music. You begin with your left foot and walk 8 steps in strict time with the music, then you take four steps in half-time, counting one-and on each side, taking a step on the flat of your left foot for the count of 1, then bringing the ball of the right foot up behind the left heel and touching the floor with the ball of that foot for the count of "and"; the same with the right foot, and so on. The complete movement being in strict time and "4-and" for half-time.

There may be eight, twelve, sixteen or sometimes twenty-four numbers, and the people are made to walk around in circular formation in time with the music, until they walk gracefully without any awkward mannerisms. Now, there will always be somebody who will start with the wrong foot. Someone will always be out of time. Some of them are born without a sense of rhythm. They don't belong in the show and they must be eliminated if you are going to make a success of the ensemble work; only people who do modern dancing well should attempt the dancing.

We go along and teach our regular routines, whatever I lay out for the show, but working on every number at the same time, doing maybe four steps for one number, four for another, and so on, until I have laid out the whole show in my mind. I never lay a show out in advance. I

do my best work on the spur of the moment. I have tried
the other way, but whatever is cut and dried is never any
good. I must be inspired at rehearsals.

When those who are going to be the principals have
learned the songs, I talk to them and try them out on a
few little test steps to see what they can do. Some of them
are usually able to do some little dance movements. Then
I make them stand behind the ensemble and do the work
I have taught them, not in front of the chorus where they
would be embarrassed if they missed a step, but behind the
lines where they can be picking up the work. Then I
eventually get them out in front, and they usually do about
the same dance as the ensemble, because if they don't the
ensemble shows them up. And you don't get your precision effect. You must always get in an effective finish to
every number, either a final picture or an exit. If you
want the chorus to get a hand, bring them on for the encore, and let the chorus exit big on the encore, but first
get your effective finish. Then you have them all back
for the encore, then exit the chorus if you like, and let the
soloist stay on and let her or him do a solo dance if it is
going to be strong enough. There are different ways to
finish a number and you have to use your own judgment.

Be patient when you handle the principals and chorus,
but persistent. Shape up the dialogue right away, and
take the entire show through as soon as you can—the first
Sunday as I suggested, if possible. Make them run
through the show no matter how it looks. They must
stand up for the ensembles and go through what they have
learned, no matter how rough it is, and the principals must
do whatever they are supposed to do to the best of their
abilities. Don't take "no" or "I'm not prepared" or anything like that for an answer. Accept no excuses; go

through with it. The more you go through the sequence the better they will be at the performance.

Along about that time I am thinking about the pictorial effects. I will have worked out a costume plot for the principals and chorus by this time. By a costume plot I mean an assignment of dresses, costumes, for both the chorus and principals. I make out two separate plots, one for the members of the chorus and one for the principals, in sequence from the opening number of the show down to the end of the show. If I have thirty-six or forty-eight members in the chorus, I put their names in and the costumes that they wear for each number, in the order that they are worn. These plots are then typewritten according to the sequence of the show. This is most important. They show every change in costume that every one of the ensemble makes during the performance. The same thing with the principals. Always figure the time you have allowed each person to change costume, otherwise you will strike a snag which may ruin the performance.

The show is taking a definite form by this time. I then start to give them formations or groupings on the scene. When the curtain goes up sometimes they are discovered on the scene. Some scenes I arrange for the purpose of obtaining a good, effective picture, according to the architecture and atmosphere of the scene, or I may give them some very effective entrance movement coming down a staircase, through an arch or gateway, or over a fence. This is influenced by the set. I sometimes arrange surprise entrances, or little surprise exits which are inspired by the lyrics or music. Sometimes I may use a personality in the ensemble and give her an entrance or exit last. I resort to any sort of producer's magic, as I call it, to get an effect or to provoke applause, always keeping the costumes and the color schemes in mind. Of course, I have my own "bag of tricks" with which I can insure the success of any musical play that has any sort of entertainment appeal, and you, no doubt, will have yours in time, with experience.

During the dialogue rehearsals, I make the principals speak the dialogue in time, the same as the dances are done in time. They are not allowed to use their own conception of how the lines should be spoken unless I think their conception is better than mine. Every syllable they utter will have to dominate the entire auditorium. That is something that the coach must understand. When the house is full, the audience makes a difference in the acoustics. Your people in the show don't know anything about that, and so you must govern the volume of the dialogue and set every inflection, attitude of the body, and gesture definitely. But never let them use gestures that are obvious.

We will next assume that up to this time we have been working in a hall. Now to perfect the dialogue it is sometimes necessary to go over one speech fifty times or a hundred times, to get a certain inflection and to set the accompanying "stage business." Stage business—all of it—creates some dramatic value for the performance. That has to be worked out, if you want to get effective pieces of "business," much depending upon the brain power and the experience of the coach, whether he is able to devise effective business or not. Sometimes you will find it indicated in the script. For a man to make a success at this business he must have inventive ability. He must thoroughly understand dialogue, how to time it and set it. They must pick up their cues, and at the proper moment, and not make "stage waits" between lines. Sometimes the line is one that calls for a laugh. Sometimes there is a line preceding it, preparing the audience for what is to

follow. We call that a feed line. Where the period comes
there should be a slight pause. We time that. The actor
counts to himself, "1, 2" before proceeding with the next
line, that gives a laugh a chance to get under way. If you
don't give a line like that a chance, it doesn't get over and
the point is lost. It doesn't get the laugh that you expect,
and it would if the coaching is done properly. Rehearsing
dialogue is very tricky work. You must be very strict
when you rehearse it. If anybody on the stage should move,
if a chair is moved or if a door is opened at the wrong
time while the dialogue is going on, it would detract from
the line and kill the play. No one can move while a line
is spoken unless it is some kind of a line that doesn't call
for a point. But if it is a comedy point that you want to
put over, or any other kind of an effective point, the characters must be still and the line must be delivered, and
after the period, after the end of the line, you can break
the picture and move.

Many a play is killed because people don't understand
how to rehearse dialogue, don't understand how to get
scenes over; amateur coaches teaching wrong business. I
saw wrong business ruin a whole show once in Baltimore.
The chorus was walking up and down stage trying to get
a lyric over, with no sense of direction. They didn't know
where they were going or why. The coach just told them
to walk up and down. The soloist's back was toward the
audience at times; she was facing right; she was facing
left; in every conceivable direction except the right one
to get a song over. Of course the number failed. The
soloist should have been in the center of the stage so the
lyric could have been heard and followed by everyone in
the audience. Get the verse and the first chorus over so
that the audience gets the idea of the song. It creates
atmosphere for the number. If you walk sideways and

your face is sideways, the audience doesn't get the lyric. When I rehearse a show the faces are at least three-quarters to the audience, when a person sings or speaks. Nobody must ever have their back to the audience when a line is spoken. If they sing a song or speak a line, everything must be done for the benefit of the audience. That must be kept in mind from the time you first begin to rehearse the company. Whether it is a professional or an amateur company makes no difference. They are trained in the same way.

Now, let us say we have finally perfected the play. They know the lyrics, they know the numbers, they know the "business" that occurs during the dialogue, and they know the "business" of the ensembles. By this time the play has actually taken form, and it is time to rehearse it with the scenery. When the scenery is added, both the ensemble and the principals who do the numbers all report in their practice clothes. Insist upon that. This insures their getting right down to business without "stalling," as nearly all people on the professional or amateur stage are disposed to do.

Go through the sets, get effective groupings so that you get the most natural and effective pictures and it all conforms to the architecture of the sets.

After you have finished rehearsing with the scenery, commence to give them the hand-props. Sometimes I use important hand-props in dialogue before I take on the scenery. That has to be carefully worked out and considered. Otherwise I work the scene rehearsals in with hand-props. You will find that most every one who has to handle a prop will fumble it, will be terribly awkward with it. If they have to pick a chair up and set it some place else, they will drag it across the floor and make a noise with it. They can't pick it up and set it down without any noise. This must be rehearsed. If they have to handle some hand-prop, they will drop it at the wrong time. Most people are very clumsy in the presence of an audience. Rehearse them with hats. Gentlemen have very often come on the stage in amateur performances and worn their hats in drawing rooms in the presence of ladies. I have seen them take them off and place them in the most ridiculous places, even in professional shows. Figure all of this out and rehearse it carefully. I have had awful times just trying to teach them to sit down and stand up properly.

After the scenery and props come the costumes. We never have any trouble unless somebody is trying to rehearse everything at the same time. Not even in an amateur show do I do that. I won't allow it. The sequence of final rehearsals is in this order; the scenery, the props, the costumes, the lights, the orchestra.

You often have trouble with your costumes unless·you get them from a good concern. There are two or three first-class establishments in New York where you can rent most anything. I have given the names of some in a preceding chapter. There is one big firm in New York that has recently bought over a million dollars' worth of costumes from the Charles Frohman Estate, including some wonderful period costumes.

I always seem to be able to get about what I have wanted for amateur productions from certain big New York establishments in this line of business; those who make costumes for the Famous-Players, Griffith, and·the very best moving picture and theatrical companies. They have made many things for Marion Davies and her Cosmopolitan pictures. I had a telegram from a girl in Minneapolis the other day. She had to have a certain costume, because her engagement depended upon it. She was to work three weeks at $150 a week, and she couldn't do it without the proper costumes. I had one of my men pick out the costumes for her. They cost her $45 for the entire three weeks. They were sent to her by parcel post C. O. D. by one of these firms.

We have an art department in our studios where we make our own designs for settings and costumes. When amateurs or professionals write to me or wire me, I am usually able to put them in touch with the right people and help to get just what they need. Any of these can be gotten at reasonable prices. The prices range from $5, $6, $7.50, $10, $12 and $15 a week for each costume, depending, of course, upon the quality of costume. I used a marvelous costume once worn by Ethel Barrymore in one production, and I think I paid $15 for the rent of it. A costume like that would cost $1500 to have it made.

After I am through with the costumes, I begin to do the lighting. I will use certain lights that will affect the sets, the scenery. Other lights will be used for the characters. I use the side lights, overhead lights, border lights, and front lights. The spot-lights are used to pick up the characters; sometimes I use X-ray border lights down stage over-head to pick up the costumes. These lights are not focused on the scenery at all. The other lights are worked to tone the scenery to the desired effect, either to obscure it or to bring it out vividly.

Be very careful of the kind of light you use on the costumes. If you have trouble with the scenery or the costumes, you can usually disguise them and make them look entirely different by some sort of trick lighting effect. I remember one time staging a production at the Winter Garden. The management set a limit of $23 for each costume; that's all they would allow. I had about sixty-four girls in that ballet, and it was staged by Theodore Kosloff, who is now in Los Angeles. He was formerly at the Empire Theatre in London, when I lived in London. He couldn't speak a word of English at that time. He had to sail for Europe before he finished staging this ballet, and he turned the ballet over to me, with a friendly request that I personally finish it for him, which I gladly did. He had explained what he wanted in costumes, and the management finally ordered some costumes made at the above price. I just wish you could have seen what came in. When you are used to spending $150, $175, and as much as $1,500 on chorus costumes alone you can imagine what we got for $23. When the girls put them on I was obliged to put colored lights on them, red, blue, dark amber, and I did finally manage to get a very beautiful effect, which you can do if you find that your costumes are not up to the mark. Experiment with your colors until you get the desired effect.

After we get through with our costumes and lights, we are ready to add the orchestra. That is the last thing of all. I bring the orchestra in for a reading rehearsal, with the composer and musical director, and we correct whatever orchestra parts there may be wrong and smooth out the music. We always have a special orchestra rehearsal without scenery, without costumes, without the principals, without the lights, without any stage hands being around, and we perfect the musical end of the show with the orchestra and company prior to the dress rehearsal.

Then we have the final full dress rehearsal, orchestra, stage hands, costumes, lights, props, scenery, facial make-ups, everything complete. We make them up for the dress rehearsal thinking that they will remember how to make up for the opening performance, but we always find that they can't do it, and about half past four or five in the afternoon of the opening performance we begin to make them up again. Then we are all ready for the opening performance, and we drive them through this at a terrific pace, not allowing anyone or anything to *slow* the performance up, which would be fatal.

* * * * * * * * *

When you sit in front and see a show going along prettily and smoothly, you little think of the amount of brain work, foot work and executive power and force that has been necessary behind the curtain to make the performance what it is!

Does it pay?

Here is a recent newspaper clipping:

"The Kansas City Junior League Follies, recently produced for a week's run at the Shubert Theatre, Kansas City, under the personal direction of Mr. Ned Wayburn, resulted in a net profit to them of $13,844.00."

NED WAYBURN

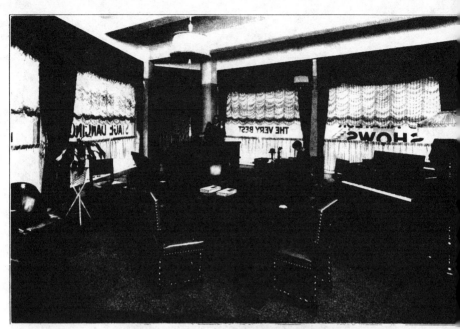

NED WAYBURN'S PRIVATE OFFICE

A CORNER OF WARDROBE ROOM

NED WAYBURN STUDIOS OF STAGE DANCING

A THIRD FLOOR CORRIDOR

ACROBATIC DANCING PRACTICE.

CHILDREN'S SATURDAY HOUR

NED WAYBURN AND TWO TINY PUPILS; HERBERT COLTON, 6;
PATTY COAKLEY, 5

PRIVATE INSTRUCTION

USUALLY our beginner pupils at the studios enter themselves i n a class, of either one or another of the types of s t a g e dancing that a r e so popular, and proceed regularly along the lines of class instruction.

Then, in nearly every class, there will be those who "eat up" the work, who advance rapidly and get ahead of the others, because of special capability or unusual capacity along the line they are studying.

Others go along at a natural pace, developing at the average rate, and in the end come out as well schooled as their speedier companions. For them the regular routine of class instruction is sufficient and effective. Their progress is safe and sane.

Still others lag. This condition is present in every walk of life, in every school, profession, trade. Some always get behind, fail to grasp the meaning of their teacher's talk, are deficient in initiative ability and so may not interpret his steps in their own actions. I do not like to think or say that any of our pupils are lazy or indifferent; ours is no place for either laziness or indifference. But whatever the reason, the fact persists, a certain small proportion of nearly every class in our studios fails to advance as rapidly as their sister mates are doing.

If this element will recognize its own shortcomings and is sufficiently ambitious to desire to succeed, the remedy lies in the direction of private instruction.

So, too, in the case of the fast learners, those who are really getting ahead of the majority of their mates; they will profit measurably by taking our private instruction.

We have special studios and special instructors for just this purpose. Professionals come to us without solicitation, for new steps, new tricks, or new touches to old dances, and a few private lessons here sends them out with new stuff to please their public. The student who has come to an impass, who finds she is not progressing in class as she wishes to, and the student who is very facile at her work and her learning, and knows herself capable of going ahead more rapidly than class routine permits—these are the two who will do well to consider the taking of private lessons. The average pupil may well be content with her class work if she is going along in good fashion, and for her, private instruction is not so essential. She may wish it later on as conditions change, but at present the ensemble instruction, with its unison work and the gentle competitions of fellow-students doing the same stunts, may be all that she requires.

Ask your instructor if he thinks you will best remain in class, or take private lessons, or do both. And ask me. Both the teacher and I will be perfectly frank with you and advise you for your own best interest.

At the desk in the main office you will learn what hours are available for private lessons, and you will be assigned an hour, an instructor and a private studio, if you and I decide that you will benefit by this course.

EXPERIENCE

IF I hadn't had many years of stage experience myself, I'd not be competent to instruct any one on the subject. I am not only a teacher of dancing, I am also a dancer, and can do all the steps as well as tell you how to do them. My experience as a stage dancer began in a store basement in Chicago, where I tried to imitate the best dancers I had seen at a Variety show. I put on wooden shoes and whistled my own clogs and jigs for hours at a time, till I brought myself by main strength, and no personal instruction, to a point where I could exhibit my home-made steps to a professional dancer. That is a hard way to get experience. You are more fortunate than you may realize in having everything that you have to do to become a dancer all worked out systematically for you, and told you and shown you by a simple method which anyone can learn, with perfect music and everything else that modern science can devise to aid you.

In the old days the beginner in dancing went direct to the stage door and stated his or her desire to become a dancer. The applicant was sometimes accorded a tryout. If he or she appeared awkward or was slow to catch the tempo, or not physically developed to please the eye, that was the end of it. There was no time to waste in helping to overcome minor defects, no personal interest shown whatever. He or she was dismissed summarily without any advice of a helpful nature.

If the candidate exhibited qualities that recommended her or him to the producer, he or she was given a stage training in chorus work following a tryout. The training was obtained in rehearsals, conducted for weeks, without compensation. The instructor might become impatient at any evidence of slowness of comprehension or execution; he might resent tardiness, absence, or slight infringement of stringent rules, and in such cases dismissal was the usual penalty.

The young lady or gentleman aspiring to become a stage dancer in that day and age paid a considerable price for the experience, as you may readily imagine.

Contrast then with now. You are acquiring this needed preliminary experience to fit you for a stage career in our courses under conditions that recommend them to ladies and gentlemen. There are no subordinates in our courses. All are equal. There is discipline, of course. You will find discipline on the stage when you advance that far. But discipline won't hurt you, not our kind. We ask for silence, attention, practice, and the conduct that ladies and gentlemen naturally observe. If you are a lady of social prominence, studying for the grace and beauty and health that our lessons impart, and not intending to favor the stage with your presence, you are accorded the same treatment that all others receive. This is a pure democracy if ever there was one.

By the old way of obtaining training and stage experience a young lady was kept for years in a subordinate place, and if she at last worked her way up out of the chorus into solo dancing, it was by "main strength," a vivid personality, aggressiveness and untiring effort.

Our first and primary instruction in the courses takes the place of the years of disappointing hard work that formerly prevailed. You are not held down. Your personality is encouraged and developed. You have to do your part, of course; we are not going to make stars of you if you don't help us do it. But the experience you must have is ready and waiting, and is based on a knowledge of things theatrical, gleaned and gathered through a series of years of personal experience exclusively in that field.

So much for the easier preliminary experience.

Now you have passed the portals of our studio, fitted and trained, a solo dancer, worthy of entertaining a public who waits to pay for the pleasure of seeing you do your turn. On the way through the courses you have had some small samples of what an audience is like. There have been the visitors' days when your work was on exhibition, and a Frolic before your fellow students in our own Demi-Tasse Theatre, or perhaps some neighborhood or church entertainments near your home. Those have all been good experience for you.

Now, as you enter upon a professional career, you must be content with a moderate start. I know how far you have advanced and what you may reasonably expect to do in your first, your starting engagement. Come to me before you commit yourself to any manager's care, if you possibly can arrange to do so.

In a small vaudeville act you may be able to command $40 to $50 a week as a beginner doing a specialty. You may have a year of doing three or four shows a day on "small-time," as it is called, which is splendid experience for you. Then you may advance to bigger time, playing two shows a day with bigger pay, and then, having improved yourself and your act as you go along, you are in line for the still higher grade theatres, where your work will get the eye of some production manager who will offer you a really worthwhile engagement in a production, as a Broadway show is called.

You cannot become a star in three or four months. It is only the foolish ones who dream of such a possibility. It takes time and experience to get on at a big time house like the Palace Theatre in New York City, which is recognized as Broadway's best showroom for the vaudeville artist. Look at the history of the stars you know. Evelyn Law worked four years before she reached her present Broadway fame. Ann Pennington has been working fifteen years, Fred and Adele Astaire nearly fourteen years —and I can name all the stars on Broadway and tell you exactly how long it took them to reach the pinnacle of their present success. So expect for yourself a moderate position on the start until experience has developed you and the public learned to like you, and then your advancement should be rapid and easy.

Do you know that as the result of my years of experience I originated all the solo and ensemble dances taught in my courses? Because of the same experience I conceive and create all of the novelties, settings, costumes, ideas and theatrical effects that are used in all the productions, professional and amateur, that I stage. There is no other school that can duplicate our service, since there is no other producing director of any standing in the theatrical world connected with such an organization as mine.

You are invited to benefit by my experience in every way. It is a part of your education here that you are not asked to pay for. I tender it freely to all who become members of my family of pupils. Not only are you dancing routines of my own constructing, and listening or reading at times to my class room talks on subjects bearing on stage-craft and showmanship, but also you are earnestly invited to consult with me about your personal ambitions and desires.

I have literally helped thousands of good girls and boys to make millions of dollars for themselves, in the aggregate, and have brought a lot of happy hours to many million people who have willingly paid their good money to see my pupils in their perfect work on the stage. Profit by my experience; let me help you with my knowledge. This will make your experience easier for you, and the more quickly fit you for the lofty position that a perfectly worthy ambition prompts you to seek.

INSPIRATION

WHEN you present yourself as a pupil it is to be inferred that you are already inspired with a desire to become a dancer of the first quality. That is good and as it should be. Without inspiration no one has ever accomplished anything worth while in any line of endeavor. Stage dancing is never a matter of luck or breeding; it is the direct result of hard work under competent instruction, with your being inspired to bring forth the very best that is in you.

All of us here at the Ned Wayburn Studios are inspired with a desire to create a career for you, if you desire one. Whether we succeed in our endeavor or not depends upon you. We will do our part faithfully, earnestly and joyfully, and furnish you such an opportunity as no other generation of aspirants for stage honors and success ever possessed. Our courses themselves, as well as our scientific method of developing you, are really inspiring to the new student with the primary inspiration of desiring a successful, honorable and profitable career.

As you approach the studio building from Broadway you note that its appearance is attractive. It is new, clean, impressive; and on the large second and third floor main windows, and on the Broadway and 60th Street corner windows, you note the signs, the lettering that stands out, to tell you that you have arrived at the haven of your dreams and hopes.

You step off Broadway and enter the corridor of the studio building through the main entrance on 60th Street, where elevators await you, to convey you the single flight up to the second floor, and you step directly into our main business office. Here is found further inspiration, for stage dancing is here treated as a business and in a business-like way, and our business office indicates that fact to the new-comer at the very first glance.

The prospective pupil approaches the long counter. She is greeted by Mrs. Wayburn, who acts as hostess, or chaperon, or it may be by some other principal or employee, whose business it is to welcome and greet the new arrivals who come to us daily. Your introduction of yourself is followed naturally by your questions as to this or that which you wish to know about our terms and methods, to confirm your own understanding of the matter. These are answered fully and courteously. Our greeters welcome your inquiries. Ask us just what you want to know, and their response will be politely given. Anyone behind the counter thoroughly understands dancing.

Are you from out of the city, and do you wish to be directed to a suitable hotel, boarding house, studio apartment or private residence for your domicile while here? We have a list of desirable and investigated places to suit all purses and all needs, and are glad to pass the information on to our students.

Your questions being answered to your satisfaction, you decide to enroll. The booking secretary invites you behind the counter, where an enrollment card and contract is made out and signed. This contract stipulates the number of lessons you are to receive and the kind of stage dancing you are to take. You take the work just as I have personally laid it out in the courses. The matter of tuition is arranged, and you, as one of us, are invited to accompany a guide to the various classrooms, studios, offices and other departments of the two large floors—and absorb inspiration for your future work from what you observe in the way of modern facilities and actual instruction being given to live classes.

There is nothing more inspiring to the new pupil than to see our various dancing classes in action. In fact, a view of our classes in progress of work is inspiring to anyone, professional or nonprofessional. The girls do their class work with a vim and snap that betokens their interest and their intention to make good. They are a smiling happy lot of young ladies that it does one good to look at. Especially is this true of the advanced classes; the beginners' classes are busy learning the A, B, C's of dancing, and these rudiments are absorbing. But to watch the beginners today, and then see the same pupils a few weeks later as they advance in ease of movement and in a completer understanding of their work, is most inspiring of all—inspiring to you who see them and to the progressing pupils themselves. If it were possible or practical to let the public in to look at our classes at work, our present large quarters would soon prove inadequate to give foot room to the great number of inspired ladies who would wish to enroll here and join in the gayeties. There is contagion in watching our best students at their "play."

Our new pupil is escorted also into my private office, there to be welcomed by me personally. A large and richly furnished room is this, its walls decorated with photographs of stage stars of universal fame who have been developed by me, and incidentally helped up the ladder of fame. Here is inspiration on every hand.

In her progress through the two floors of the studios our newcomer is absorbing inspiration continually. To enumerate some of the features that make an impression on her receptive mind as she proceeds from room to room:

There is the Call Board in the main office. Now in the theatre the Call Board is an established institution, placed handily to the stage door and inspected daily by all members of the company for such information as the management wishes to impart. Our Call Board serves a similar purpose, and we encourage its daily perusal by all the students. We post thereon press notices that our graduates send us of their own success as reported in the newspapers; also notices of my own producing activities in many cities; the date of the next makeup classes; information of every nature that concerns the studio or its clientele.

There is the Grand Ball Room, the most complete room for its purpose that was ever constructed; its floors clear-maple, its walls full-length mammoth mirrors; its windows large, its ventilation perfect and easily regulated; its double rows of practice bars; its clocks regulated and wound electrically by the Western Union Telegraph Co. every hour, striking to announce the opening and closing of the class instruction.

In this Grand Ball Room, the large Ballet studio, the various class-room and private instruction and rehearsal studios, the gymnasium, and especially in the Demi-Tasse Theatre, which is a corporate part of our studios,—in all these there is accumulated a fund of inspiration that suffices to start the new student with a hopeful and expectant spirit of future accomplishment that is a prime essential to her success.

On the day in which instruction is to start, the pupil returns to the studio and is assigned to a dressing room. Here she finds expert maid service, the maids being on continuous duty during all instruction periods. She is accommodated with a locker, if one is required, with her indi-

vidual key. She is introduced to the row of modern
shower baths, and finds accompanying them every form
of up-to-date sanitary appliances and fixtures. She is
now "at home," a full-fledged member of the "happy family," and her education in her chosen art is about to commence.

She takes her seat in her first classroom. She finds herself surrounded by a number of other young ladies who,
like her, have come here imbued with the laudable ambition to advance their interests in health, beauty, accomplishment of grace, and to fit themselves for an independent and lucrative career, not one of whom is any more
advanced than she is. Her inspiration is furthered by
this contact with those who are to become her fellow class-
mates. She takes note of the heavy felt floor-pads beneath
her feet, the practice bars along the wall, etc., and is thus
assured that every care is being taken here for her security
from harm as well as for her comfort and advancement.

Her instructor, she finds, is a professional dancer of
wide stage experience, who knows every one of the actual
steps he is teaching, for he executes them before her, aid-
ing her eyes by a living example, while he at the same time
informs her understanding by telling her what each step
and motion is and why it is done. His every word and
action is inspirational. She feels now that she is on the
highroad to success.

Presently, I enter the room and proceed to organize the
class for service, following which I address them on matters concerned with their courses, seeking to instill into
each prospective star an ambition to reach out for perfection. And from this hour the inspiration is enhanced with
each new day's progress.

As I often say, in one of my class talks, "Inspiration
plus perspiration equals one good dancer."

ATMOSPHERE

ATMOSPHERE is something that one feels but cannot see, Atmosphere on the stage is created by means of stage settings, costumes, electrical lighting effects, music, orchestration, and certain stage decorations as properties, all combined into one complete whole.

Every attitude of the body that one assumes in front of an audience on the stage creates a certain dramatic atmosphere. Every gesture, every expression of the face, every move of the body aids to create atmosphere. Characteristic attitudes of the body, characteristic walks, characteristic dancing also creates atmosphere. In order that a solo and an ensemble dance may get over with an audience it must have atmosphere. This atmosphere must be figured out in a scientific way. It requires unusual creative faculties to produce anything original or atmospheric in the way of a solo or ensemble dance for the stage today. No novice without experience can properly create perfect atmosphere, for it requires a thorough knowledge of stage-craft and showmanship, as well as of stage dancing and the technique of the stage, to create an atmosphere in which a solo or ensemble dance, or a song number will live. Without atmosphere the dance becomes all perspiration and no sense. There must be a definite idea behind a dance or underneath it. Everything must be done to embellish the theme or general idea. No idea must be overproduced; just enough must be done in the way of creating atmosphere for a dance to allow it to get over properly. In other words, it must be fully realized and produced properly, in a skillful, artistic way.

The first step in creating atmosphere is the selection of proper music, which will give real inspiration. Without inspiration nothing worthwhile is ever accomplished in the way of stage dancing. Machine-like dancers never get over. One must learn to inject one's own personality into each dance, in order to radiate an atmosphere that will bring success. This important subject of atmosphere is taken up in all our courses, and practically and thoroughly demonstrated and taught. Great care must be exercised that a dance is not overproduced, because if the scenery, costumes, in other words, the background, is allowed to dominate the dance itself, the dance will fail. The pupil must always dominate the costume and the entire stage setting or surroundings in order to get the dance over. Lavish production and accessories of any kind sometimes will interfere with the success of the pupil, or dancer. In other words, a too lavish production will detract from the dance itself and from the one who is performing the dance. So it really takes a person of artistic perception, who has become practical through actual experience, to set a dance properly and surround it as it should be surrounded. Many a novice will have good ideas, perhaps, for atmosphere, but through lack of experience will not be able to get those ideas over on the stage. It takes, therefore, practical stage direction to realize all the possibilities of stage atmosphere in a practical way.

The subject of atmosphere as it relates to the future success of our students, is given proper attention in our courses. I personally present it before the classes in talks from time to time, and demonstrate its meaning and purpose practically, by use of settings, lights and properties on the stage of my own Demi-Tasse theatre, connected with the studios.

The recognition of atmosphere and its need in connection with stage performances is a mental process, an idealization that not every material mind is capable of grasping readily. Probably no pupil would think of enrolling in a course that had atmosphere for its sole subject; yet it is an important matter to all students of the stage, and my plan of introducing it incidentally in my classroom talks, and at the same time showing them by a practical stage demonstration just what it means to them personally, has put it before our pupils in such an interesting and material way that they cannot fail to absorb some knowledge of its benefits.

Every producing stage director must possess an innate or an acquired sense of what we designate as atmosphere, in order to put on a production in a perfect, pleasing and profitable way. My many unqualified stage successes demonstrate my possession of this essential element, which I try to unite with originality and artistic perception, as well as a sure conception of what a fickle public will welcome and approve by its patronage. Hence, my talks on atmosphere are of more than usual value.

DANCING CHILDREN

WHEN you are teaching a child something that suggests play, and that at the same time is beneficial to health and beauty, and is also the real foundation for a future career, you are accomplishing much in an easy and pleasing way.

The activities in our Saturday classes for little tots do all of this. They are called dancing classes, and they become that, but the gradation from romping play into systematic dancing instruction is accomplished practically without consciousness on their part, and thus they learn the rudiments of stage routine almost without knowing it.

I don't know of any bunch of children anywhere that have a happier time than do our littlest pupils in their dainty lessons in the studios. They love every bit of the "work." In the first place, it is adapted to their years, and their instructors are both competent and kindly; and while it is quite a problem to handle a roomful of little folks bent on mischief, and direct their playing along systematized lines, we do it, and before they know it the little feet are stepping in unison to bright music, and gradually there is awakened a pride in perfect performance, and the little playmates become little dancers, each trying his best to equal or excel his or her fellows.

I go on record as saying that the age of eight years is the most favorable for the beginning of a dancing career, for then the young pupil has a mind sufficiently developed to easily comprehend instruction, and a body readily responsive to training. Yet we take children from four to seven years of age for specialized training which prepares them properly in the fundamentals and technique that is so necessary. Occasionally some five-year-old dancing marvel is discovered. Young years are learning years the world over, and right training in foundation work for the future great dancer, as taught in our studios, is so attractive in itself and so suggestive of real "fun" to the little learner, that both child and parents give it their hearty approval.

Dancing teachers in other cities send promising children to New York to study for professional careers; mothers bring the little dancers to New York, anxious to put them on the stage at once. But that is not possible, as a state law prohibits any child under sixteen from appearing before a paid audience to sing or dance, while permitting them to go on for dialogue parts only, if they are past ten years. Producers demand birth certificates and live up to the law. There is in New York City a Gerry Society, which controls the situation and is sharply on the alert.

Here in New York City there is a professional school for stage children, which many attend.

The great majority of the children who come to our studios for dancing instruction are from families who do not want the children to take up stage careers, but wish them to be properly and thoroughly trained in every type of dancing, which incidentally brings out all the natural grace in the body, develops health, poise, charm of manner, personality and symmetrical bodies. Parents naturally desire to see their little ones graceful, accomplished, pleasing in deportment, and able to exhibit a few clever steps in home or amateur entertainments—a parent's proper pride. Others, especially professional stage people, active or retired, enter their young folks in my courses with a view to their ultimately becoming professional stage dancers. They know the emoluments. They know that one daughter on the dancing stage is worth ten in the parlor—financially. They know, too, that old adage "as the twig is bent," and the rest of it, so they start their twigs straight and in fertile soil with faith that in this way their child's future is well and happily provided for. A knowledge of stage dancing is a life insurance policy that pays big dividends during one's lifetime. The dancer is her own—and perhaps her parents'—beneficiary.

We have tots here in the studio at our Saturday classes as young as four. Usually, however, they are five, six, or over. In their primary work we give them all sorts of jolly exercises—walking, running, galloping, and for the tiniest we have "skipping special," "baby work," body building and dancing games.

Our Junior class for children (ages four, five, six and seven) devotes half an hour to very mild physical training and limbering and stretching work on the heavy felt pads, and then there is half an hour of dancing games. The hour thus passes all too quickly with our interested little pupils.

As they show proficiency in this work we give them the actual dancing steps which are arranged in effective routines. All of the technique is necessary and beautiful and they love to go through it before the big wall mirrors and see themselves in graceful poses.

Those whose little bodies are especially adapted to it are allowed to take up so-called acrobatic dancing, and it is not surprising that the heels-over-head idea appeals as it does to the juvenile mind. It is action such as they crave, doing "cart-wheels," "splits," "back-bends" and many showy "tricks," and they just love it. They are never forced in this work, but really accomplish it themselves under painstaking instructions. Children eight, nine, ten and eleven years of age are assigned to the intermediate classes, beginners or advanced, according to the proficiency or talent that they show me. Those twelve, thirteen, fourteen and fifteen years of age are placed in the Children's Senior Classes, either beginners or advanced. I, personally, grade them and supervise all of their instruction. When they reach the age of sixteen, the girls are put in the adult girls' classes and the boys at sixteen are given private lessons from then on. There are no mixed adult classes.

One thing we are very careful and considerate about is, putting a child on her toes in the ballet work. We find cases where teachers elsewhere have forced this too soon, before the child's feet and ankles were prepared for it. Mothers are sometimes to blame for that, for they are eager to see their little daughters do this pretty work; but we insist upon proper foundation work first, developing the child gradually, and then, when the strength is there, we know we should be able to do the rest not only without danger of permanent injury but with assurance of pleasing and perfect success.

Children thus gradually get instruction in five basic types of dancing, i. e., musical comedy, tap and step, acrobatic, ballet, including classical, character, toe, interpretive, and exhibition dancing. They may develop best along one of these types, and choose to follow that one out to a real professional quality, or they may acquire a good working knowledge of all and thus have a diversity of accomplishments. Then when they reach the age limit of sixteen that permits them legally to enter upon the profit-taking period, they are ready to respond.

I watch the little folks with their instructors every Saturday. They are graduated according to their ages at first, and then graded according to ability, usually at the end of each term (every twelfth or thirteenth week). The youngest group gets one hour's work, all their little bodies can stand, while those between eight and fifteen inclusive get two hours instruction each Saturday. Their mothers, guardians or governesses are in a spacious waiting room.

We are making a lot of children happy, and at the same time laying a foundation for their health and beauty, and perhaps for their financial prosperity. The future great dancers of the next two decades are somewhere in this lot of little ones; which ones it will be is unknown to them or to us, but all are given an equal opportunity, and many will make good.

DANCING HANDS

IT IS not only the rhythmic movements of the feet and legs that constitute a dancer. Every stage dancer employs as well her face, hands and arms in giving expression to grace, beauty, and the many interpretations of her pantomimic art. Watch the next dancer or group of dancers you see at a show, and it may surprise you to discover how much the hands and arms have to do in adding to the effectiveness of the presentation. It is a compliment to the dancer's artistry that you have been absorbedly pleased by the complete effect, with no thought on your part of analyzing the structure in detail.

But let her put her hands and arms out of the picture and note the disastrous result. You then realize emphatically how much the motions of the entire person, of the limbs and the torso and head, are interdependent to create the grace and rhythm that complete the perfect dance.

The various functions of the hand as detailed are:

1, to define or indicate; 2, to affirm or deny; 3, to mold or detect; 4, to conceal or reveal; 5, to surrender or hold; 6, to accept or reject; 7, to inquire or acquire; 8, to support or protect; 9, to caress or assail.

How these several functions are naturally evolved from the various movements of the hand will be readily understood when one reads the definitions:

1. (a) To define: first finger prominent; hand moves up and down, side to earth; (b) to indicate: first finger prominent; hand points to object to be indicated.

2. (a) To affirm: hand, palm down, makes movement of affirmation up and down; (b) to deny: hand, palm down, makes movement of negation from side to side.

3. (a) To mold: hand makes a movement as if molding a soft substance, as clay; (b) to detect: rub the thumb across the fingers as if feeling a texture held between them. (A movement often made when following a train of thought.)

4. (a) To conceal: bring the palm of the hand toward you, the fingers at the same time gently closing on palm; (b) to reveal: reverse the above movement, exposing palm.

5. (a) To surrender: closed hand opens, palm down, action as if dropping something on the ground; (b) to hold: the hand closes as if to retain something.

6. (a) To accept: fingers close on upturned palm as if receiving something; (b) to reject: fingers unclose from down-turned palm as if throwing something away.

7. (a) To inquire: a tremulous movement of the outstretched fingers as in the blind; palm down; (b) to acquire; hand drawn toward you, fingers curved toward down-turned palm.

8. (a) To support: palm up, making a flat surface as if supporting a weight; (b) to protect: palm down; a movement of fingers as if covering what you protect.

9. (a) To caress: a movement of stroking up and down, or sideways. If sideways, one caresses the animal nature; (b) to assail: palm down; the fingers make a convulsive movement of clutching.

In other words, the hands give expression or emphasis to the thought that it is desired to convey, both in speaking and in the pantomime of the dance and the screen.

Learn, therefore, to use your hands correctly in every dance. There is an idea to be put across in every step from your entrance—your first greeting to your audience —through the measured cadence of your dance steps, to the final exit—your appeal for approval. While you acquire the necessary dance steps to make you a perfect dancer, also learn the hand and arm movements that complement your steps and perfect the picture into its most pleasing possibilities, movements that shall develop the idea of the dance you are portraying and carry it across the footlights.

As soon as you get command of your foot work and master the technical steps of your routine, put your hands and arms into action and develop their connection with your dancing steps so that both shall coördinate as one, and thus your dance will grow into a complete and perfect expression in the easiest way.

Do not neglect your hand-action. It is a positive necessity to successful dancing, and the time to give it attention is while you are learning the rudiments of your art. This work is taught in the Ned Wayburn Modern Americanized Ballet Technique.

DANCING FEET

GOOD dancers will take good care of their feet—the tools of their trade. They are essential factors in your salary-drawing power. Treat them kindly, and they will thank you and remain your meal ticket for many years.

A hot foot bath followed by a careful pedicuring it seems unnecessary to recommend, for that is a daily habit with all dancers and other ladies.

If your feet are tired and cry aloud for care, prepare a bath for them of common baking soda and warm water, using two tablespoonfuls of soda to a bowl of warm water. This will reduce the swelling of the feet and ease them greatly. Now rub them with a cut lemon. This freshens them and also makes them white and pretty. Allow the lemon juice to dry on them, then apply cold cream and massage them thoroughly. Now wipe off all surplus cream and dust them with talcum powder. Put on soft house shoes and you will feel like a new person.

Massage with olive oil is splendid for tired swollen feet; soaking them in salt water is also good.

Here is a favorite foot balm you can have put up at the drug store: Calomel, ten grains; carbonate of zinc, one dram; oil of eucalyptus, five drops; ointment of rose water, one ounce.

First bathe your feet in cold salt water, then rub in the balm, massaging it well into the feet at night, and powder freely with talcum in the morning.

When the feet swell from long standing or tedious rehearsals, relief can be had by dissolving the following powder in the foot bath: Borax, two ounces; rock salt, two ounces; alum, one ounce.

If your feet are tender, soak them in this bath for ten minutes, and then dry thoroughly: Hot water, five quarts; boric acid, 200 grams; tannin, five grams.

For removing callous spots, soak the feet in hot water for ten or fifteen minutes, then take a piece of pumice stone and rub the callous spot. Do this every night. During the day keep a piece of cotton which has been covered with cold cream on the spot to keep it soft. This will remove any callous in a short time.

Can you think of a dancer with corns? What torture the idea suggests! A limping, crippled dancer would be distressing to gaze upon, and even a minute corn could create this condition. It simply isn't done. For a dancer to tolerate a corn is a confession of carelessness, of personal neglect, and indifference to everything concerning her art.

To prevent corns and most other foot troubles, wear shoes that fit your feet. A too loose shoe makes corns just as quickly as does a tight shoe, for when shoes are too large there is a constant friction, which develops a corn. And see to it also that your stockings fit your feet. A short stocking cramps the foot, and a loose stocking wrinkles and rubs in spots.

The first thing to do for a corn is to relieve it from all pressure. The druggist has an abundance of corn cures, most of which are effective, but if you choose to have one made up to order, here is a sure cure: Salicylic acid, twenty grains; alcohol, one-eighth ounce; flexible collodion, one ounce. Mix and apply to hard surface of corn with a small brush. Do this once or twice daily for three days, then soak the feet in hot water, and a layer of skin will come off. Repeat till corn is gone.

Tight shoes two sizes too small for you do not make your feet look small; in fact, they make the feet look larger, and you haven't freedom to walk or dance. Tight shoes and high-heeled shoes are injurious to the health. The circulation of your whole body is interfered with by wearing them, and cold feet, corns, bunions and many other painful troubles result.

Wear comfortable shoes if you would have freedom in dancing and all other exercises. Whatever shoes you wear, have them comfortable, so you can forget your feet as you step joyously forth to trip a measure in your chosen profession.

DANCING SHOES

EACH type of dancing demands its own fashion in footwear, and the novice while learning and rehearsing requires a foot covering differing materially from that to be worn later in the perfected dance on the professional stage.

It is very desirable for the newcomer into the dancing world to acquire knowledge of the correct shoes to be worn to facilitate action, make the learning as easy as possible and keep the feet in perfect condition.

In taking up this subject I shall tell in simple language what is the best and most practical way to dress the feet for the various occasions that arise in dancing. One general rule can be laid down for everyone and all occasions: *Have your shoes fit your feet.* Do not simply "buy a pair of shoes." Ascertain the size and width of shoes that correctly fit you, and ask for your shoes by these specifications. Go to a first-class shoe dealer. Don't buy a shoe merely because it is pretty. Cheap shoes are often the most expensive, and if poorly made may injure the feet.

The above advice applies to every shoe you buy, for house, sports, street or evening wear, as well as for dancing.

For the courses, consider the type of dancing you are taking and dress your feet with shoes suitable for that kind of work.

If your foot is short and fat, buy a short vamp shoe; if your foot is long and narrow, get shoes with a long vamp. Stiff soles being bad for the arches and hard to work in, be sure to get flexible soles.

For the toe dancer there are toe shoes which have a padded box toe. These come in black and white kid and in pink satin. This toe shoe and the regular soft ballet shoe, which is used for ballet technique, should both be a perfectly snug fit, the toes of the foot coming to the very end of the shoe. To do this requires a shoe about two sizes smaller than one's regular street shoes.

Nothing is better for the limbering and stretching foundation technique, as given in the Ned Wayburn courses, than the soft ballet shoe with a quarter-inch lift at the heel.

For acrobatic dancing this type of shoe is also recommended, though many prefer an elk sole cut out sandal, which is also the choice for Oriental ballet dancing. These sandals if too large will bulge at the sides, hence care in their fitting is desirable. The most commonly used shoe for girls doing acrobatic and soft shoe work and one that is excellent for this purpose, is a black kid flat, as it is known, which has a low heel and flexible sole; a sensible, comfortable shoe, such as your feet thank you for.

For tap and step dancing there are several types of shoes, the most common being that known as the "Mary Jane" or juvenile shoe with ankle strap and button or buckle. Another favorite is the laced low shoe, known as the oxford, made for both men and women. The solid clog shoe has a full wood heel, arch and sole, and is used for very advanced clog dancing; not to be worn by beginners, but only the most accomplished professional solo dancers. There is also a low show for "Tap" dancing called the "Split-clog" shoe, used by very advanced pupils only, never by beginners, the half-sole being wood and the heel wood, as well, but most professional dancers prefer what is known as the "Haney" metal plate on the end of the shoe to bring out the "taps," or else a wood-fibre half-sole, but no beginner should be worrying about this. Just remember, that you must never try to learn to dance in a French, Cuban or military heel, as they act as a handicap or "brake." No one can learn with them because they pitch one forward at the wrong angle and impair the health.

There are several attachments, called "jingles," "taps," fiber half soles, and the like, that the expert dancer in this type of work will wish to have on his dancing shoes, and I shall tell you about them here, but it is best to avoid their use while you are learning the dances. After you have mastered your stuff

Fibre Toe

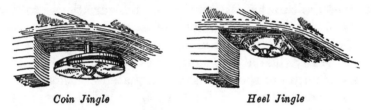

| *Coin Jingle* | *Heel Jingle* |

and qualified yourself without them, then have them put on, but not until after you have become a real dancer.

There is a "coin jingle," as it is called, a brass disc about the size of a quarter of a dollar set loosely on the shoe shank, that sounds like two coins striking together at every shake.

The heel jingle is a brass plate set into the shoe near the heel with a loose disc inside it from which extends a plug that as you step falls and hits the floor.

The regulation stage shoe has a very flexible shank and a French heel. It is not a desirable shoe for the student of dancing because of the heel. But for high kicking and similar types of stage dancing after one has acquired a knowledge of the art, it is very satisfactory. Be sure it is comfortable and fits well.

There are other shoes that come naturally into use on the stage for certain types of dancing. There is the low ballet shoe of the Greek type, and a similar one in the high ballet type.

What is known as the Russian boot finds its place in some dances. It is often red, green, or white, to match the costume. Variations of this boot are the Spanish, Gypsy or Hungarian, Cowboy, and others.

There is also a high-laced close fitting boot with a very low heel and soft sole used by men, as a rule, in certain kinds of acrobatic dancing.

When you get into theatrical footwear, there is practically no limit to the possibilities and the variations. Period shoes of all times and nations—Grecian, Roman, Egyptian, etc.,—make the list almost endless.

But really the only dancing shoes you will first concern yourself with are those I have designated as belonging to the learners' work for foundation technique, acrobatic, musical comedy, tap and step, ballet and toe dancing.

In the exhibition dancing the usual ball room shoes are preferred. If the dance is done in character, that will determine the style of the shoes.

I want to sound a warning about French-heeled shoes and high-heeled shoes in general, such as ladies find so fashionable.

A pretty female foot is charming, and one's feet should be dressed in the most becoming manner. But high-heeled shoes do not make a pretty foot. It is impossible to walk gracefully or safely in them, and as for dancing, no one can ever hope to become a dancer who wears such clumsy foot-gear while attempting to learn the art.

The persistent wearing of high-heeled shoes does much to bring about female troubles. It is conducive to ill health, crooked figures, weak ankles, and many internal ills. There are crippled ladies of mature years whom I know, who frankly admit that their condition is due solely to the wearing of high-heeled shoes in their younger years, "to make their feet look pretty."

I want to make my abhorrence of high French heels as strong as I can. You cannot wear them in my studios. I will not permit them, for to wear them indicates that you will never learn to dance, and there is no use in wasting your time in trying. After you have learned, in suitable and proper shoes, how to do your dances, then a shoe with a baby French heel will be permitted for musical comedy dancing, and a shoe with a low common-sense (not necessarily ugly) heel for tap and step dancing.

Fortunately, it is not necessary to wear French-heeled shoes in order to have pretty feet. There are an abundance of attractive shoes on the market that one can choose with assurance of enhancing the beauty of their feet, without this deforming heel. If one uses the words "sensible" or "solid comfort" when speaking of shoes—women's shoes especially—it suggests something sloppy and unattractive, and some young women will have none of it.

There is no intention to advocate the wearing of such shoes, nor any others that are not attractive and good looking. Get becoming shoes for every occasion, by all means, but see to it that they do not have the fatal, high French heels. Before you take a single lesson in the dancing art, dress your feet with proper shoes properly fitted, and thank me for starting you right.

Most large cities have shoe stores with dancing shoe departments, but if you are not able to supply your needs locally, write to the Ned Wayburn Studios for information and it will be forthcoming. But please bear in mind that no shoes are dealt in at the studios and no direct orders for shoes will be considered.

THE QUEST OF BEAUTY

EVERY person desires health, vigor, grace, poise—and I know of no woman who would object to personal beauty of form and face.

Beauty of face may or may not consist of bewitching features and perfect complexion; many a woman is admired for her good looks while her features may not be considered classically correct. The quality of one's complexion can be improved by exercise and correct diet, and, for stage or social purposes, by the proper makeup.

Beauty of form is a matter of training. The "female form divine" can be improved and kept at the "divine" standard if the possessor wills it, goes at it right and persists in the effort. Bodily health is a factor in all beauty. Get your body healthy, and the rest of the way to beauty is easy.

When I state that stage dancing, as taught in the Ned Wayburn courses, is a developer of health and vigor, a sure road to grace, poise and personal beauty of form and face—in a word, a maker of beautiful and attractive women—I am making a statement of fact that is irrefutable, based on actual and frequent occurrence. You never saw a properly trained dancer who was not in perfect physical condition.

Many ladies learn my dances for the benefits to be derived from the training; young ladies and others not so young; the stouts and the thins, especially, and both profit alike by the health-producing activities they find in our courses. These ladies neither need nor desire a stage career; what they do want is freedom from awkwardness, a bit of pleasant reducing or filling out of hollows, a lasting development of the foundation of beauty. They come from professional, industrial and social circles. An hour a day, except Saturdays and Sundays, for a few weeks, and we have their blessing forevermore.

And while on the subject of beauty, here is another thing:

A girl has a pretty face. On the strength of her beauty she thinks she would make a success as an actress. (Hollywood is overflowing with this type of girl.) She is a good home dancer, and surely dancing on the stage is no different! Perhaps she is right in her estimate of herself, and then again she may be mistaken, for it requires more than mere physical appearance to be a top notcher in anything outside of an exclusively beauty show. Not that any lady's pulchritude is a handicap to a stage career or in any way undesirable. On the contrary, the stage has always welcomed beautiful women, and will continue to do so.

But, here is another girl in the same social set who makes no claim to being a beauty, and does not think of herself as being of a type that lends charm to the stage— and this Cinderella may possess the very qualities that go to make the professional actress and dancer, and yet let the opportunity pass because of her failure to recognize her own value. Her face, with proper makeup under our skilled direction, with the correct treatment of its features, consideration of the stage lighting, and her hair becomingly and appropriately dressed, may far outclass that of the pretty girl who has only aspiration without the necessary qualities to back it.

In other words, beauty of the street and the home is a vastly different thing from beauty on the stage behind the footlights. So do not worry at what your mirror tells you. If you have the other qualities that make for professional success, my courses will instruct you fully as to the way to look your best, and you will be surprised at the latent possibilities for personal beauty that we will discover for you.

BELLE BAKER

CHARLOTTE GREENWOOD

CLEO MAYFIELD

JANET STONE AND NICK LONG, JR.

WHO'S AFRAID!

I HAVE never known a graduate of our courses to have a bad case of stage fright. This doubtless is attributable to the fact that our pupils are thoroughly grounded in all their stage work before going before a critical audience. They know their steps and routines perfectly, have mastered the physical side of dancing. Their first dancing is done before their class, their instructor and myself. Once a month we have Visitors' Day, for relatives and friends, here in the studio. Our students appear in action before them, and at other times before some neighborhood or church benefit audience. They are properly dressed for their part, and their makeup is right when they go "behind the footlights" for their first professional performance—all of which gives the necessary self-confidence that carries the dancer through the trying ordeal of a first appearance.

STAGE FRIGHT—WHAT IT IS AND HOW TO OVERCOME IT

When you step out upon the stage to do your turn for the first time, you will be very grateful to me for having instilled into your mind the necessity for doing your work over and over till it has become second nature to you. You will thank me, too, for the long series of foundation work, limbering and stretching exercises, that you have gone through, that have kept you from being muscle-bound, given you confidence as well as ability, and left you without fear of not being able to go through with what you have undertaken. This and the knowledge that your costume and makeup are perfect, are of the greatest help in begetting that confidence that overcomes the danger of stage fright, not only on a first but also on all subsequent appearances. Knowing that you look right is half the battle; the other half is the certainty that you know what you are about to do and know it perfectly.

Stage fright is the uncontrollable fear of an audience. It is the result of excessive nervousness. The orator, the actor and the singer experience this dread more often than does the dancer or the instrumental musician. The mouth becomes dry and the throat contracts as the speaker or singer attempts to get his voice across the footlights and out to the audience. One's voice becomes faint and unnatural, weak and uncontrollable. Those who afterwards have become the world's great actors and singers have many of them been overcome with stage fright, and even left the stage on a first appearance. Richard Mansfield was one of these. He fainted from stage fright at his first appearance, yet he afterwards became one of the greatest dramatic stars in the world.

The stage dancer does not have this difficulty with her voice, and if trained right while acquiring her art should never be subjected to the bugaboo of fear. But I am going to lay down some general rules here for the prevention and control of stage fright that will give you confidence and also serve to instruct you how to act if the worst does happen and nervousness gets the best of you. In chorus work, of course, there is little danger. Your mates will carry you along if you miss a step or break your routine, and you'll soon get back all right. In solo work, don't try to look at your audience nor single out any individuals.

Don't glue your gaze on the orchestra leader, though he alone is the audience of which you have any right to be at all conscious. He and his baton are your friends and are giving you your tempo. Be aware of them incidentally but not conspicuously, and forget the rest of the folks in front entirely. Forget yourself, forget everything but the music that fills your ears, and let your dancing absorb you completely. Radiate an air of conscious certainty in all you do. Smile. Look happy. Your dance is a good one and you know how to do it well. You know you do. Pretty soon a ripple of applause starts. It grows and fills that big half-dark place down there before you. That is a tonic. Your stage fright or your fear of it is gone for good. Your audience has accepted you. Now you glow with the happiness that is yours by every right. Applause is to you and your art as the shower and the sun are to the flowers. You live on it. Without it you are a failure.

Suppose you had let your fear master you. Suppose you had quit cold, got cold feet, let yourself be scared out of your wits, and not braved the thing you feared. That would have been a calamity. Your promising career would have ended before it began, after all your expenditure of time and money for lessons. Don't let anything scare you. Go on when your turn comes. Keep going. No matter what happens, don't give up—keep right on till you get your nerve back.

I saw a young singer come out in front of a large audience once, get her cue from the orchestra, and stop dead. She looked out over the crowded auditorium. The leader held his baton suspended in air. "Wait," she said. "I've forgotten it." The audience was dead silent, understanding just what had happened, and very sympathetic. The orchestra leader spoke a single word to her.

"Oh, yes!" she smiled, and her voice swelled out into the song she had so nearly forgotten.

Did she get a hand? I'll say she did, and a couple of encores and a press notice next morning that told all about it, and her career was launched. She had presence of mind and control of herself. Cultivate this by first gaining perfect control of every muscle in your body, by persistent practice of all of your dancing exercises, technique and dance routines; great confidence in your ability will come with this.

I am going to advise you to do as I have always done, and that is, write your routines down and keep them. Each has a name. Ask your instructor, he can tell you the name for every step. Write these routines in sequence, and remember each one. Go through each one every day, no matter how many you collect. The more of them you have the richer you are, for they are valuable. You will be a solo dancer one of these days and with this list you have you can make up your own routines,—take a step from this one and that one and build a new dance for yourself. After a year or two you'll find this easy to do, and it gives you a chance to work in your own personality. In writing down the routines in the first place, while still in the courses, as I have advised, you are helping yourself become fit, so fit and so familiar with your work that you couldn't get stage fright if you wanted to. So in doing this you are really accomplishing two very important things, enlarging your dance vocabulary and making yourself stage-fright proof.

Always go on the stage with the firm conviction that you are going to do well and make a hit. Say to yourself with deep feeling, "I shall do well tonight. I shall have a big success. Everything will go just as I want it to."

This is called auto-suggestion, if you want to know, and it is a self-starter, too, and makes the wheels of success go 'round. Step on it! It is good for every performance.

Be satisfied with small beginnings at first. Exhibit your work in public whenever you can, to gain confidence and experience. Keep your eye on Broadway and work toward that great thoroughfare, of course—all dancers do that—but don't think of making your first appearance there. The farther away from Broadway you make your first appearance the better it will be. Learn the art of costuming yourself for your part, and learn the art of makeup. They come next in importance to the actual dances themselves that you are patiently practicing. When you start out, take with you a knowledge of dress and makeup as well as of dancing, and when you are mistress or master of these three arts and make use of them properly, you can go on the professional stage without dread of being overcome by stage fright. No real artist ever is, although any great artist will be a little bit nervous perhaps before making the first entrance in a new play on an important first night. But the sight of the audience cures that.

THE DANCE
AND THE DRAMA

THE art of acting as it has been known for thousands of years, derives from the dance, and is a direct evolution from the representation of the emotions as portrayed by the primitive dancers. Joy, anger, love, jealousy, hatred, revenge, triumph and defeat were all interpreted in the Grecian dances of the period antedating the introduction of the speaking actors, who told in words and gestures the stories that had formerly been conveyed through the dance. The victorious warriors returned from battle danced to show how they had fought and destroyed the enemy. The hunter described in a dance how he had slain wild animals. The traveller who had visited what to him were distant lands, told of the strange people he had met by imitating them while he danced. Gradually there was evolved the addition of spoken words supplementing the action, accompanied by appropriate gestures and facial expression. Man had discovered his ability to become for the moment another. person, and to interpret certain emotions more vividly than through the medium of the dance. The stage became the opportunity not only for the representation of elemental forces and actions, but also for the principal creations of the imagination.

While the slowly developing drama departed widely from the limitations of its origin, there has, nevertheless, remained an association with the dance that will continue for all time. Especially is this true of the lighter branch of the drama, comedy, and the modern combination known as musical comedy or comic opera. In the popular stage entertainments of the day dancing forms an important feature of a large percentage of all productions that appear in the leading theatres. In many of the classical plays, by great dramatists, that are annually chosen for revivals, the dance appears, and the actor or actress who cannot dance misses many opportunities for profitable engagements. There has always been a kinship between the dance and the legitimate drama, and many prominent stars began their apprenticeship for the stage in the ranks of musical comedy or as vaudeville dancers. With few exceptions it will be found that the men and women who have achieved success on the stage are enthusiastic devotees of dancing, and they will agree that to those intending to make acting their life work a thorough training in the art of the dance is an essential part of their education.

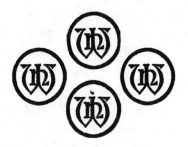

PERSONALITY IN THE DANCE

EVERY individual possesses something that for lack of a better word is termed "personality;" something elusive and evasive, that cannot easily be defined or explained, but nevertheless remains the essential quality that distinguishes its possessor from every other human being. But while all may have the potentiality for some distinct and special attribute, unfortunately for by far the greater number this is never developed or expressed, and they pass through their uneventful, monotonous existence, without even realizing their capacity for being or doing something outside the routine of their daily occupations.

In this era of the newest of sciences, psychoanalysis, which is attracting the study and investigation of millions, much attention is being given to the explanation of the failure of so many persons to find an outlet for hidden capacities by the well-worn "inferiority complex." The flower of personality, we are told, is born to blush unseen because of an individual's belief that he or she is in some way inferior. Despite all the books that have been written, and the good advice that has been given, urging the development of self-confidence as the starting point for worthy accomplishment, there is still all too prevalent an attitude of timidity and hesitation that says in effect: "I can't be what I would like to be, so what's the use of trying."

This inability or unwillingness to believe in one's self; the disposition to doubt one's powers, to admit defeat before trying, is nowhere more clearly apparent than in the attitude of many persons who possess the physical and mental qualifications that with proper training would bring distinction and profit as exponents of the dance. They admire the successful dancers; they feel that they too are capable of expressing themselves through this art. But,—and here comes the cold water that quenches the spark of their ambition,—they are timid; afraid of failure; they fear that they haven't the persistence and capacity for application that is needed to assure success. Perhaps they do make an attempt, but the work is hard, they just know that they won't be able to stick it out, and after a few futile efforts they give it up, and spend the rest of their lives wondering what they might have accomplished if they had persevered.

To these too easily discouraged persons the message of the dance is: "What others have done you can do. You have the physique, or at least it can be developed. You have the intelligence to accept instruction. You have the patience needed for the continued repetition of movement that makes perfection. You have an individuality that can be expressed in the subtle shadings and delicate touches that growing skill will enable you to show in every graceful movement. You have in you the capacity for artistic and harmonious expression of your personality. Why not develop it?"

I cannot emphasize too strongly the importance of *personality* in a successful stage career. Along with the actual mastering of the dancing steps and the acquisition of health and a beautiful body, comes just as surely the development of one's personal qualities. And because each person has an individuality which is distinctive from that of everyone else, all must select the type of dancing which is best suited to their own personalities. That is why the performance of stars like Evelyn Law, Marilyn Miller, Ann Pennington, Gilda Gray and Fred and Adele Astaire leaves a lasting impression. Every step, every movement is designed to drive home the characteristics of their individuality.

Even more important than the actual dancing steps they do is the manner in which they execute them—the individuality that they express. It is the almost indefinable factor called personality which lifts one out of the ranks of the chorus and makes the solo dancer. In this book I am trying to help you develop your personality, in the same way that I have discovered and developed that quality in so many of today's theatrical stars.

Most emphatically I want to impress upon you that it is not "chorus work" you are learning in my courses. It is professional and individual dancing, that when mastered gives one that certain something that one lacked before, a feeling of having accomplished assurance of success.

Anyone who masters the dances takes on a certain confident feeling in time, after exercising great patience in practice. With this confidence, the happy pupil radiates a new magnetic personality which the audience feels—but more about this later on, when you will learn just how one's self is injected into the dances, until they are vitalized and become the living embodiment of the emotions and spirit of the dancer. This is putting one's own personality into the dance, and is one secret of every great artist's success, which we seek to instill into the minds of all our students.

DANCING AND EASE OF MANNER

MAN is a gregarious animal, and eagerly seeks the company of his fellows. In civilized society men and women gathered to dine, to converse, to dance, to play games, to watch others indulging in various sports or pastimes. Out of this intermingling at social gatherings there has gradually developed an accepted code of conduct termed "good manners," which are as stringently binding as any law enacted by a legislature. And there are penalties for violation of this code, that are surely imposed upon the luckless offender, ranging all the way from a snub, a sound or gesture of disapproval, to social ostracism.

"Manners maketh man" is an ancient aphorism that has a very wide application. While the forms and standards of what constitute good manners change with the times, their essential basis is always the same—a deference to, and consideration for, those with whom one is thrown in contact. Courtesy, politeness, helpfulness, and other evidences of good breeding and careful training, are the outgrowth of a desire for eliminating selfish instincts. The rude man or woman is an egotist, seeking to assert his or her individuality without regard for the sensibilities of others.

Aside from the willful violation of those unwritten laws that have come to govern social intercourse, there are many who err because of excessive self-consciousness, which makes it difficult or impossible to put themselves at ease among those with whom they would like to associate. They are painfully aware of their own surplus ego; they are constrained and awkward; they feel that in some way they are outsiders, that, as the slang phrase puts it, they do not belong. It is probable that more social failures are due to this trait than to any other cause.

Against this self-conscious attitude a thorough training in the dance is a most effective remedy. The shy, constrained, awkward boys and girls mingle with their companions on terms of ordered freedom and equality. They are taught grace of movement; the spontaneous expression of their individuality is modified by contact with their associates; they acquire a graceful walk and carriage. To follow the various movements of the dance in harmony with the music takes their thoughts away from themselves, and provides an escape from the dread self-questioning: "Am I doing the right thing?" Success in mastering the technique of the dance brings assurance and poise, and adds immeasurably to the capacity for adjustment to environment that marks the well-mannered members of what is in the true sense of the word "good society."

DANCING AND CIVILIZATION

SOLEMN professors are discussing the question "What is Civilization?" the answers ranging all the way from an increase in man's power over material things that add to his comfort and happiness, up to the development of higher ethical standards of personal conduct. To one the civilized man is he who has brought to his service the hidden forces of nature, and by steam and electricity has girdled the earth, vastly increased the production of wealth, and by superior methods of transportation has brought all regions of the globe into close contact. To another the mark of civilization is the diffusion of valuable knowledge, the spread of popular education, and the sharing by a whole people of the culture and scholarship of the great creative minds. To yet another the real test of civilization is in the cultivation of a greater capacity for enjoyment of all that life has to offer. And a fourth affirms that only those are truly civilized who have learned the laws of right living and conduct, so that in seeking the fullest development and expression of their natures they are careful to avoid infringing on the rights and welfare of their fellow men.

Leaving the definition of civilization for future settlement, it may be taken for granted that a civilized society is one in which order and individual rights to life, personal liberty, and lawfully acquired property are respected; in which the rule of brute strength is supplanted by the higher law of reason and social justice and in which the people are free to develop their artistic and aesthetic tastes into a complete and harmonious whole. Applying this standard to the world's history there are found great civilized communities that at various periods have emerged from primitive barbarism, have flourished for ages, have left their records of high achievement in architecture, sculpture, painting and other arts, in imperishable literature, and in religions that phrase the highest exaltation of human thought and ideals. Such are the civilizations of ancient Egypt, India, Greece and Rome, where the conditions attained were as greatly in advance of those prevailing at the time in practically all the other regions of the earth, as are those of modern Europe and America compared with the black tribes of Africa.

To the student of social customs in various ages it is significant that the peoples of the most civilized countries were eager in their search for the higher enjoyments, and that among them the dance was regarded as one of the most important forms of self expression. Along with the greater accumulation of wealth; the erection of great palaces, temples and other enduring movements; the mastery of form, line, and color by the sculptor and painter; the progress in music and literature toward higher levels, came the recognition of the dance as one of the greater arts, worthy of encouragement by rulers and statesmen.

The fact that at the period of highest civilization in the four countries referred to the dance was held to be an important and honorable art, is testimony to its inherent value as a means of satisfying the universal desire for human expression of the beauty of form and harmonious movement. It is not a mere coincidence that the most enlightened peoples of all ages have regarded the dance not only as an amusement or diversion, but as exemplifying the eternal laws that bind mankind to its earthly environment. Poets, philosophers, scholars, leaders and teachers of men, have at the times that they have been most highly regarded because of their special qualities or abilities, joined in rendering homage to the dancer as an interpretative artist.

Coming down to modern times and our own country, it is found that as America has vastly increased in population, wealth, knowledge and material comfort, along with the widest extension of popular education of any great nation on the earth, there has arisen a greatly increased and steadily-growing interest in the dance, both as means of individual enjoyment, and as an artistic entertainment ranking high among all forms of creative effort. With the growth of great cities and industrial centers social activities have been greatly multiplied, and of these the dance is easily the most popular. At all seasons; at the winter resorts of the South, or the seashore, and in the mountains in summer, the story is the same; dancing is the one diversion that never palls, and is constantly engaged in everywhere. Golf, with its hundreds of thousands of devotees, has brought with it the country club, where the dance flourishes until the wee sma' hours. In the home, in hotels, restaurants and supper clubs, the dance reigns supreme. Learning to dance has become a part of the boy's or girl's education, along with the ordinary school studies. Not to dance is to be distinctly outside of practically all social circles in American cities and towns, and each year finds the number of one's dancing acquaintances increasing. From the select few who are assumed to be "smart society," down to the multitudes who make no social pretentions, everyone dances, and enjoys it. If a poll could be taken of the population over twelve years of age in any American city, asking for their favorite amusement, it would doubtless be found that dancing comes first.

In the field of public entertainment dancing holds an equally prominent place. The musical comedies, vaudeville acts, and other theatrical productions in which the dance is the chief or an important feature, testify to the popular appreciation of the highly skilled and highly paid artists who delight the public eye.

The motion picture is reputed to have seriously affected the prosperity of the legitimate drama, but it does not appear to have lessened the interest of amusement seekers in shows of which dancing is an essential part. The percentage of theatrical productions in which dancing figures has in recent years steadily increased, and the financial success of so many of this class of entertainments proves that the public knows what it wants, and is getting it. The enthusiastic crowds attracted by the great dancing artists also testify to the growing appreciation by the American people of what is distinctively the product of advanced culture and the higher civilization. As population grows, and as the percentage of urban residents, as compared with the dwellers in rural districts, increases, there will be an ever-increasing interest taken in the dance and all that pertains to it.

DANCING AND CHEERFULNESS

"FOR the good are always the merry," says William Butler Yeats, Ireland's foremost living poet, in "The Fiddler of Dorney." This is an old truth, too often ignored or forgotten. There are, unhappily, many persons who have conceived the strange notion that goodness means a gloomy outlook toward the world and those who inhabit it. To them this earth is a vale of tears; everything is evil and steadily growing worse; if every prospect pleases it only emphasizes their conviction that man is vile. Natural instincts that prompt mankind to rejoice and be glad, to lift up their voices in cheerful songs, or to express their abundant vitality by joyous dances, are to them evidence of sin and depravity. If they could have their way they would abolish every manifestation of happiness, and carry their conviction that man is doomed to endless pain and woe into the life beyond.

That this peculiar idea of the relation of goodness to happiness at one time represented the prevailing sentiment of what are termed the enlightened peoples, is undeniably true. Yet always there has been a saving remnant that protested against the solemn, serious, and sad railers against mirth and merriment, and at last these dissenters are finding that they are rapidly becoming the majority. No longer are normal men and women ashamed to show that they are glad to be alive; that they believe that they were meant to be happy and should seek happiness; that they do not agree that goodness means repression of natural impulses. Perhaps they are less concerned with abstract standards of conduct than were their ancestors. For them life is a joyous adventure, and they wish so to live that they may experience to the full all that it has to offer.

Not the least encouraging sign of the changed and changing attitude of humanity toward the old repressions and fears, is the world-wide extension of interest in all forms of popular amusement. People no longer think that to be good—or moral—whatever those words may mean, is to be a doleful machine, wearily going the rounds of earning a livelihood. They question the authority of those who try to inflict upon them their narrow standards of life. They ask questions. They want to know many things. Why, they ask, should it be a virtue to wear a gloomy face, to shun pleasure, to avoid their impulses to sing, play or dance? They have capacity for enjoyment. Why should they starve their natures, and go without pleasures that are rightfully theirs? It has often been said that Americans have not as a rule known how to play. They are changing all that, and as the level of education and intelligence rises, as wealth accumulates and is more widely diffused, as old inhibitions lose their force, this country is destined to become the great playground of the world. The American people are above all else cheerful and optimistic. They know what they can do because they know what has been done, ever since their brave pioneer forefathers cleared the forests, subdued the wilderness, spread out across the wide prairies, and established the mightiest empire of the earth. The present and all coming generations that enjoy the fruits of pioneer labor and sacrifices have a right to be joyous. They are free, prosperous and filled with vitality, vim, pep and go. They want more from life than any other people. There are among them no country peasants, or city proleteriat, no class distinctions, no artificial aristocracy. Strong, confident, fearless, they work not merely, as the masses in other lands, for a bare existence, but as a means for providing the comforts and pleasures to which they feel they are entitled.

Whether people are cheerful because they dance, or dance because they are cheerful, may not easily be decided. One thing is certain, that if from an assemblage of men and women there should be selected those with smiling, happy faces, by far the greater percentage would be found to be dancers. "For the good are always the merry," the lighthearted, free from care and worry, who sing, or dance, or play because of their superabundance of vital energy, and because in so doing they are in harmony with the primal laws of being.

DANCING AND COUNTRY LIFE

FOR more than a generation the problem of checking the steady drift of the young people from American farms into the cities has occupied the attention of statesmen, able editors, farm leaders and economists. It is universally agreed that agriculture is the basic industry upon which the prosperity of manufacturing and commerce depends. When the farmers are prosperous their demands for all kinds of manufactured goods sets in motion the wheels of industry, labor is fully employed and merchants find increased sales to the rural communities and factory workers. When, as happened five years ago, there is a widespread depression among the farmers, it is felt by manufacturers, railways, merchants and industrial workers in every field. Today, as one hundred years ago, when Thomas Jefferson wrote that agriculture was the most important of all industries, the welfare of the American people as a whole is indissolubly bound up with the existence of a large and prosperous agricultural interest.

President Roosevelt twenty years ago recognized the importance of keeping on the farms the young and vigorous American men and women who are needed to maintain the enormous food supplies required by the vast populations of the great cities and industrial centers, and

appointed a Country Life Commission to investigate and
report on the conditions that were making life on the farms
unattractive as compared with the cities. One of the reasons found by the Commission for the increasing flow of
country youth cityward was the lack of social activities
and amusements in the rural districts, and the consequent
desire to migrate to localities where a denser population
brought wide opportunities for social diversions. Curi-
ously enough, the dance as a means of promoting soci-
ability among the farm population was not discussed,
possibly because of an old-fashioned prejudice against
dancing that still prevails in many rural regions. Why
certain good people should object to the dance, innocent,
joyous and beneficial as it is in practically all its mani-
festations and associations, can only be explained on the
grounds given by Lord Macaulay from the British Puritan's objection to the sport of bear-baiting. "The Puritan
condemned bear-baiting, not because it gave pain to the
bear, but because it gave pleasure to the spectators."
There was a time when it was considered frivolous and
wicked to be happy, and dancing and many other innocent amusements were put under the ban. This narrow
view of life is, fortunately, becoming outgrown, and no
power is now invoked to prevent pleasure-seekers finding
diversion in sports, games, or the dance.

With the gradual disappearance of the ancient view of
pleasure as akin to sinfulness, there is no good reason why
dancing should not become as popular in the rural districts as it is in the cities. The automobile and good rural
roads have combined to make possible social gatherings in
central localities that would have been impossible twenty
years ago. Improved farm machinery and implements
have shortened working hours on the farm, so that the evenings are no longer devoted to finishing up the day's work.

Then there are the long winter evenings when the heart of youth calls to youth, and when in every village or country hamlet there should be assembled joyous groups, finding in the dance an escape from the routine of daily cares. Picnics and outings would take on new attractions, and under the spur of rivalry the simpler forms of dancing would evolve into its more artistic branches. There would be something to look forward to outside the family circle; new acquaintances and agreeable companions. With the dance would come a wider knowledge and love of music that would stimulate its study and practice. In many thousands of farm homes the radio is now installed, and programs of dance music are arranged that make it possible for millions to join in moving to the strains of the best metropolitan bands and orchestras.

The contrast between the city residents and their "country cousins" is in no respect more marked than in their walk and carriage. Watch the city crowds, as with heads up, chins in, and shoulders back, they step out briskly along the sidewalks. They know how to walk. They may be going somewhere in a hurry, or sauntering to see and be seen, but in either case they carry themselves as individual personages. They have been taught grace of movement, and their self-confidence expresses their individuality. Compare with them a group of rural walkers. Too often the latter slouch carelessly and drag limbs that are awkward and aimless. They are frequently bent and listless, as though walking were hard labor imposed as a penalty. They do not know how to hold their arms to keep them in accord with their bodily progress. It is not an injustice to the country folk to say that by their walk they can nearly always be distinguished from the city resident. Instruction in even the simplest forms of the dance, and practice in their movements, will bring about a far-reaching change. The country boys and girls will learn to hold themselves erect, they will quickly see the difference between the sort of progress by what has been described as a process of falling over and recovering one's balance, and real walking by a coördinated entity. They will take pride in well developed bodies, and will show in every movement the results of the training that has enabled them to become proficient in the dance.

Is it not possible that the answer to the old query: "How you goin' to keep them down on the farm?" may be found in the advice: "Teach them to dance"?

Perhaps you are asking yourself, "What has country dancing to do with stage dancing?" And I will answer you:

Just this: The city has no monopoly of talent in any field. The candidate for dancing honors and emoluments comes as often from rural communities as from metropolitan. But first, whether in city or hamlet, there must be present in the aspirant the true love of dancing as an art, a sense of rhythm, an urge to step to music,—and these he or she discovers only as the ballroom dancing in the home community develops them.

This is no lure; it is a true word: There are young ladies and gentlemen in all localities who, if they but knew it, could rise to heights worth while, because possessed of genuine talent needing only correct training to develop its possibilities to the full.

The country-bred girls and boys in our courses have equal opportunity with their city cousins, and both are thriving alike.

DANCING AS A SOCIAL ACCOMPLISHMENT

SOME years ago the editor of a great New York newspaper, who was nationally known as one of the foremost personalities of his era, invited a group of his friends to his home to enjoy a performance by the then celebrated Spanish dancer Carmencita. After the plaudits of the delighted guests had died away, a lady eminent in society inquired of her appreciative husband: "Why didn't we ever think of arranging for something of this kind?" And her worser half agreed that for the future they would follow their host's example, and make dancing by great artists a feature of their social entertainments.

Ever since that time there has been an increasing demand by those whose wealth, culture and good taste have made them the dominant force in American society, for the services of the leading exponents of the creative art of the dance. To the ballrooms of the great mansions that adorn every city of any considerable size there have come brilliant assemblages of the men and women who by reason of their special qualifications are recognized as social leaders, to see, enjoy and appreciate the charm and beauty of "woven paces and of weaving arms." The hosts whose invitation includes the announcement "special dances by Miss—or Mr.—" know that there will be few declinations because of other engagements. The fortunate ones who are able to command the presence of any of the well known stars in the dancing firmament at a social gathering, are assured that their guests will carry away with them only pleasant recollections of a delightful occasion.

Even to those who may have often seen the artist in public performances, there is an additional charm in the dances as given in the more intimate conditions of a private gathering. The knowledge that the audience appreciates every detail, down to the slightest touch, stimulates the dancer to the highest mood of artistic endeavor. "Art," wrote William Morris, "is the expression of man's joy in his work." Emphatically is this true of the dancer's art, and the exaltation of joyousness into perfect harmony of motion comes only when the artist knows that the message conveyed is understood by the onlookers.

To those who wish to make their impress upon society by distinctive gatherings, the artist affords an ever new and always pleasing entertainment.

As knowledge of the illimitable possibilities of the dance expands, there is certain to be a growing demand for the types of dancers whose gifts make them peculiarly adapted to the exercise of their art at social functions.

UNIVERSAL APPRECIATION OF THE DANCE

THE chief reason why dancing as a public entertainment will always maintain its present popularity, and will be in even greater demand in the future than in the past, is to be found in the fact that to appreciate and enjoy to the fullest degree the work of the creative dancer requires no special knowledge of the art itself on the part of the spectator. There are many who do not understand or appreciate classical music. To many others the speaking drama makes no appeal. Still others care nothing for the motion picture, and cannot be induced to witness a performance on the screen. But everyone—men and women, young or mature, can enjoy the beauty, harmony, and exhilaration of a well conceived and well executed dance. There is something in the nature of us all that responds immediately to the message that the dancer conveys. Perfection of form, grace of movement, harmony of action with appropriate music, all combine to make up a spectacle that thrills and inspires. To slightly paraphrase Robert Browning:

> "Others may reason and welcome,
> But seeing the dance, we know."

As was said of the Athenians of old, the American people are always looking for something new. They are
quick to take up this or that fad in dress, games, sports
or amusements, and after a brief time throw it aside.
There is nothing of the fancy of the hour in the popular
acceptance of the dance, either for personal practice, or
as a stage entertainment. What has been seen in all the
American cities during the past ten or twenty years—the
steady growth in popularity of the dance in all its forms
—is no whim that will presently pass. On the contrary,
nothing can be more certain than that each year will find
a greater increase in dancing, both by the people themselves, and for them by the artists of the profession. It
was said for a long time by visiting foreigners that Americans had not learned how to enjoy themselves. This may
have been true at one time, but it is not today. The chief
object of life, it has been discovered, is to live abundantly
and joyously. Everything that helps to make living more
cheerful, healthful and agreeable; that satisfies aesthetic
needs; that ministers to the sense of beauty and harmony,
will be encouraged and developed, and as one important
means to these ends, the dance must of necessity flourish
and endure.

GERTRUDE LAWRENCE

RITA OWEN

ADA MAY (WEEKS)

AL JOLSON.

THE MELTING POT OF THE DANCE

A GREAT deal is being talked a n d written about changing the millions who have come to this country from foreign lands, or are the children of immigrants, into 100 per cent Americans. So far as the advocacy of measures for this purpose is based on a sincere desire to bring home to everyone living under the national flag a knowledge of the essential principles of our government and instituions, this is worthy of the encouragement and aid of all patriotic citizens. There is, however, another aspect of the Americanization movement, that is not so admirable. This is the attack on ideas, manners, customs and amusements peculiar to certain foreign peoples, not because they are necessarily wrong, or antagonistic to genuine Americanism, but merely because they are different. According to some of these self-constituted authorities the way to instill patriotism and love of country into the benighted aliens is to persuade them to abandon all that links them with the land of their ancestors, and become exactly like the prevailing type of Bangor, Maine, Augusta, Georgia, or Portland, Oregon.

Oliver Wendell Holmes tells how when he was a boy living in Cambridge, Mass., there was a constant warfare between the boys of his district and those who lived down by the water front, who were regarded as foreigners, because they seemed to be in some way different. He concluded that most of the racial antagonisms and hatreds that so often lead to quarrels and war are due to the same notion; that the foreign man is inferior because his ways are different from ours.

Against the narrow ideas that would reject many things of great value because they are of foreign origin, there is need for a wise and discriminating selection of the best that all regions of the earth have to offer in the domain of science, literature, music, painting, the dance, and other arts, and their combination with the results attained by American creative effort.

In no respect is there a more urgent need for the development of a truly American art spirit than in the wide field offered by artistic dancing, yet it would surely be a mistake to ignore all that has been learned and accomplished in the long experience of other peoples. A foolish prejudice against foreign dances should not be allowed to prevent the incorporation of their best features into what will ultimately be the distinctive American school.

That there assuredly will be an essentially American type of dancing in all its branches, that will reach heights far above that yet achieved by any other country, cannot be doubtful. As the increase of wealth, not only for a few, but for the great mass of the people, gives more leisure, creates new desires, and brings increased capacity for enjoyment, it is inevitable that more and more will the public appreciation of the dance call for still greater advances. As the various races from other lands have mingled their several qualities and gifts, and have produced the highest civilization on a broad scale that the world has ever seen, so will the creators of new and more beautiful dance forms utilize the characteristic dances of all nations in achieving what will be the 100 per cent American dance.

YOUR OPPORTUNITIES

THOSE of you who are perfecting yourselves for a stage career are naturally giving consideration to your future as you advance in the courses, and are wondering just how you will go about it to get well placed in your chosen line of work.

I am going to tell you how some have tried to do this, and then tell you the best, surest and safest way. And do not for a moment think that I am guessing about what I tell you. I know the theatrical world and theatrical ways and methods, and I know the managers, the producers, and all the principals connected with our profession, and they know me. So I am not guessing when I say that your personal interests in all matters connected with the stage will be best conserved by entrusting them to me.

In our classes here in the studio there is apt to be one or more dominating spirits who become anxious to go around the booking offices and seek for a try-out and an engagement.

It is true that to go to any office and say that you are a recent or prospective graduate of the Ned Wayburn Studios is a good recommendation, and you may get a hearing and a try-out on the strength of it. But please be advised by me and let me give you the try-out first when I am sure you are ready for it. Your teacher should first be given a chance to see what you can do individually. His advice is invaluable and impartial. When he reports that you are advanced sufficiently to deserve consideration for a solo role, then come and dance for me. I am glad to have you do this, and shall always give you my decision honestly and fairly, and let me add, freely—no charge whatever. If I see that you are deficient in any way, I will be frank and tell you so, and will also suggest what you should do to correct your fault. In other words, you will get constructive criticism, and kindly advice, in my office, whereas anything short of perfection shown to a booking agent or possible employer would be apt to insure abrupt dismissal. They would give you no helpful advice, and you would prejudice yourself, for your effrontery, in their eyes for any future engagement you might seek.

So be advised by me. I respect an ambition that prompts you to go out and hunt an engagement, but, believe me, yours is not the best way. There are agents and agents. Some would do right by you, and perhaps some would be unscrupulous. I am not going on record in this book with any details that would seem to reflect in the least on anyone, so I'll not enlarge upon this subject here. But I will tell you more about this if you come to my office and ask me to.

Now if any pupil in the school asks you to go around the theatrical agencies, please don't do it, but come and tell me. Perhaps some day you both will come to me and say "Thank you."

Oftentimes we send out groups of our students, two, four, six or eight, to go on the professional stage for something special. Sometimes they are paid; sometimes it is done gratuitously; but the experience alone is worth money to them.

The regular theatrical season opens about Labor Day and lasts till around Decoration Day. Summer engagements begin about the first Monday in June and end about the last Saturday in August. Calls are sent out about the middle of April for summer work, and about the middle of July for the winter or regular season. If you are able to qualify, you will get the benefit of these calls for dancers, and when you go with my recommendation, it will be only to the best managers.

I will inform you fully as to the best forms of contract for you to sign in every case, and make no charge for this. You know, when you engage to go with a show, you do not simply take the manager's word for it that he will employ you for so many weeks at so much a week, nor does the manager simply take your "Yes, I'll come," and let it go at that. This matter of entering his employ is a business affair, a transaction of importance to you both, and calls for a signed agreement that binds him, the manager, as to his responsibility to you, and binds you as to your duties to him. It is a legal document, binding on both parties, the manager and you—and let me tell you right here, you feel mighty big with your first stage contract duly signed and delivered, and in your pocket, and while you may in future seasons get contracts that specify much larger salaries than your first one does, no contract will ever *seem* so big and important to you as this first one, the start, the goal of your ambition. I love to see my pupils with their first professional contracts! They are so happy and hopeful; the world opens up new delights for them; they have arrived. The reward of their untiring exertions here in the courses is at hand, and they have earned it and deserved it. "Good for you!" I feel like saying; and I am truly happy to think that I have been in some degree instrumental in bringing this about.

My experience has been paid for. I have learned to profit by my own mistakes, and I can and will save you all the risk in closing deals that involve so much—perhaps your entire future stage career. I can and will do this, if you let me.

STAGE-CRAFT

WHEN my pupils become professional dancers and "sign up" for their first stage engagement they will wish not to be or appear ignorant of the marvelous mechanism that is the modern theatrical stage. Not that they will learn it all from any book, but my knowledge of things back stage will be of help, and I have jotted down here some of them for that purpose. The rest of it the new entrant upon the real stage will absorb in time, but with the help of my condensed explanation herein no one who reads need appear lost or totally bewildered in the new environment back of the curtain line.

Let me tell you some of the important things that every pupil of mine who contemplates a professional career should know about the theatre, the building itself and the stage upon which you expect to present your offerings to the public.

Proscenium Arch, the Frame of the Stage Pictures

In the first place, the theatre building is divided into two parts, the auditorium and the stage. The dividing line is known as the curtain line. In stage parlance the auditorium side of the dividing line is the "front of the house," or "out front," and the stage side is always "back stage."

The proscenium arch of the stage makes the frame for the pictures on the stage. "The opening" means to the professional the width across stage at the proscenium arch, and varies according to the size of the auditorium and the line of sight of the auditors. It may be thirty feet, forty, or even more, as is the case in the New York Hippodrome and other large city theatres. The height is sometimes the same as the width, or slightly less, the complete frame of the arch being usually of an oblong shape, possibly thirty-five feet wide and twenty-five feet high.

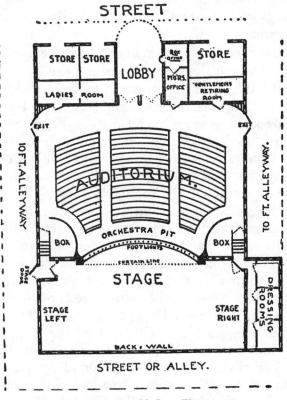

Diagram of a Modern Theatre

The fire laws require a fireproof curtain, which is on the outer or audience side of the two or more curtains that hang on the stage side of the proscenium arch. Next to this asbestos affair is the "act curtain," that raises and lowers, and is usually painted on fire-proofed or heavy duck canvas. There may be used instead or in addition to the act curtain, what is known as a tableau curtain, that works in a traveler above, which can be drawn straight off stage, both ways, parting in the middle, or be pulled to a drape at each side. This is always made of material and sometimes painted in aniline dye; if painted in water color or oil it would crack.

There is never any curtain in front of "the arch" or proscenium. The footlights and the apron are in front of the fireproof curtain. The apron may be deep or shallow, and at its front edge is the footlight trough and a masking piece, fireproof always, to shield the eyes of the audience and reflect the footlights onto the stage. The footlights follow the front curvature of the apron, when it is curved, as is usually the case, although many of the modern stages have no apron at all, the footlights running in a straight line across, sometimes within a foot of the fire curtain.

The stage itself extends from the curtain line to the back wall of the theatre, and from left wall to right wall. Under the roof of the stage, anywhere from sixty-five to ninety feet above the floor, there is a horizontal lattice work of steel or iron covering the entire spread of the stage, and known as the gridiron. The space on top of the gridiron is called the rigging loft. The roof of the stage over the rigging loft is a huge skylight, opened or closed from the stage. The skylight is made light-proof for matinee performances. On the gridiron are rigged the blocks and pulleys through which pass the lines attached to all the scenery that goes up in the air, or "up in the flies," which is the name given the space between the top of the proscenium arch and the gridiron. To take scenery up, is "flying it," in stage language, leaving the sight of the audience; whatever goes up "flies," and whatever is carried off to one side or back is "struck." The stage manager, when he wants the scene taken away, gives the order "strike" to the stage hands, or "grips," as they are called, who are on the stage level, and he pushes a button for the head-flyman in the "fly-gallery" to fly whatever scenery goes up.

There is a "fly-gallery," as it is called, usually ten to fifteen feet wide, some twenty-five to thirty-five feet above the stage level and extending from the front to the back walls of the stage on one side, against the side wall, usually of steel and concrete. Then there is the "paint-bridge," perhaps five feet wide, extending across the stage at the back wall from side to side, on a line with the "fly-gallery." Sometimes there is a "paint-frame" attached to the back wall on which scenery is painted. It is movable up and down. Sometimes twenty to twenty-five feet above the stage level is a light-gallery, on each side of the stage running parallel to the fly-gallery, but under it. These galleries are for the purpose of holding calcium lights and operators. Running from the back wall of the stage to the proscenium wall all the way of the fly-gallery on the front edge nearest the stage is the pin-rail, very strong and imbedded in the wall front and back of the stage; it holds all the scenery that goes aloft. When the scenery is raised, the "lines," as the ropes or cables are called in stage language, are pulled down and tied off to this "pin-rail." These lines attached to the scenery are usually in sets of three, sometimes four, and extend straight up through the blocks in the gridiron and across the gridiron down to the pin-rail in the fly-gallery. As they are usually fastened to three or four different points on each piece of scenery they are necessarily of three or four different lengths, but the lines are tied and handled as one at the pin-rail, and pulled all together. In a set of three lines, the line nearest the pin-rail is called the "short line," the next one the middle line, the far one the long line. "Trim it," you hear the order given. This means to "level" whatever piece of scenery it is. "Tie it off" is the way they direct that the lines be made fast to the pin-rail. In rainy or damp weather the ropes get longer; in dry they shrink; then it is necessary to "trim the drops," letting out the lines and tying them over before the performance. This is done under the direction of the master mechanic or stage carpenter. Often there is a counterweight or bag attached to the lines above the fly-gallery to help carry the weight of the heavy scenery as it is sent aloft to its resting place in the flies, out of sight of the audience and out of the way of everybody on stage.

The various drops are known on the stage as "solid," "cut" or "leg" drops. Borders about forty feet long by twelve feet deep, hung horizontally, mask in the top of all scenery, and hide the "flies" from the audience on the lower floor, and may be interior, exterior, foliage, straight, arched, or sky borders (plain blue). In troughs hung across the stage by steel cables from the gridiron, their height regulated from the fly-gallery, are the various border lights, each usually in three circuits, red, white and blue. These are hung at intervals of about six feet, the first being about that distance back of the act curtain and the others spaced about every six feet to the back wall of the stage. On the average practical modern stage there will be anywhere from four to seven border lights. On the stage, between the curtain line and first border light, are the first entrances, known as left first entrance and right first entrance. The right and left of the stage are always the dancer's right and left as she or he faces the audience. About six feet back of this is located the second entrance, and about each six feet interval is a successively numbered entrance, as "third entrance," etc. In a "full-stage" setting the last entrance to the rear is called "upper entrance." A scene in the space covering the entire first entrance is spoken of as being "in one"; in the second entrance, "in two." When one passes out of sight of the audience he is "off stage." The various entrances and exits are designated in writing and print by characters that carry their meaning plainly, as RUE (right upper entrance), L2E (left second entrance). So, too, with spoken directions on the stage. When you are told to "exit LUE," for instance, you are supposed to know that you are to go off stage at the left upper entrance. No one in the theatre ever speaks of standing "in the wings"; always it is "in the entrance."

The prompt side in a theatre is usually the left first entrance, though sometimes it is on the other side, where are located the electric switchboard controlling every light in the building, under the personal direction of the chief electrician, and a series of buttons above a shelf or prompt desk attached to the wall about the height of a bookkeeper's desk, where the stage manager makes his headquarters during each performance, the stage manager being like the captain or skipper of the ship. All signals are given by the stage manager, the buttons usually placed immediately above or at one side of the prompt desk, within easy reach controlling buzzers, lights or bells that tell as plainly as shouted words could do what is to be done and who is to do it. Sometimes lights flash to give directions and warnings, instead of the buzzer sounding. Every action of the stage hands below and aloft is directed in this manner from one central point of control by one master mind, the stage manager of the show.

The orchestra usually has a music room of its own somewhere under the stage or in the cellar of the theatre, where the musicians congregate before the performance

and during their "waits." A buzzer or bell warning
to them is said to "ring the orchestra in," and they are
usually allowed about three minutes to get into their
places in the orchestra pit after it sounds. There is
also a "drop" signal buzzer or light to give the head
flyman in the fly-gallery the signals that indicate when
to raise and lower certain "drops," or hanging pieces. A
bell would be heard by the audience and detract from the
performance. A curtain buzzer or light gives the "warning" and "go" signals to the stage hands in the fly-gallery
who are called "flymen," for raising and lowering the curtains or other scenery, like "drops," "borders," and any
other pieces of scenery that have been "hung" to fly. In
some modern theatres the switchboard and its operator are
raised some ten feet above the stage. In such a case a buzzer signal from the stage manager's prompt desk directs
the manipulation of the lights for the guidance of the chief
electrician in his elevated perch, these signals being given
at a certain "cue" in the performance, and he knows from
his cue sheet, always before him, just what lights are required on each succeeding cue.

Stage dressing rooms are by law required to be separated from the stage proper by a permanent wall. Access
to them is usually found near the front wall of the stage,
seldom along the back wall. In modern city theatres dressing rooms are in tiers, as in the New Amsterdam Theatre,
New York, where there are seven floors of dressing rooms
reached by a private elevator used for no other purpose.
The modern stage dressing rooms in city theatres have
every known arrangement for comfort, sanitation and con-
venience.

Stage artists have no business in the front of the house,
nor, conversely, have those whose employment is in the
front of the house any business on the stage. Both keep

their separate places at all times. Artists are always required to enter and leave the theatre through the stage
door. All first-class managers forbid the artists to be
seen in "the front of the house." Members of the company
usually are required to report for matinee performances
about 1:30 P. M. and for evening shows about 7:30 P. M.,
but always before the "half hour" is called, which is thirty
minutes before the overture is played. The stage watchman, known as the stage door tender, is always at the stage
door before and during a performance and permits none to
pass in who are not directly connected with the stage end of
the theatre, the day stage door tender being on duty
usually from 7 A. M. to 7 P. M., and the night stage door
tender from 7 P. M. to 7 A. M. The night watchman goes
his rounds regularly throughout the night at required intervals, registering on a time-clock from different stations
throughout the theatre building; all outer doors and windows are locked about one-half hour after the evening performance.

No messages, calls, telegrams or information of any
character from outside is permitted to enter the theatre
for any actor or actress who is inside and hence secluded
from all outside contact and purely in the realm of the
playhouse. This and absolute exclusion of all interlopers
is one of the strictest rules of the theatre, and woe to him
who attempts its violations, or to the doorkeeper who permits it. Any messages received are given to the artist
after the performance. No person who is not a member of
the company should ever be permitted to visit a dressing
room during a performance, only afterwards; such a contact takes the mind of the artist off her or his work.

Men who have obtained wrong ideas about members of
the theatrical profession and have boldly sought to force
their presence onto the stage have been summarily dealt

with before now—and in some cases I have helped in the good work myself. Sometimes, after the performance, relatives, friends or escorts are permitted to enter the stage door and there await the street-clad and departing performers. But strangers and would-be "stage-door Johnnies" are always barred out.

There is no "green room" in the modern American theatre. We have all read about a meeting place in the rear of the stage that went by this title in the old English novels and biographies. They may exist still in some foreign theatres, I am not sure—but I doubt it. What I am sure of is that the American stage is sacred to its artists, principals and subordinates alike, and to its stage manager and the stage hands who keep things moving behind the curtain line.

It is a business and not a game. A theatrical life is taken seriously by all who wish to succeed in it. No triflers need apply nowadays.

After every performance the stage is cleared of all obstacles, scenery and everything else. The last member of the company out of each dressing room is required to put the light out, lock the dressing-room door and leave the key to the room with the stage door tender who is held responsible for the contents of the rooms. The act curtain and the asbestos curtain are raised. A single electric bulb or pilot light on a portable iron stand about three feet high is placed centre of the stage near the footlights, and casts its beam across the stage and throughout the auditorium. The show is over and the fire-laws are obeyed.

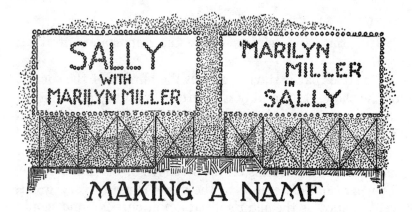

MAKING A NAME

ONE may see big electric signs carrying bright-light messages similar to the above placed conspicuously over theatre entrances in all cities of any magnitude. Such signs convey to the passing populace the interesting information that here is located a certain play, and also that in this play a certain person appears as a main attraction.

Now to the passerby whose knowledge of things theatrical is merely cursory, scant or non-existent, the two signs given above may have exactly the same meaning, bear the same message in both cases. But to all those "in the know" as to stage matters the two signs tell two entirely different stories, and the location of the names of the play and the actor convey important information in the theatre code that the wise ones interpret at a glance.

Here are the two readings as the stage-wise render them, and when I have told you about this you will catch the point at once and ever after be able to "read the signs" with a clear conception of their import:

The name at the top of each sign is "starred"; the other is "featured." In one, the play is given the star position and Miss Miller is featured; in the other, Marilyn Miller is starred and the play featured.

"Well, what of that?" you ask.

Just this, and here is where the importance of it all comes in:

The one that is starred carries the burden of the success of the show. If the play is starred, its failure does not reflect on the person featured; but if the actor is starred and failure follows, the actor and not the play is considered responsible, the actor not having proven a *magnet,* not having drawn business on the strength of his or her name. The personal difference to the actor is really very great, yet "to star" is the actor's great ambition. No one should ever be starred unless popular enough to attract plenty of patronage and thereby insure "packed houses."

This applies not alone in the signs over the door, but also in all the theatre's publicity. Pick up today's newspaper, and look at the stage announcements. "Mary Pickford in—" you don't care what the play is when you see the star's name. The star carries the play, in such a case. "Rose-Marie, with Mary Ellis and William Kent." You are glad to go and see the featured pair, but in this case the play is given the star position, it having registered success, the profits from this musical play having been as high as $18,000.00 per week during its run in one New York theatre.

Now the point of all this, that has to do with the stage dancer, is, "How did Marilyn Miller get a name that entitled her to this conspicuous exploitation, and how can I go about it to become equally well-known and famous, myself?"

You are wise to ask this question seriously early in your stage career, and if you have or develop the quality that makes for stardom you can read this chapter with confidence that it is an accurate and correct account of how many a stage celebrity has progressed from an unknown and unheralded place in the theatrical world, to one where Broadway producing managers have solicited the privilege of elevating her or his name over the doors of their playhouses.

Bear in mind that your name is to you what a trademark is to a manufacturer. And, to continue the analogy, you cannot establish a name in a day or two, any more than the manufacturer can make his trademarked goods universally known in a short period.

You are starting out now with the laudable ambition to make a name for yourself, and have still to seek your first engagement. You know your dances, are continuing your practice, and have confidence in your ability to make good.

Don't hurry to get yourself before any producing manager until you have had a little experience in some hideaway place, like at a church or charity benefit performance, some local entertainment, or club affair, anything of this nature, that will enable you to try yourself out before a small or friendly audience, test your ability to overcome stage fright, and get hold of yourself before a crowd. Having done this away from Broadway and gained assurance, then an appearance in some regular theatre, preferably at some benefit performance, usually given Sundays, should come next, where the dancer is sure to be seen by someone who has the authority and position to offer an engagement. Any sort of an engagement with a reputable management is a good beginning and should be accepted without expectation of a fancy salary, an opportunity being what one always needs in order to prove one's ability.

If you do not succeed in creating a demand for your services at appearances like this, do not become discouraged; make up your mind to keep on trying until you do attract the attention of the right manager. Always be willing to make any sacrifice as far as remuneration is concerned for an opportunity to appear to advantage, and be everlastingly grateful to whoever gives you your first opportunity, or foothold which enables you to establish yourself.

Send a brief letter to the offices of various managers announcing your forthcoming appearance. Enclose a good full-length photograph, preferably in stage costume, the best you can afford, i. e., taken by the best photographer you can get. Some of these managers or their representatives will be there and see your performance. Be sure you are "making good" before you try to interest any of the big managers. It is better for you to be seen by the manager before an audience than in an empty theatre.

Be satisfied to make a small beginning for the experience, provided you get a chance to do your best dance. This will help you establish yourself, but it is going to take a long time to prove your ability. Travel, and make territory for yourself. Go in a vaudeville act, if offered such an engagement. Keep on "small time" for a year, if necessary, and get your name known in a certain territory for a pleasing entertainer. Get on with some act, big or little, as a solo dancer, at a reasonable salary, and expect the first two weeks to be at half salary, as is usual. Do not demand a large salary until managers are clamoring for your services—make it an inducement for someone to employ you in the beginning.

When you start on a road tour your first inquiry of your company manager will be for a "copy of the route." You want to know where you are going, what towns your itinerary takes you to, so that friends can be advised in advance of your location day by day, and letters and communications reach you with certainty.

To the trouper, a town is a "stand." A week's showing in a place is spoken of as a "week stand"; the first and last half of the week is each a "three-day stand," or "four-day stand," or the "first" or "last-half." Then there is a "two-day stand" and a "one-night stand," which are self-explanatory. A "run" is a greater period than a "week stand," and you hear of a "two-week run," an "eight-week run," "six months run," and "one year run," etc.

There is a solid season, a theatrical year of forty weeks, of travel, experience and development, beginning about Labor Day and ending about Decoration Day, and a summer season beginning about the first Monday in June and ending about the last Saturday in August. Your work and progress is being watched unknown to you at every performance. The manager back home finally knows all about your work through "reports" which are kept in the main booking office and to which he and all other managers on his particular circuit have access.

Now you are ready to try for something bigger and better, ready for "big time" vaudeville, perhaps in your own act; if not that, then in someone else's act. Your second year's advancement is based on the weekly report that has been sent to headquarters regarding your reception by the public and the way in which your act has got over. Big time may mean Chicago, Boston, Philadelphia, and any or all the larger cities on the various "circuits." It may include the Keith-Albee Palace Theatre in New York, the Mecca of all vaudeville artists. It is at the Palace that you know you and your act are seen by every revue, musical comedy, or dramatic manager casting director whose business it is to pick and engage artists.

There is no school like vaudeville for the dancer, singer, actor or actress in any line of musical work. Most of the brightest stars in the theatrical firmament have graduated from vaudeville into greater things, and many of them return to the vaudeville stage for a flier now and then. It is there that you come in contact with different wise audiences in different cities and learn how to handle them. You watch your fellows in their various acts, note the bills as they change every week, or usually twice weekly, and your audience with them. You are in two, three or four shows a day in your short time, and learning how to get over better at every show. The vaudeville audience knows what's what. You can't fool them. You've got to do your best for them all the time—and you will, or you will not remain in vaudeville, where you have to "make good" every performance. It is an invaluable experience, your first stage years, and you will gather lasting benefit from your active vaudeville appearances. You must not complain of the number of shows you are required to give daily—the more you give the more practice you get before a paid audience, and remember you are gaining experience while being paid for it.

You may follow a season of this with a road show over your former territory another year, and you will find your old friends in the audience ready to boost you. You are on the right road to the "making of a name," which after all is what you are after. For although they will not remember your name yet, if you really pleased them they will remember your offering; about your third trip around they will learn your name and never forget it—provided you "make good." If you fail, the audience will forget you; but *not* the manager. Once you fail in his opinion, he will never forget or forgive it. He will never give anyone who fails a second chance. That is "show business."

Your fourth year should find you in a New York production in some good company. For New York is always the objective point, since the best and most opportunities are always there. There follows naturally a year on the road in the same company, as the show abandons New York for a tour of the larger cities. Always make the road trip in order to create territory for yourself, to establish a following, to make a still bigger name and demand for you, which means a larger salary eventually. You are sufficiently established now, after five successful years, to be able to expect another New York engagement, under the same management in all likelihood but with a new vehicle. This New York engagement and another year on tour with the same play puts you seven years along the way to a name in the big lights, and your name has been growing day by day, until it is now known in good territory, and consequently, through wise exploitation—publicity—it has become a magnet and attracts patronage.

When the time comes that your name is to go up in front of the theatre, choose to be featured at first rather than starred. If anything must fail, let it be the show, and not you. Don't risk failing to "draw business" to the box office.

There will come a time somewhere along in your progress to fame when you will need a business manager or an agent versed in all matters of a theatrical nature, favorably known to all the large producing managers, and able to advance your fortunes materially by protecting and looking after your interests. He is entitled to receive ten percent of your earnings from whatever source, and the services he can render you are well worth it.

Nearly every successful actor and actress has a manager. Stage celebrities have not the time, let alone the experience and ability, to promote their own business interests, watch for opportunities to secure the choice engagements, and attend to the very necessary publicity and negotiations for contracts for the future. The reputable agent or artist's manager is always on the ground and in touch with the best managements and things theatrical daily. But no such representative worth while will bother with you until you have made good.

The best artist managers or agents know in advance what is being planned for the coming theatrical season. They are in close contact with the very high-ups in the theatrical world, men whose contracts you hope to sign on the dotted line soon. A good agent may save you several years' time in advancing to a stellar position. He knows the value of publicity, which often is half the battle in getting yourself before the public. You must have publicity, whether or not you secure a representative to attend to it for you. Interesting newsy stories about you, with effective art studies of yourself in costume accompanying them, are gladly accepted by many newspapers and magazines. The rotogravure sections of Sunday papers contain many pictures of theatrical folks. A beautiful picture will usually carry a story, and you are wise to get a few good ones rather than many cheap prints. Every first-class theatre has its own press agent, and every production of any size its own press representative. Both are glad to coöperate with you if you have real ability, and help you with the preparation of your stories and photographs and getting them into the daily newspaper. There are also many publicity concerns who make it a business to keep your name and picture in the public eye at a moderate charge. But you must be able to *make good* first.

Neither publicity nor anything else will avail to establish a permanent name for you unless you are prepared to deliver the goods. Duds and dumb ones never make a big noise in the world. There is no star name awaiting the inferior person in this profession. All the front-page publicity in christendom won't do the trick if you haven't back of you real talent and something the public is clamoring for. And you cannot hope to fool the wary producer by any false representation or exaggerated claims.

You are not wasting your time while on the way to the bigger things. Seven years may seem a long time to wait, but you are not starving on the way, and you are really not "waiting" at all. You start with a reasonable salary that advances from year to year and engagement to engagement, as you deserve it. You must build all the way on solid rock, then the structure that you finally rear, because of its firm foundation will endure forever.

Build up a public interest in yourself if you expect any producing manager to pay you what you are worth. Perhaps he will never pay you what you think you are worth, but if you bring money into the house he knows he must pay you well in his own interest. And believe me, he knows whether you are an asset or a liability to his show. You have simply got to prove to the box office that you are producing—not stage money—but the real stuff.

There is such a thing in stage lingo as an "overnight hit." Someone suddenly "stops the show" in a town; that is, gets an unusual number of recalls. But wait a while before you decide that you are ready to star on the strength of that. Your next audience or the audience in the next town may not be so enthusiastic over your act. An "overnight hit" is seldom continued beyond the single performance. It is pleasant while it lasts, but it doesn't last long. You must perform consistently and "make a hit" at every performance, with every audience.

Be patient, you who would star and see your name go up in the bright lights on the Great White Way. Do not get discouraged. You will meet with obstacles on the route to fame undoubtedly, as others have done, and, like the others who have finally arrived, you must overcome them one at a time as they appear, by sheer force of will-power, determination, pluck or whatever you desire to call it. If you are a weakling and lack strength of character do not ever take up a stage career, for you will get many a bump; so be prepared to stand it. For only those who are determined to succeed will ever reach the top, where there is plenty of room always.

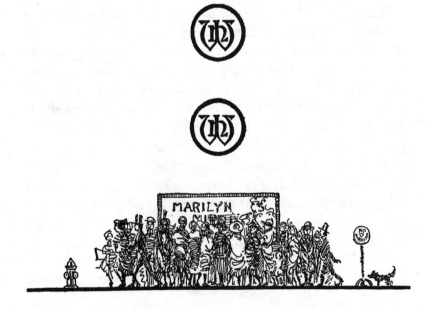